"Ethics and Attachment: How we
Every scholar and researcher conc
ity should read this scientifically sound, theoretically innovative, and gracefully written volume. While applying insights from psychoanalysis, attachment theory, and neuroscience into the morality field, it opens up new avenues of research on the contribution of child's attachment experiences to moral judgments later in life. I thoroughly enjoyed this book as both an attachment researcher and a person concerned with moral wrongs and the promotion of a more just and harmonious world."

Mario Mikulincer, Professor of Psychology,
Interdisciplinary Center (IDC) Herzlyia, Israel

"Govrin explores a revolutionary thesis with tight logic and irrefutable evidence, revealing that even our most complex moral judgments have a surprisingly simple beginning—the dyad of caregiver and infant. Through discussions that range from psychology to philosophy, ethics to evolution, Govrin leaves little doubt that he is a true scholar of morality, and that the elegant "Attachment Approach" to morality helps explain much about our judgments of good and evil. A must-read for anyone interested in moral psychology."

Kurt Gray, Associate Professor of Psychology
and Neuroscience, University of North Carolina
at Chapel Hill, USA

"Drawing on sources as diverse as psychoanalysis and neuroscience as well as philosophy and attachment theory, Dr. Govrin discerns in the earliest years of life the basic cognitive and affective structures undergirding the complexity of moral life. He combines a careful analysis of moral conflicts with a sensitive and thorough exploration of how we evaluate them, both consciously and unconsciously. *Ethics and Attachment: How We Make Moral Judgments* is a masterpiece of creativity and scholarly integration that will be required reading for anyone interested in the psychology of moral judgment."

Ronald C. Naso, psychoanalyst and clinical
psychologist in independent practice, Stamford, CT,
USA; current President, American Board and Academy
of Psychoanalysis

Ethics and Attachment

Why are we disgusted when an elderly woman is robbed but sympathize with the actions of a Robin Hood? Why do acts of cruelty against a helpless kitten bother us more than does the trampling of ants?

In *Ethics and Attachment: How We Make Moral Judgments*, psychoanalyst and philosopher Aner Govrin offers the attachment approach to moral judgment, an innovative new model of the process involved in making such moral judgments.

Drawing on clinical findings from psychoanalysis, neuroscience and developmental psychology, the author argues that infants' experience in the first year of life provides them with the basic tools needed to reach complex moral judgments later in life. With reference to Winnicott and Bowlby, the author examines how attachments affect our abilities to apply to make moral decisions.

With its wholly new ideas about moral judgments, *Ethics and Attachment* will be of great interest to ethics and moral philosophy scholars, law students, and psychoanalytic psychotherapists.

Aner Govrin is a clinical psychologist, psychoanalyst and a director of a doctoral program in the Program for Hermeneutics and Cultural Studies at Bar-Ilan University, Israel. He is a member of the Tel Aviv Institute for Contemporary Psychoanalysis (TAICP).

Philosophy & Psychoanalysis Book Series
Jon Mills
Series Editor

Philosophy & Psychoanalysis is dedicated to current developments and cutting-edge research in the philosophical sciences, phenomenology, hermeneutics, existentialism, logic, semiotics, cultural studies, social criticism, and the humanities that engage and enrich psychoanalytic thought through philosophical rigor. With the philosophical turn in psychoanalysis comes a new era of theoretical research that revisits past paradigms while invigorating new approaches to theoretical, historical, contemporary, and applied psychoanalysis. No subject or discipline is immune from psychoanalytic reflection within a philosophical context, including psychology, sociology, anthropology, politics, the arts, religion, science, culture, physics, and the nature of morality. Philosophical approaches to psychoanalysis may stimulate new areas of knowledge that have conceptual and applied value beyond the consulting room reflective of greater society at large. In the spirit of pluralism, *Philosophy & Psychoanalysis* is open to any theoretical school in philosophy and psychoanalysis that offers novel, scholarly, and important insights in the way we come to understand our world.

Titles in this series:

Ethics and Attachment

How We Make Moral Judgments

Aner Govrin

Routledge
Taylor & Francis Group

LONDON AND NEW YORK

First published 2019
by Routledge
2 Park Square, Milton Park, Abingdon, Oxon OX14 4RN

and by Routledge
711 Third Avenue, New York, NY 10017

Routledge is an imprint of the Taylor & Francis Group, an informa business

British Library Cataloguing in Publication Data
A catalogue record for this book is available from the British Library

Library of Congress Cataloging in Publication Data
Names: Govrin, °Aner, 1966- author.
Title: Ethics and attachment : how we make moral judgments / Aner
   Govrin.
Description: 1 Edition. | New York : Routledge, 2018.
Identifiers: LCCN 2018026481| ISBN 9781138079779 (hardback) |
   ISBN 9781138079786 (pbk.) | ISBN 9781315114286 (Master) |
   ISBN 9781351627252 (Web) | ISBN 9781351627245 (epub) |
   ISBN 9781351627238 (mobipocket)
Subjects: LCSH: Decision making. | Psychology—Moral and ethical
   aspects.
Classification: LCC BF448 .G69 2018 | DDC 153.8/3—dc23
LC record available at https://lccn.loc.gov/2018026481

ISBN: 978-1-138-07977-9 (hbk)
ISBN: 978-1-138-07978-6 (pbk)
ISBN: 978-1-315-11428-6 (ebk)

Typeset in Times New Roman
by Swales & Willis Ltd, Exeter, Devon, UK

To my mother, Nurit Govrin

Contents

Preface

This book calls for a conceptual revolution in our understanding of morality.

It presents a novel theory, the attachment approach to moral judgment, which explains what stands behind most of the moral judgments we reach. Many attempts have been made to explain the intriguing process of moral judgment. This has produced a variety of answers, some clashing, from a range of disciplines. In what follows, I will attempt to show that a less apparent truth underpins the process of moral judgment and that the explanations so far offered resolve only part of the puzzle.

My main thesis is that moral judgments are based on a unique social cognition. The cognition is so simple that one wonders why no one has identified it until now. In fact, my book only puts into words what every human being knows in their heart of hearts from a very early age, an unconscious relational knowledge, like music that has been playing all our lives without our noticing it.

This provides an answer to an array of seemingly very divergent and baffling questions: Why does cruelty towards a helpless kitten bother us much more than trampling ants? Why are we disgusted when an elderly woman is robbed and yet admire a Robin Hood? How can it be that people who share a general moral code are poles apart when it comes to judging the morality of abortion or capital punishment? Moreover, the principle proposed in this book also addresses such theoretical questions as: What is the nature of ethics? Does it rely on reason or emotion? What is evil?

The theory in a nutshell

People perceive all moral situations, however different, using the same set of parameters. These universally shared criteria enable us to easily identify moral situations and differentiate them from other non-moral events. At their core, moral judgments require us to *judge relations between two parties*. Moreover, moral judgments are not limited to judging one isolated, single component of a moral situation, such as intentionality or the extent of harm caused, but rather require an assessment of an entire relationship that is held up to our prior expectations of how relationships of this type should be handled.

One of the most important factors in judging relations is assessing the asymmetry of power between the parties.

This is why although robbery is in itself deemed to be wrong, we will unequivocally condemn a thief robbing an elderly woman, but maybe less so someone who defrauds his insurance company, and we might even salute a Robin Hood.

The intent is the same, the action is the same and the damage is the same: an unlawful appropriation of someone else's property. And yet these are three different dyads with three different relationships between victim and thief, resulting in three different judgments.

The picture becomes still more complex when different observers evaluate the same dyad. The thief's mother in the first event is likely to reach a different judgment than will the son of the old woman, and both will differ from the third judgment reached by an independent judge. Thus, three judges, each with differing interests and perspectives, will assess the relations between the sides in a different manner.

Nonetheless, I will argue that even though they reach different conclusions, the three judges are engaged in the same mental actions, using the same parameters, evaluating the same data. Moreover, the three judges are able to reach widespread agreement as to the nature of moral judgment, which enables them to communicate and understand one another. For example, they all agree that one must not steal, and certainly not from the poor, the sick, the oppressed and so on.

The meaning of a moral situation is a function of the meaning of its parts and of the dyadic rules by which they are combined. We break the moral situation down into its most basic component parts. Within the dyad, we identify relations between two sides: strong/weak, dependent/independent, helpless/in control.

We have a range of expectations as to how the strong party to a dyad should and should not behave towards the weak side. We perceive moral failure when, as observers, we believe that the conduct of the strong towards the weak has violated our expectations. This social cognition is universal. We always expect the strong to protect the weak or at least cause them no harm. This expectation stands behind every person's moral judgment in every culture. In the book, I explain in detail the differences between individuals and between societies related to moral judgment. A side identified by one observer as "weak" will be considered "strong" by another. And yet, even though they reach contradictory conclusions, the two observers analyze the moral situation using the same parameters. They are engaged in the same cognitive calculation: detect a dyad, quickly identify the weak and strong parties, and assess whether and to what extent there was a violation of expectation.

However, even though the cognitive calculation is universal, our relations towards each of the sides, the sympathy and hostility we feel towards them, constitute an unstable and variable set of factors that differ from person to person and from culture to culture.

In this book, I argue that our moral intuitions originate in our expectations regarding the position of the weak. We have this knowledge intuitively, it is accessible to us effortlessly and directly, and we feel that it requires no justification or explanation. One of my main arguments is that this intuitive knowledge is based on our earliest experience, from the first year of life, when we were ourselves part of a dyad in which we were the weak side and our life depended on the devotion, care and protection of the stronger side.

This book's main thesis is that in the first year, a powerful early organizing process takes place that eventually enables the infant to abstract what is common to all moral situations. Thus, we tend to intuitively view moral situations as a perceived interlocking dyadic system of childlike and adultlike parties. Let me explain.

From the moment of birth, and for a considerable time thereafter, we are all nurtured and nursed by a caregiver. Strip humans of all their personal life stories and cultural practices, and you are left with one pivotal formative experience that humans have shared for as long as *Homo sapiens* has inhabited our planet. In the early years of life, every child goes through a period of total dependence, which, if the child is to survive and grow, requires relations with a caregiver. We are born into a dyadic situation: two human beings who, at the nonverbal level, influence each other in a moment-by-moment coordination of the rhythms of behavior, emotion and cognition. The two parties are merged with one another though their functions are distinct: only one of the two is dependent on the other in sustaining life and growth. This long phase of dependency forms a *unique social cognition, the prototypical dyad*: infant/caregiver, dependent/ independent; the relationship between one who has all the power and another who lacks any form of power, one who is needy and one who is resourceful, one who is responsible and one who is not, and so on. Moreover, the prototypical dyad determines not only how these two parties differ; it also provides a clear understanding of their preferred interrelations. The perceived independent ought to be committed to the welfare of the perceived dependent and responsible for the dependent's welfare. The dependent is not obliged to do the same.

In certain dyads, the obligation is total, as in the first primary dyad, between caregiver and infant. In other situations, it may be partial, as in a teacher/pupil dyad or a psychotherapist/patient dyad. Sometimes the obligation is limited to a specific responsibility such as the obligation a policeman has towards a citizen. And sometimes the obligation is simply not to harm, or to be very careful, as in the car driver/pedestrian dyad.

From birth, culture will pull this basic structure in diverse directions. Cultures differ from each other in the objects they define as dependent and independent – what is considered moral in one culture is considered transgressive in another. But there is a unity in the cognitive processes that lead people to interpret and judge moral situations, even though the results may widely vary.

The fundamental structure of this social recognition is innate and becomes activated during early childhood, just like other capacities such as language acquisition. The infant has an innate disposition to participate in a dyad in which a caregiver supplies his or her basic needs. When this innate disposition is brought into contact with a realization that resembles it – a real caregiver who is motivated to meet the infant's needs, even in a minimal way, just to maintain life – this social cognition starts to evolve. One of the ways it evolves is by learning to extend its application to situations outside the dyad, to other group members and even strangers.

Lakoff and Johnson (1999) write:

> Brains tend to optimize on the basis of what they already have, to add only what is necessary. Over the course of evolution, newer parts of the brain have built on, taken input from, and used older parts of the brain.
>
> (p. 43)

Paraphrasing Lakoff and Johnson's theory, we can ask if it is really plausible to suggest that if the infant/caregiver system can be put to work in the service of a parent protecting his or her child, the brain would build a new system to duplicate what it could already do in other social relations?

All humans are capable of distinguishing between good and bad. In saying that, I am asserting that every human possesses the necessary knowledge to reach moral judgments. Apart from those with serious mental handicaps, we all have the ability to break down a moral situation into its basic component parts, identify who is the dependent and who is independent, and analyze the relations between them in terms of violations of expectations.

To perform these mental functions, a person does not need additional instructions, practice or physical bodily development. The natural environment in which the child is raised is sufficient. The infant simply needs to be a part of asymmetrical relations in which someone cares for him or her and ensures that he or she is able to survive at the most basic level. Even an infant to a depressed or abusive caregiver has been given enough care to survive.

None of this infers that education and social interaction are of no importance. On the contrary, the basic innate moral skills expressed reflected in learning the dyadic rules only constitute an initial platform through which the developing child is able to understand and bestow meaning to moral education.

The attachment approach to moral judgment rests on the notion of a "moral intuition" that is unconsciously enacted and automatic. However, just because it is automatic does not make it moral. Moreover, moral intuitions can be entirely relative and subjective based on desire and emotional prejudice.

Morality is typically thought of as a developmental achievement, not something innate, hence it requires socialization and self-consciousness, which an infant does not have.

I do not distinguish between moral judgment and the intuitive capacity to discriminate between good and bad because in my view it is difficult to know where the border between them lies. In this book, I argue that the moral thought which uses principles of justice and morality, such as that applied by a judge in a juridical system based on democratic and liberal principles, also uses the fixed universal parameters that serve our intuitions. Such principles put a constraint on the computation result, but they do not change the computation process. Thus, in this sense, we are not talking about two separate systems as many mistakenly thought.

*

The book is in two parts. The first part, "Conceptual and empirical foundations," outlines the rationale of the new theory.

In Chapter 1, "Why we need a new psychology," I present a critique of moral psychology as it is practiced mostly by the followers of either Kant's or Hume's philosophies. Moral psychology has so far mainly tended to be dedicated to proving that the essence of morality is either "cognitive" or "emotional." But because both emotion and cognition should be considered equally central to moral psychology, any dichotomizing account will necessarily miss their content. In the final section of this chapter, I describe two theories in moral psychology that took the latter course without pitting cognition against emotion – universal moral grammar (UMG) (Hauser, 2006; Mikhail, 2007, 2012) and the theory of dyadic morality (Gray et al., 2012b; Schein & Gray, 2017).

In Chapter 2, "Morality and early interactions: main theories," I survey the modest body of thought, gleaned mostly from disciplines outside of moral psychology, according to which the origin of our moral capacities resides in the early interactions between infant and caregiver.

Chapter 3, "The moral skills of infants," cites extensive evidence according to which an infant possesses a minimal set of skills required for moral judgment already in the first 12 months of life. It describes the many works of research that relate to infants' ability to understand others' intentions, motivations and desires, to prefer people who resemble them, and to reach basic moral decisions. Such studies offer us an unparalleled opportunity of discovering humans' socio-moral anticipations at the very beginning of life.

The second part of the book, "The attachment approach to moral judgment," describes various aspects of the attachment approach to moral judgment.

Chapter 4, "The building blocks of moral judgment," discusses questions such as: What characteristics do different moral situations have in common? How do people recognize moral situations and identify regularities within them? What are these regularities? My assumption is that we deal with moral situations in the same way we deal with other objects or events. We categorize the situation as moral and then judge it according to which *pre-existing representation* it most closely resembles. I present the formula A → C as representing the building blocks of all moral situations.

Chapter 5, "Decoding moral situations," shows that we represent each of the parties in ways that are comparable to our fundamental representation of children (or infants) and adults. All our efforts are geared to construct the reality of the moral situation in terms of a child/adult dyad. We also evaluate the relationship between the adult-schema and child-schema parties in terms of their relations (→). We possess a schema for the dyadic relation, centered on our knowledge of adult obligations to children.

Chapter 6, "Variance and consistency in moral judgment," explores the fixed as well as the more variant foundations of moral judgment. The ability of supporters and opponents of abortion or of the death penalty to communicate and understand one another stems from the fact that the moral arguments used are subordinate to fixed and uniform parameters. Disagreements (i.e. different judgments) arise from the different weight that the two opposing sides assign to the fixed parameters. The chapter also provides a coherent account of how we construe moral justifications. It shows that any attempt to change a moral judgment through a rational argument must focus on the perception of the childlike and adultlike features. This holds true not just for concrete cases, but also for moral principles. Extensive feedback loops and robust top-down constraints operate in a way that any information about these features influence the entire gestalt.

Chapter 7, "The like-me criterion and turned-off dyads," describes the subjective nature of moral judgment. We encounter many moral failures around us, but they often leave us indifferent and lacking emotional involvement. The chapter describes the conditions in which the moral judgment is charged with a motivational/emotional component. Through people's attitudes to different animals (some fortunate to possess human characteristics) the like-me criterion is described as the decisive criterion in the process of reaching moral judgments. *Turned-off dyads* are construed when an observer recognizes the moral failure without difficulty and yet the suffering of the victim fails to arouse any emotional or motivational component in him or her.

Chapter 8, "The prototype of evil," implements the attachment approach of moral judgment, to the perception of evil. I suggest that the perception of evil consists of four salient features: extreme asymmetry between victim and perpetrator; a specific perceived attitude of the perpetrator towards the victim's vulnerability; the observer's inability to understand the perpetrator's perspective; and insuperable differences between the observer and perpetrator's judgment following the incident, which shake the observer no less than the event itself. I then show that the perception of evil involves a cognitive bias. The observer is almost always mistaken in his or her attributions of a certain state of mind to the perpetrator. The philosophical and evolutionary significance of this bias is discussed, as well as suggestions for future testing of the prototype model of evil.

The Epilogue suggests how the insights of the attachment approach to moral judgment might help us to enhance dialogue with people who support conflicting moral views.

The fact of my being a psychoanalyst has had an enormous influence on the writing of this book. In their daily work, analysts always put the dependency and vulnerability of the patient, together with the asymmetrical relations between them, at the center of their understanding and technique. Perhaps more than in any other discipline, psychoanalysis has taken a huge interest in the inner world of infants. In the attempt to understand people and human suffering, psychoanalysis attaches great importance to the fact that we all come into this world in an utterly helpless state and completely dependent on a caring parent.

The child/caregiver dyad is perhaps the most under-theorized domain in moral psychology. Though there is a vast body of literature showing the link between patterns of early attachment and moral behavior (Chugh et al., 2014; Mikulincer & Florian, 2000; Robinson et al., 2015), the subject of parenthood in infancy remains on the margins, exiled by moral psychology's long-standing cultural bias against it and ignorance of the subject's importance.

Researchers working in multiple disciplines have been a source of inspiration in the writing of this book (see Chapter 2): John Bowlby (psychoanalysis), Donald Winnicott (psychoanalysis), Carol Gilligan (feminist thought), Anton Dijker (social psychology), Darcia Narvaez (psychology) and Patricia Churchland (philosophy). These theorists were the first to reveal how psychic life in infancy paves the way to our moral capacities. While all these theories are well known and understood in their respective fields, very few of them have played a part in, or influenced, moral psychology.

In this book, I offer critiques of other thinkers in the field of moral psychology. Chapter 2 in particular makes me uneasy because there is always the possibility that I have not properly understood their ideas. In my defense, I can only say that I have done my best to offer a fair summary of a whole family of ideas that I found to be too restrictive.

This book aims to show how behind a vast variety of opinions, similar cognitive processes are at play. Always, moral judgment involves moral calculations, and these in their turn – no matter how complex the situation at hand – hark back to the same basic parameters experienced by each and every human being during the first year of life.

The attachment approach to moral judgment is an overarching theory that explains distinct domains of morality that seems unrelated. To expose the laws and working principles that appear consistently across organizational levels from the largest to the smallest, and to discover regularity behind phenomena that appear to be disparate and dissimilar, is the grand objective of science.

Of course, we must continue to honor the uniqueness of every field, since the formulation of principles at the simplest level is not always sufficient if we are to understand the more complex moral phenomena. I hope that researchers in the fields of psychoanalysis, moral psychology, moral philosophy, anthropology, neuroscience and sociology will continue to expand the meeting ground between cognition, emotion and attachment. Conceivably, this encounter will lead to change in each of the separate fields of research, will shed new light on them all, and broaden the domain in which their findings can be implemented in a way that goes beyond their original objectives.

Acknowledgments

I gratefully acknowledge the advice and assistance of Oren Harman, Mordechai Nisan, Golan Shahar and David Bar-Gal, who read sections of the book and offered their wise comments.

Kurt Gray, whose ideas have been inspiring in the writing of this book, invited me to write a chapter on moral psychology in a book he jointly edited with Jesse Graham titled *Atlas of Moral Psychology* (Govrin, 2018). That invitation encouraged and stimulated me to write this book. Prof. Ed Greenstein and Prof. Elda Weizmann from Bar-Ilan University have been friends and a tremendous source of support throughout.

Part of the thesis presented here was published by *Frontiers in Psychology* (Govrin, 2014a, 2014b, 2018), and I thank *Frontiers* reviewers and editor Prof. Rafael Malach from the Weizmann Institute of Science, Israel, Rina Lazar from the Sackler Faculty of Medicine, Tel Aviv University, Israel, and David Smith from Robert Gordon University, United Kingdom, for their helpful comments and suggestions.

This book would not have been published without the support and encouragement of Jon Mills, editor of the Routledge series. For me, Jon has been a source of inspiration, guiding me in making rich and fascinating links between psychoanalysis and other fields of study.

A special thank you to Mirjam Hadar, who helped me with the editing of the book, offering me her rich experience and wisdom. My thanks to Dan Gillon, my long-standing translator, who worked on the book with exceptional devotion, and Noga Galor-Ariel, my research assistant, who worked tirelessly and professionally in preparing the book for publication.

I want to thank Kate Hawes of Routledge, who provided a fast and generous response to every question. It is a great privilege for an author to work with a publisher who believes in the books they publish. My thanks also to Charles Bath of Routledge, who accompanied the text at every stage of production with great care and devotion.

My good friend Baruch Many showed great interest in my ideas and supported me in moments of crisis.

I thank my wife, Osnat, and my children, Or and Yonatan, who are the joy of my life. Over many years, I have had countless conversations with Osnat about the internal structure of moral situations, which clarified many aspects of my theory and helped me to improve it.

I owe my mother, Nurit Govrin, to whom this book is dedicated, a debt greater than I am able to describe here. Her unswerving support of my writing and the way in which she was always there for me enabled me to be creative and write.

I was able to discuss the ideas in this book with my beloved father, Shlomo Govrin, before his death. He was a source of inspiration, support and encouragement throughout my life, in addition to the many insights he offered me in my writing.

Part I

Conceptual and empirical foundations

Chapter 1

Why we need a new psychology

The last decade has witnessed significant progress in the field of moral psychology. Recent research in moral psychology has produced strong evidence to suggest that moral judgment is intuitive, and is accomplished by a rapid, automatic and unconscious psychological process (Damasio, 1994; Greene & Haidt, 2002; Hauser, 2006; Mikhail, 2000; Shweder & Haidt, 1994). This line of research challenged the long-dominant cognitive development paradigm conceived by Kohlberg (Kohlberg, 1969; Piaget, 1932/1965; Turiel, 1983, 2006), according to which moral judgment is the product of conscious, effortful reasoning.

Nonetheless, most theories in moral psychology remain general and undefined, leaving key questions unanswered.

There is, for example, considerable disagreement and confusion as to what moral intuitions are and how they work: What exactly are the underlying cognitive processes of these judgments that "operate quickly effortlessly and automatically, such that the outcome but not the process is accessible to consciousness?" (Haidt, 2001, p. 818). How are moral situations represented in our minds? What cognitive processes intuitively glue together different moral situations to one category?

Most theories did not usually concern themselves with these questions. It is my strongly held view that, with very few exceptions, up until recently all the parties currently engaged in debating the central issues in moral psychology are captive to the eighteenth-century controversy between rationalists and sentimentalists. Indeed, many theories of moral psychology expressly associate themselves with one of these two major moral philosophies.

Astonishingly, moral psychology is still overshadowed by a dispute that dominated this field of study 200 years ago.

Philosophical views about morality understandably affect those whose main occupation it is to develop a theory of moral psychology. Any theorist's explanation of morality is of necessity marked by his or her views about how morality works, and these views were mostly defined by the long tradition of moral philosophy.

Theories in the relatively new, almost fledgling field of moral psychology therefore unsurprisingly refer to key issues raised by philosophers.

One problem, however, that has been the outcome of the relative wealth and depth of the philosophical discourse on the subject compared to its psychological counterpart is that the problems of moral psychology have remained static over time, and so, of course, did the solutions.

In many ways, the main questions have not changed since the publication in 1751 of Hume's *An Enquiry Concerning the Principles of Morals* (1751/1998), in which he noted that: "There has been a controversy started of late much better worth examination, concerning the general foundation of morals; whether they be derived from reason, or from sentiment" (EPM 1, p. 3). This debate, according to Hume, questions whether we can "attain the knowledge of" moral distinctions "by a chain of argument and induction" or whether we must experience "an immediate feeling and finer internal sense" (EPM 1, p. 3).

Kant, by contrast, posited the universal nature of moral judgments. What one ought to do now, or what one thinks to be right or wrong now, is what one should always do, or consider right or wrong. Moral judgments are applicable beyond the specific case, in a way in which emotions are not. The specific judgments are a product of invariant moral principles. And these are derived by and from reason. Only humans are rational and can have principles, though some animals can have feelings and even express them.

Why have most philosophers and psychologists assumed that it is important and appropriate to stress the reason/emotion binary when addressing moral judgments? The answer is that this binary reflects a very profound trait of morality – its dual nature.

Moral judgments depend on cultural and social contexts. They vary over time and from one individual to another. They bear a direct connection to the emotions. Considered from this perspective, moral judgments may appear subjective, arbitrary and very similar to aesthetic judgments or even to our preferences in taste in matters of food. When we compare different cultures or different historical eras, we witness the enormous variability in terms of morality. This easily leads to the conclusion that there is no regularity or consistency in the domain of moral judgment.

We may, however, choose to describe moral judgments in an essentially different manner. For they don't *feel* at all the same as aesthetic judgments, say of a painting or of a certain dish. In the case of moral judgment, people are not merely affected by their feelings or by the common values of his or her social setting. Often people feel they are unequivocally right, and that their stance is non-negotiable. People believe they are acting on the strength of an objective principle, which holds over and beyond the particular case at hand, to any other situation or question of a similar kind.

No moral philosophy or psychology is complete without a thorough discussion of this duality. The dichotomy between reason and emotion is a reflection of this problem.

However, sticking to it left too many problems unanswered.

For example, throughout this chapter, I will show why premises of followers of each approach – such as "Moral judgments are strictly cognitive and uninfluenced by emotions" or "We cannot form moral judgments without moral emotions" – are inconsistent with empirical findings.

This line of questioning suggests that the two views, when taken in isolation, leave something out – just as rationalists left out emotion, so sentimentalists fail to include cognition.

As I will show, the dichotomous – and often antagonistic – view of emotion and cognition is under increasing challenge. Moral judgments cannot simply be slotted into compartments of the brain related to either cognition or emotion. In the process of reaching moral judgments, affect is neither independent of nor prior to cognition. In the making of an ethical judgment, it is likely that perception and cognition are directly and powerfully influenced by information with affective or motivational content.

The cognition versus emotion debate led most researchers to neglect the patterns and regularities of moral situations and to overlook such important issues as, for instance, how moral situations are represented in our minds and what kind of information the brain encodes and computes when making right/wrong judgments.

Following a brief survey of the controversy between those who support the primacy of cognition in decision-making and those who promote the centrality of emotions, I shall discuss a number of key theories in moral psychology representative of either side of this divide.

The present aim, then, is to illustrate that neither one of these approaches is sufficient, and to show why basing a moral psychology on the underlying binary offers us answers and results that are too restricted.

This chapter does not merely review the main theories in the field, but also shows how the model I propose responds to various theoretical lacunas in this area of study. The paradigm suggested in this book joins a modest tradition of theories that refuse to think of moral judgment as emerging from a binary split between emotion and cognition, and instead search for deep structures that apply specifically to morality.

In the last section of this chapter, I will describe two theories in moral psychology that took the latter course without pitting cognition against emotion – universal moral grammar (UMG) (Hauser, 2006; Mikhail, 2007, 2012) and the theory of dyadic morality (Gray et al., 2012b; Schein & Gray, 2017).

Emotion versus cognition

The emotion versus cognition controversy is at the heart of an old and sometimes passionate debate. It is a polemic that brings to mind the ancient argument as to whether emotion *precedes* and is *independent of* cognition, or whether all forms of emotional expression rely on, or are embedded in, prior processes of thought. In the history of Western thought, reason and affect were viewed as two deeply intertwined yet separate domains. They were thought to be in competition, at times verging on outright antagonism.

But new findings on the cognitive unconscious that takes part in almost every cognitive process, including those at work in complex decision-making, have subverted the common distinction between emotion and cognition. An early version of such a theory is to be found in Leventhal and Scherer (1987). In their view, affective responses, on the one hand, and involuntary, instinctive, non-conscious responses, on the other, should not be differentiated. Leventhal and Scherer regard emotion as the product of an amalgam of components. They argue that the link between emotion and cognition needs to be seen within a theoretical framework that includes a multiplicity of processing components, and which views affect as the product of a combination of these elements. They believe that we no longer need to preoccupy ourselves with defining emotion and cognition separately. Instead of asking "What is emotion?" and "What is cognition?" we need to identify the part played by certain specific processing components involved in a particular emotional experience.

This early model demonstrates that the split occurs, rather than between emotion and cognition, between emotions *in conjunction* with automatic, non-conscious, pre-reflective processes, on the one hand, and cognitions that stem from controlled processes, on the other.

Research in cognitive science over the past 20 years or so has led to a new view of the unconscious as being capable of functioning in areas previously considered the exclusive domain of conscious thought. These areas include such functions as complex information processing, behavioral patterns, the pursuit of objectives and self-regulation. In his groundbreaking paper "The Cognitive Unconscious" (1987), John Kihlstrom described how early models of human cognition based on the modern high-speed computer had viewed the unconscious as a reservoir of pre-attentive perceptions and dormant traces of memory. According to Kihlstrom, these models erred in assuming that complex mental processes required conscious awareness. Unlike the psychoanalytic unconscious, the cognitive unconscious includes no inherent drives seeking satisfaction. According to Kihlstrom, when compared to the intensity and illogicality of psychoanalytic drives and conflicts, the cognitive unconscious is somewhat unimpassioned, seemingly rational and lacking motivation. Kihlstrom (1987) thought that "conscious awareness . . . is not necessary for complex psychological functioning" (p. 1450). His model of the cognitive unconscious is mostly concerned with affect, motivation, and even control and metacognition. The cognitive unconscious includes the causal nature of phenomenal experience, of intentionality and free will, and the attribution of these qualities to others as well. As Uleman (2005) put it, "the list of psychological processes carried out in the new unconscious is so extensive that it raises two questions: What, if anything cannot be done without awareness? What is consciousness for?" (p. 6).

The interaction between affect and cognition

The question, then, is about the nature of the interaction in the mind between automatic, rapid, unconscious processes, and slower controlled cognitive processes. Are they antagonistic? Pulling in different directions? Or do they, in fact, complement one another?

This dichotomized view of the brain is currently under challenge by an approach that places the emphasis on the deep integration between regions of the brain, and suggests a holistic model in which none of the brain's regions is categorized as uniquely cognitive or affective (Feldman Barrett et al., 2007; Ochsner & Gross, 2005; Pessoa, 2008).

Recent research such as Goldberg et al. (2014) takes what has been termed a "constructionist" approach, with the central idea that knowledge and meaning are "constructed" from experience. The theory posits that numerous functional networks across the brain are reciprocally activated, giving rise to a gamut of emotional states (Barrett & Bar, 2009; Lindquist et al., 2012). The suggestion that there is a connection between a broad range of cortical functions and emotion is not new. This link is reflected in theories that contend that when emotionally processing an event, an individual's responses are akin to "preparation for action." Indeed, the word "motivation" derives from the Latin *emovere* (literally: to move out). The theory links emotional processing to "action preparation." The claim has been supported by a number of behavioral and physiological studies (Cacioppo et al., 1986; Davidson et al., 2000; Frijda, 1986; Lang et al., 1990; Lang et al., 1997).

Emotional processing therefore does not only involve isolated and separate emotions, but consists of a kind of plan of action – a plan in which both emotions and cognition feature. Luiz Pessoa (2013, 2015) is one of the most prominent advocates of the approach, asserting that cognitive and emotional processes are not separate and dichotomous.

The core argument of his book *The Cognitive-Emotional Brain* (2013) is that cognition and emotion are integrated and highly interdependent. In Pessoa's view, the classical model of a dichotomized brain has been unhelpful to neuro-scientific research. According to Pessoa, a new way of thinking is needed that, instead of dichotomizing brain functions, views them as complementary, each defining the other, and most importantly as not mutually exclusive. Understanding it as a network implies that the mind-brain is not an organ whose functioning can be split between emotion (or motivation) and cognition. Which is to say that emotion and cognition should be viewed as neurally controlled less by properties inherent to particular regions of the brain and more by communications between and among numerous areas within it. From this perspective, affect and cognition are operationally integrated systems that constantly impact on one another.

For example, Pessoa challenges the neuro-scientific literature that attributes a central role to the amygdala as a pivotal node in processing emotion, partly because of the "low-level" properties ascribed to the subcortical pathway. Based on empirical evidence covering humans as well as rodents, Pessoa argues that the amygdala's functions far exceed the domain of emotion. One of its central functions, he believes, is in information selection. If behavior is driven by affect, the selection of information for further thought is a major task (Grossberg & Levine, 1987). The amygdala has a crucial role in processing the question "What is this?" and therefore is instrumental in determining what is important to the observer (Pribram & McGuinness, 1975).

According to Pessoa, the amygdala also participates in resolving the issue of "What is to be done about this?" Important to Pessoa's view is the contention that the amygdala is also involved in the expression of both positive and negative valences, as well as in making decisions. Whalen (1998) posits that "information gathering" would be a better term to describe the amygdala's various functions. He believes it is probably best to avoid looking for too tight a definition of the functions of this complex region, and simply accept that the amygdala has a highly significant impact on the brain's mechanisms and behavior.

Another example is the medial prefrontal cortex (PFC). This brain region has been traditionally implicated in planning complex cognitive behavior. However, more and more studies show that the compartmentalization of the medial prefrontal cortex (PFC) is an unsupportable model, and that we must instead regard the PFC as a region shared by cognitive and emotional domains. This view allows the PFC a mediating role that supports the adaptive control of complex behaviors (Pessoa, 2008; Shackman et al., 2011).

By way of an alternative, Pessoa suggests that we view the interaction between emotion and cognition, rather than in terms of push and pull, as a reciprocal relationship resulting in processes and signals that are neither wholly cognitive nor entirely emotional.

In short, those regions of the brain that have always been viewed as hubs of emotional processing would seem to be profoundly and extensively "connected" to regions traditionally associated with cognitive processing, suggesting that at times they have significant "near global" roles, and that this may be a pivotal feature of their group.

Moral psychology and moral judgment

Various theories in moral psychology, stretching back to the end of the 1950s and up until most recent work, have participated in the debate over the nature of moral judgment. Most of them assume the existence of two dichotomies, namely between cognition and emotion and between rapid automatic and controlled conscious processes of thought.

The domain of moral judgment "invites" such dichotomization more than do other fields of studies. The complex moral situations we encounter actually involve several levels of thinking, and their often conflicting tendencies create discord in the mind of the observer. For example, it is easy to think that the judgment "it is wrong to physically injure a rapist when caught" is a conflict between emotion ("hurt the bastard") and cognition ("even rapists have rights, they should be put to trial and people are not allowed to hurt them"). It seems that where we are confronted with complexity, we are tempted to reach easy binary solutions to disentangle the apparent knots. As I will show, each judgment involves a level of integration between cognition and emotion.

The mental function that accompanies moral judgment is fueled by emotional, cognitive, conscious and unconscious factors simultaneously.

How the emotion/cognition debate has haunted moral psychology

Piaget and Kohlberg

Moral psychology has its origins in the writings of Piaget and Kohlberg. Their theories emphasized the centrality to moral judgment of conscious rational processes and the ability to provide reasoned justification for decisions taken.

They viewed cognitive development as the essential precursor of moral development. Neither Piaget nor Kohlberg considered emotion to be central to moral judgment.

Because moral judgment depends on a high level of cognition, children under the age of 9, in the view of these theorists, are unable to make complex moral judgments.

Piaget's concept of "structural parallelism" (1954) included the idea that progress in the ability to make moral judgment was an indication of an altered cognitive state, and similarly that the increasing sophistication of an individual's moral judgment was the product of progress in his or her cognitive development. Having observed that children often exhibited different proportions of both compliance and cooperation, Piaget (1932/1965) reached the conclusion that moral orientation evolved through phases that, "broadly speaking, follow one another without, however, constituting definite stages" (p. 195). He suggested that small children's morality took the shape of obedience to their elders because of the egocentric and concrete nature of their perspective and because their social world is dominated by a variety of seemingly all-powerful and ever-present adults. Older children tend to link morality to cooperation among equals. They have acquired the cognitive ability to understand the viewpoint of the other, and understand such abstract and complex concepts as reciprocation (cf. Carpendale, 2000; Youniss & Damon, 1992).

In Piaget's view, children in the first few years of life, when making a moral judgment, are unable to attribute intentionality to an individual's harmful action. Rather, their judgments are entirely based on the extent of harm resulting from the incident. Piaget argued that once they understood intentionality as part of a moral judgment, at what he called the post-operationalist stage, children should be able to develop an intention-based morality.

The next turning point in theorizing about moral judgment was the work of Lawrence Kohlberg (1969, 1981; for recent studies, see Kurtines & Gewirtz, 1984; Rest, 1984). Kohlberg was influenced by Piaget's developmental theory as well as by Kant's moral philosophy. Kohlberg expanded on Piaget's theory by suggesting that stages in moral development follow a stepwise invariant order of six irreversible stages, structurally defined and content-free.

Kohlberg's method of evaluating an individual's moral development was to interview his subjects on a series of dilemmas. Subsequently, he examined the justification participants offered for decisions taken in a number of highly complex moral situations that they were presented. Among the more famous dilemma posed by Kohlberg is the Heinz dilemma: Should Heinz steal medication he cannot afford to buy in order to save his very ill wife? Because Kohlberg and his followers analyzed the justification rather than the decision itself, they appeared to believe that moral decisions are tantamount with their justifications.

Based on his findings, Kohlberg (1969, 1981) developed a stage theory of moral thinking that goes well beyond Piaget's initial formulations.

Unvaryingly, Kohlberg, like Plato, supported a rationalist model that allows for emotion to be taken into account by cognitive reasoning. However, in the final analysis it is reason, and not affect, that is responsible for moral judgment:

> We are claiming . . . that the moral force in personality is cognitive. Affective forces are involved in moral decisions, but affect is neither moral nor immoral. When the affective arousal is channeled into moral directions, it is moral; when it is not so channeled, it is not. The moral channeling mechanisms themselves are cognitive.
>
> (Kohlberg, 1971, pp. 230–231)

Gibbs (1995) described this very well when he argued that for Kohlberg:

> The construction of moral meaning . . . generates motivating feelings such as logical necessity or sentiments of justice – but such affect is secondary in the sense that it owes its motivational properties and indeed its existence to constructive processes.
>
> (p. 42)

Kohlberg's theory of moral development is rooted in three key assumptions: (a) the most important element enabling moral development is the level of sophistication of moral judgment reached (Colby & Kohlberg, 1987, pp. 1–2); (b) moral judgment is formulated in "structures of the whole" (Colby & Kohlberg, 1987, p. 8), that is, the stages are not just isolated responses, but are *general* patterns of thought that will consistently show up across many different kinds of issues; and (c) the novel moral structures children form in the course of development entirely alter and replace earlier formed structures (Colby & Kohlberg, 1987, p. 7). Kohlberg found that participants scored at their prevailing stage across nine dilemmas about two-thirds of the time. This appears to be a fair amount of consistency, suggesting that his stages may reflect general patterns of thought.

Kohlberg, like Piaget, dwelled more on moral judgment than on moral behavior. His finding that as people mature they acquire new forms of moral reasoning that "transform and displace" earlier structures (Colby & Kohlberg, 1987, pp. 6–7) led Kohlberg to the conclusion that all humans go through stages of moral development in exactly the same way. Later structures, he argued, were more cognitively complex, integrated, reasoned, and well ordered than the structures they replaced. Judgments made when the capacity to see things in perspective has expanded reflect a greater determination to achieve universality, logical validity and impartiality (Krebs & Denton, 2005).

Haidt (2000) discusses the advantages and disadvantages of the cognitive orientation for the study of moral judgment. On the plus side is cognitive approaches' deep interest in the structure and mechanism of moral reasoning and the connections between moral and other cognitions. On the minus side, Haidt mentions the fact that such studies have neglected the link between moral behavior and moral judgment, and/or any inquiry into the social context in which the process of moral judgment occurs.

Two important findings linked to moral judgment support a strong objection to Kohlberg's theory. Research has shown that people are often unable to verbalize their reasons for some of their most strongly held moral views (Haidt et al., 2000; Cushman et al., 2006; Hauser et al., 2007; Mikhail, 2000). These findings led a number of researchers to the conclusion that, contrary to Kohlberg's cognitively based theory of moral judgment, such moral views in fact evolved intuitively via psychological processes that are rapid, automatic and unconscious (Haidt, 2001; Hauser, 2006; Mikhail, 2000; Shweder & Haidt, 1993; see also Damasio, 1994, pp. 165–201).

This questioning of Kohlberg's theory is joined by the claim that moral judgment is mainly a function of emotional responses to a given situation (Blair, 1995; Damasio, 1994; Greene & Haidt, 2002; Shweder & Haidt, 1993). This view, too, challenges the cognitivist position that in any given case, moral judgment must be based on the reasoned application of clear moral principles. The empirical evidence for the prominent role of affect in the process of reaching moral judgments comes from research carried out in the rapidly expanding field of neuroscience (Borg et al., 2006; Ciaramelli et al., 2007; Damasio, 1994; Greene et al., 2001, 2004; Koenigs et al., 2007; Mendez et al., 2005).

What led Kohlberg to attach such importance to rational, conscious and logical thought processes at the expense of intuition and emotions?

In the same way as today's moral psychology can be seen to hark back to David Hume's philosophy, Kohlberg, for his part, adopted a Kantian orientation. This was his intellectual framework, and it was supported by the trend of mainstream cognitive psychology of his time, according to which cognition is primary and independent of emotion.

Take, for example, the centrality Kohlberg attached to the reasoning behind moral judgment and his lack of interest in the moral judgment itself. Most of the participants choose the right answer, that Heinz was right to steal the medicine for his dying wife. However, the participants in the Heinz dilemma were not awarded points for merely reaching the right decision. Those points were only given if the participant reached the judgment in the way prescribed by Kohlberg. As the participants distanced themselves from the personal view and focused on the general rules of morality, their score went up, as did their ranking in terms of "moral development." This approach is typical of Kantian thinking, with its focus on the supreme principle of morality. The act is less important than its source and motivation.

Kant (1785/1959) argued that rationality and universality are the two key concepts yielding the categorical imperative in its different formulations. For a line of reasoning to be considered rational, it must in the first place be impersonal. Kohlberg adopted this view.

There can be no doubt that Kohlberg had an idealistic view of morality and justice. He truly believed well-honed thinking skills can yield a moral insight and that this can be achieved by every child. Universal justice from a Kohlbergian standpoint is thus a matter of the correct kind of cognitive development. In his view, anyone who understands rational moral principles will know how to act in line with them.

In his article "The Child as a Moral Philosopher," Kohlberg noted that:

> In the higher post conventional levels, Socrates, Lincoln, Thoreau and Martin Luther King tend to speak without confusion of tongues, as it were. This is because the ideal principles of any social structure are basically alike, if only because there simply aren't that many principles which are articulate, comprehensive and integrated enough to be satisfying to the human intellect. And most of these principles have gone by the name of justice . . . The man who understands justice is more likely to practice it . . . In our studies, we have found that youths who understand justice act more justly, and the man who understands justice helps create a moral climate which goes far beyond his immediate and personal acts. The universal society is the beneficiary.
>
> (Kohlberg, 1968, p. 30)

In contrary to this approach, one can think that even if we should try to base our judgments on universal moral principles, we cannot avoid our subjective selves.

It is one thing to say that we should try our best not to allow our subjective viewpoint to determine our moral judgments. It is quite another matter to suggest that a mature moral judgment has to be devoid of any subjectivity. Though important and possibly indispensable, the ideal of objectivity and independence from personal and subjective preference is almost impossible to achieve. Furthermore, a purely rational principle will not motivate us to act. It would leave us cold and detached. And if we could be emotionally apathetic to morality, we might fail to act morally (Prinz, 2007). The claim that mature moral judgment can be objective, rational and affectless is simply false, and might lead to a sterile and useless view of morality. As we will see in some detail later on, moral judgments, even if they stem from a universally accepted principle, include irreducibly subjective components.

Post-Kohlbergian approaches took moral psychology in the very opposite direction. Many researchers in the field argue that moral judgments are entirely a function of emotion and emotional intuition, and that cognition plays a minimal role in moral judgment. Alternatively, it is argued that emotion and cognition "push and pull" in opposing directions. Let us review some of these models.

The social intuitionist model

The fundamental claim of Jonathan Haidt's (2001) social intuitionist model is that moral judgments are the outcome of rapid moral intuitions. Thus, moral judgments become assessments of the good/bad aspects of an individual's actions or character, regarded by a culture or social group as binding. Haidt's claim is that the reasoned justification for the judgment only follows subsequently if it is somehow required. In his view, moral intuition can be defined as "the sudden appearance in consciousness of a moral judgment which includes a determination of right/wrong/good/bad/like/dislike judgments that have been reached in the absence of any conscious awareness" (Haidt, 2001, p. 821). If so, moral intuition could be said to be akin to the psychological process discussed in the eighteenth century by Thomas Reid and the Scottish School of Common Sense. This process somewhat resembles aesthetic judgment, where perception of an object triggers a spontaneous sense of "like" or "dislike."

Haidt's model concedes that there are those rare occasions when people do change their initial judgment. Most often, this occurs when the immediate intuition is felt to have been weak. In such cases, reasoning obviously plays a role in the formation of a judgment. However, in other instances, where, for some reason, the cognitively reached judgment conflicts with a strongly held intuitive conclusion, the individual's attitude will be split (Wilson et al., 2000). Publicly, he or she will express the reasoned judgment while privately continuing to hold firmly onto the intuitively reached conclusion.

According to Haidt (2010), the expression of one's moral reasoning is motivated by a need to publicly justify an already privately settled moral judgment. Generally speaking, moral debates are famous for rarely succeeding to persuade others – though there are, of course, exceptions. Because a person's adopted moral stance invariably includes an element of emotion, the theory suggests that reasoned explanations succeed not as a result of the logical argument presented, but rather by activating a new emotionally valenced intuition in listeners (Edwards & Von Hippel 1995).

According to Haidt (2001), the moral stance of the vast majority of people is inextricably linked to group norms. Consequently, according to this model, it is sufficient for friends, allies and even mere acquaintances to have reached a moral conclusion in order for other group members to follow their example without reference to a reasoned argument. Though in some instances responsiveness to the group norm may be only for the sake of appearances (Asch, 1956), there is evidence to suggest that people's privately held judgments, too, are molded by the judgments of others (Berger & Luckman, 1967; Newcomb, 1943; Sherif, 1935).

Haidt (2010) was challenged by Mallon and Nichols (2010). They claim that consciously controlled processes are to a large extent in charge of intuitions and emotions. To support this, they cite a voluminous literature relating to unconscious implicit racial attitudes. A person can, in indirect tests such as the implicit association test (IAT), display racial prejudices even though their reasoned account may not show a trace of racial bias. In the most common task in this experiment, participants are presented with black and white faces paired with either a positive or negatively valenced phrase. Typically, white participants in such tests find it easier to perform the task when the positively valenced words are paired with white faces and the negative wording is linked to the black faces. This is the case even when, in a questionnaire written ahead of the test, participants seem to be racially unprejudiced. According to Mallon and Nichols (2010):

[The] literature seems to show that that conscious controlled processes exert substantial control over explicit verbal responses and behavior, and that as these processes become overtaxed or exhausted (by increasing cognitive load or by so-called ego depletion) verbal responses come to align more and more closely with implicit attitudes.

(p. 301)

Research undertaken by Richeson and Shelton (2003), for example, shows that when consciously controlled processes are overloaded and weakened by increasing pressure on the cognitive domain, verbal explanations and behavior increasingly reflect implicit attitudes. Thus, white subjects exhibiting anti-black/pro-white prejudice in an IAT test and then interacting with an African American confederate performed less well in assignments calling for effort and attention such as a Stroop task (Richeson & Shelton, 2003). According to Mallon and Nichols (2010), interacting with the African American confederate made a claim on further controlled resources (to suppress automatic anti-black responses), which in turn depleted a resource that would be needed on subsequent tasks. Mallon and Nichols (2010) argue that these results demonstrate that intuitions "do not run the show, only to be served by ex post facto reasoning" (p. 302).

The experiments just cited provide us with significant empirical evidence that in the real world, racial prejudice is held at bay by controlled processes. As far as Mallon and Nichols are concerned, this casts serious doubt on Haidt's model of moral judgment.

Moral sentimentalism

The two most prominent contemporary advocates of moral sentimentalism are the philosophers Jesse Prinz (2007) and Shaun Nichols (2004). For Prinz and Nichols, our emotions and desires play a prominent role in constituting moral judgments. In their view, the study of morality as such (meta-ethics) is best served by moral sentimentalism as it is more aligned to the known empirical facts about moral psychology than are other rival theories. Citing recent results of experiments in the field of moral psychology, they argue that emotions play a central psychological role in shaping our moral ideals. Their version of sentimentalism is in fact part of a broader movement in philosophy that seeks to bring the ethical domain more into line with empirically observed facts about the natural world.

Nichols' (2004) "sentimental rules theory" contends that moral judgments are made up of two components: a normative theory and an affective system. While the normative theory generates rules and regulations, the affective system changes their disposition, and reinforces and motivates them. In Nichols' view, moral judgments can be reached through either emotion or cognition, and typically include an element of both. Normative theories deal with what is moral and what is immoral. They guide us of what should and shouldn't be done. Such rules have no emotional content. According to Nichols, the rules only gain an emotional dimension when linked to the affective response system. Nichols' sentimental rules theory suggests the existence of a non-emotional set of rules and regulations that operates together with an emotional inclination to feel concern, especially when the norm is violated.

According to Prinz's (2007) emotional constitutional model, emotions are an indispensable part of moral judgment because they underlie concepts such as "good" and "bad." Here, his view echoes Hume: "We do not infer a character to be virtuous, because it pleases: But in feeling that it pleases after such a particular manner, we in effect feel it virtuous" (Hume, 1739/2000, III:I:II). He argues that representations of such emotional concepts as "moral" and "immoral" contain an element of emotion in much the same way as "funny" may be thought to be amusing. In practice, Prinz argues, a joke is judged to be funny if the listener is amused, just as an onlooker would judge an act immoral if he or she is infuriated. He concedes that our emotional attitudes are often accompanied by affect-free propositional representations. Prinz maintains that when we judge that something is wrong, we tend to verbally express that judgment out loud or in inner speech. For example, when we see a pickpocket, we may think to ourselves, "That is wrong." Prinz admits that such verbalized thoughts can occur in the absence of emotions. But he insists that these verbalizations get their meaning from underlying emotional states. Verbalized moral judgments simultaneously express how we feel and how we represent things. When we say "That is wrong," we convey our feelings and also aim to assert a fact. "Pickpocketing is wrong" represents the fact that such an act has the property of "wrongness." Moral wrongness is first and foremost the property of being the object of condemnation. According to Prinz, this is tantamount to saying that wrongness is a secondary quality.

Haidt and Nichols have their differences with Prinz's view. Both Haidt and Nichols believe that moral judgments can be formed without the participation of emotion. They see a much looser, more casual connection between moral judgment and emotion than does Prinz. Rather than being intrinsic to moral judgment, emotions, for them, merely back up such judgments. In contrast, Prinz argues that emotions, constituting token instances of concepts such as right and wrong, *are* a component of moral judgment. Prinz and Nichols support Hume's sentimentalist model precisely as Kohlberg was committed to Kant's moral imperative. In both cases, a powerful philosophical commitment dictates these authors' divergent perceptions of moral psychology.

Dual-process theory of moral judgment

A more balanced approach to moral judgment has been offered by Joshua Greene and his colleagues (Greene, 2005; Greene et al., 2001). The dual-process theory of moral judgment is a notable example of an approach, based on data derived from neuroimaging, in which emotions and cognition function as separate, and occasionally antagonistic, systems (Greene 2007; Greene et al., 2001, 2004).

Greene attempted to attenuate the sharpness of this division. He proposed that deontological judgments are elicited from a region of the brain associated with affective responses, whereas utilitarian judgments are triggered in regions of the brain related to cognitive control. At times, the affective bias of deontological judgments may divert the observer from carefully considering important aspects of a given moral situation. However, in certain circumstances, the observer may be able to overcome such instinctive responses by viewing the situation in more rational and functional terms. What we see, then, is a dual process in which deontology and utilitarianism come to a clash – a mirror image of the conflict between emotion and cognition. According to Greene et al. (2008), the deontological/utilitarian conflict should be viewed as a mutually suppressive relationship. Greene describes the broad characteristics of two distinctive processes that mold moral judgment. One is marked by a carefully considered arduous process that draws on a set of abstract principles and applies those principles to specific real-life moral situations; the second is characterized by a fast process of moral judgment that produces emotional responses to a given moral situation based on mental processes that are inaccessible to conscious thought.

Moral dilemmas in which participants are faced with a conflict between the general principle of avoiding direct harm, and a utilitarian plan that involves relatively moderate harm in order to prevent greater injury, form the basis of Greene's theory.

One of the most popular dilemmas in contemporary moral psychology involves a runaway trolley that, if not stopped or diverted, may kill five people. The question is whether it is morally acceptable to redirect the trolley away from the path of the five people, and in doing so risk only one person being killed. A majority of people responding to a large-scale poll conducted through the Internet stated that such an action was morally permissible (Hauser et al., 2007). A very different result was obtained in an altered version of the dilemma in which a fat man is standing on a footbridge overlooking the tracks between the approaching trolley and the five people in its path. The five can only be saved by pushing the fat person off the footbridge onto the track, killing him but saving the other five. The majority of those polled concluded that to do so was morally unacceptable. It would seem that most people are prone to judge the first case on the basis of its consequences, and accept that sacrificing one life in order to save the lives of five others is acceptable. In the second case, the judgment was typically deontological in the sense that the participants concluded that causing harm in any set of circumstances is wrong, irrespective of the consequences.

Together with others, Greene attempted to identify the roles played by emotion and controlled cognition in people's responses to such moral predicaments (Greene, 2007; Greene et al., 2001, 2004). Greene and his colleagues suggested that the idea of actively harming a specific individual, as in the case of the footbridge, elicits a negative emotional response, leading people to regard such an action as wrong and morally repugnant. In Greene's theory, this affective response nullifies consideration of any possible positive outcome, such as saving five lives in exchange for the life of just one person. Redirecting the approaching train, on the other hand, lacks the personal dimension, and was therefore thought to be morally permissible, and this made it possible for the majority of respondents to focus on the consequential moral reasoning about the act – the saving of five lives. It may thus be concluded that the divergent judgments reached in the two cases may not reflect inconsistencies in one psychological system, but instead a conflict between two contrasting systems.

In empirical tests of this conceptualization, Greene at al. (2001, 2004) surveyed participants' patterns of neural activity as they responded to personalized and non-personalized moral predicaments. The findings showed an increase in such activity when the harm was personal. The brain regions examined included a region of the medial prefrontal cortex. By contrast, Greene et al. found that areas of the brain traditionally linked to controlled cognitive processes, such as working memory and abstract reasoning, showed an increase in activity when people were responding to "impersonal" moral dilemmas, such as pulling the lever to divert the trolley onto the side track, where it would kill one person.

A critique of sentimentalism

This comprehensive survey confirms that numerous theories in moral psychology from Kohlberg to Haidt deal with the question of morality by reference to only one axis, namely cognition versus emotion. In doing so, the tradition assumes, falsely in my view, that the study of moral psychology is forced to choose between cognition and emotion.

I would like to argue that it is more plausible that body, emotion, conscious reasoning and unconscious mental operations form one continuous mutually informing field of moral judgment. Since all these components interlock, we should perceive moral judgment as a whole system. In this sense, most moral psychologies erred when they assumed these components are isolated and bounded.

The conflicted moral judgment implied by many moral situations does not arise from mutually incompatible emotional and cognitive processes. Rather, as I will show, it reflects the stream of conflicting and inconsistent information about the *moral situation itself*.

In this sense, cognition is no different from emotion. If you hear that somebody has been murdered, you may be outraged. But if you then hear that the killer acted in self-defense and that the victim threatened him first, you may calm down. This shows how emotion was influenced by cognition. When cognition changes, the anger may fade. Emotions are hugely affected by cognitions, and cognitions are no less influenced by emotions.

That there is convincing empirical evidence confirming the central role of intuitions and emotions in moral judgment does not mean that conscious rational thought is of no significance. Having dwelled on the role of the emotions in moral judgment, let us now examine the empirical evidence that points to the importance of reasoning.

Recent studies have shown that though people cannot offer principle-based justifications for some of their own moral judgments, they are quite able to do so for others (Cushman et al., 2006). Moreover, some initially intuitive moral judgments change when the people who made them are asked to provide a reasoned argument (Pizarro et al., 2003). Other studies, using brain imaging (Greene et al., 2004) and reaction time data, show that reasoning processes are indeed involved in moral judgment.

Sentimentalist theories claim that emotions establish moral judgments. But we know that moral judgments, moral conceptualizations and thoughts about moral situations can arise in the absence of any emotions.

Let us examine the statement that Prinz (2007) offers as an example: "Stealing is wrong" (p. 17). Prinz posits that the judgment that certain acts, such as theft, are wrong is stored in one's long-term memory. Our feelings about theft constitute a rule: thou shalt not steal. When the notion of stealing enters the observer's mind, it activates those feelings. This is merely an initial stage, argues Prinz, the retrieval of a long-stored rule. In this primary phase, the feelings are not yet experienced as an emotion.

There can be no doubt that the sentence "Stealing is wrong" expresses a moral judgment. But does it really involve emotions? To argue that it does would be difficult because there is no reference in the sentence to either a victim or an aggressor; nor, for that matter, does it involve a human story that could engage our emotions. The sentence that stealing is a prohibited act is a determination devoid of emotion. To have feelings, we need to identify with the suffering of a living creature. However, many moral judgments are general, abstract and contain no images of the incidents and/ or the interpersonal relations that they may have involved.

Another case in point is that we can also "block" our emotions if, instead of using descriptions of real people, we denote them as X or Y: X was harmed by Y. Even in these cases, we can make moral judgment easily and effortlessly.

How does Prinz explain this? In his view, stealing is something about which the observer has a moral sentiment in his or her long-term memory. His or her sentiment towards stealing constitutes a rule. When the idea of stealing enters his mind or her, the rule activates the sentiment (Prinz, 2007, p. 97). This, Prinz argues, is a rule retrieval stage, at which point the sentiment has not yet been experienced as an emotion. Thus, a person can understand that his or her sentiment vis-à-vis, say murder, is negative, without at the same time experiencing a negative emotion. This, however, raises the question of whether a negative sentiment without emotion shouldn't in fact be termed a cognition.

Prinz's distinction then between sentiment and emotion is not clear: In what situations are we to use the notion of "sentiment," and when is the word "emotion" the appropriate term? If it is possible to experience a sentiment without having the feeling that accompanies it, why is it not possible to make a moral judgment without feeling anything?

This line of questioning suggests that sentimentalists are leaving something out. Just as Kohlberg left out emotion, so sentimentalists fail to include cognition. Moreover, though in many moral situations the judgment that has to be reached is clear, the emotions aroused are not.

For example, in 2006, a serial rapist escaped from an Israeli jail. People all over the country panicked and women stayed indoors after dark. In the end, the rapist was caught in the backyard of a house, weak and hungry. The arresting police officers beat him and filmed themselves as they surrounded the injured rapist much like the US soldiers in Iraq's Abu Ghraib abuse photos. In this situation, as is the case in many complex incidents of this type, people may reach a clear moral judgment: police officers must not beat a helpless person. At the same time, observers' feelings may not be cut and dried. Many felt a sense of satisfaction that such a cruel rapist was beaten and punished. That said, a person can reach a moral conclusion that runs counter to his or her feelings. For example, having witnessed the event, one may say:

> When I read that the policemen had beaten the heartless rapist, I felt sort of pleased, even though morally speaking I felt bad about what happened. Morally, I know that police officers should not become involved in unnecessary acts of violence.

The moral judgment here, as is often the case, is reached with mixed feelings.

Complex moral situations such as this involve a great deal of ambivalence. Most serious moral dilemmas resemble the case of the beaten-up rapist rather than that of diverting the oncoming trolley. The popularity of the trolley dilemma among psychologists and philosophers is in reverse proportion to its occurrence in daily life. Most moral dilemmas do not merely involve conflict between emotion and utilitarian considerations. Instead, they evoke conflict of the following kind: the aggressor is also a victim; the victim is also an aggressor. This messy situation leads to confusion and ambivalence. A good moral psychology should reflect the complexity and specificity of the moral dilemmas we encounter in everyday life. However, most sentimentalists' accounts say very little of such dilemmas.

Psychopathy

Researchers who argue that emotions trigger moral judgments time and time again investigate a mental disorder known as psychopathy. People suffering from an antisocial personality disorder (ASPD) are characterized by a combination of glib and superficial charm, pathological lying, manipulativeness, lack of remorse or guilt, impulsivity, and lack of responsibility (Hare, 1991). The disorder is likely to lead to breaches of the law, getting into trouble, yet without showing any feelings or regrets. ASPD sufferers are likely to lie and behave violently. Psychopaths are people who seem cognitively intact. The patient may be suffering from a deficit in moral motivation accompanied by a deficit in moral competence, but he or she is capable of making moral judgments. For sentimentalists, this suggests the primacy of emotion: they maintain that the deficit in moral comprehension is a direct result of an emotional deficit.

Most of the arguments advanced by sentimentalists in relation to this disorder are based on the work of R. J. R. Blair. Blair compared psychopathic and non-psychopathic subjects' ways of dealing with moral versus so-called "conventional" tasks. In the psychological literature, the capacity for moral judgment has perhaps been most directly approached empirically by exploring an individual's basic ability to distinguish between moral violations (such as hitting another person) and conventional transgressions (such as chewing gum in class). Blair found that subjects with psychopathy were significantly less likely than others to treat moral violations as distinctive (Blair, 1995, 1997; Blair et al., 1995). For example, children with psychopathic tendencies were more likely to judge moral violations as authority-dependent; in other words, individuals suffering from psychopathy treat moral rules as if they were about conventions. In a psychopathic view, conventional and moral transgressions are permissible, as long as accepted authority does not oppose such violations. As far as sentimentalists are concerned, this demonstrates that in psychopathy, moral and conventional wrongs are perceived to be in the same category.

In the sentimentalists' view, the fact that psychopaths fail to master the moral/conventional divide suggests that there is no way of making the distinction without experiencing emotional responses. In addition, these subjects seem able to comprehend social and moral rules, and they typically do not appear to have impaired reasoning abilities. Damage to the limbic system, which is responsible, among other things, for emotion and behavior, is correlated with psychopathy. This is consistent with the fact that psychopaths show diminished affective response to cues of others' suffering. Such damage does not imply any particular cognitive impairment (Kiehl, 2006).

However, not everyone agrees with the sentimentalists about impaired moral capacity in psychopathy. According to Blair (1995), children with psychopathic tendencies did not make significantly fewer references to the welfare of victims than did children without psychopathy. Moreover, there were no significant differences between the groups in their understanding of what was and what was not permissible, or of the gravity of certain judgments.

Recent experiments (e.g. Cima et al., 2010; Koenigs et al., 2012) found that APSD subjects, like other people, when presented with personal moral dilemmas (such as the trolley dilemma) also regard killing as *less* permissible than killing in impersonal moral dilemmas. If moral judgments were driven only by emotions, psychopaths who have emotional deficits would judge that causing harm in personal and impersonal moral dilemmas are *equally* permissible. It might be argued that psychopathic subjects just imitate the moral decisions of people who have no psychopathy. But since the scenarios of moral dilemmas such as the trolley dilemma are not every day occurrences, imitation of normative behaviors can hardly be what persons with psychopathy rely on in this case. Because subjects suffering from psychopathy, who have emotional deficits can regard personal harm as less permissible than impersonal harm, it is reasonable to assume that they gain access to such information by a nonemotional, cognitive process. It seems reasonable to suppose that it is the cognitive representations of the morally relevant features of an action that are responsible for a pattern of moral judgments (Banerjee et al., 2010; Dwyer et al., 2010; Huebner et al., 2009; Mikhail, 2007). Because level of intelligence is not correlated with psychopathy, we are inclined to believe that non-psychopaths also appeal to such non-emotional, cognitive mechanisms to make (at least some) moral judgments. This leads us to assume that emotion is not an essential causal factor in the moral judgment of normal people (Zhong, 2013).

According to Cima et al. (2010), "emotions are like a gain function, moving our judgments up and down a scale from very bad or forbidden to obligatory or required" (p. 65). But that is a long way from arguing that emotion is causally necessary in all moral judgments. It seems that emotion is not causally necessary for moral judgment, but may *determine the severity of moral judgment* (see also Cima et al., 2010; Huebner et al., 2009). We should keep an open mind and allow for the possibility that a judgment lacking any form of emotion might nevertheless be a real moral judgment (Zhong, 2013).

Moral development

Another issue that triggers opposition to the sentimentalist approach is linked to the fact that this approach has no full and convincing explanation for the emergence of our moral inclinations. Why do moral failures lead to negative feelings and to right/wrong judgments in the first place? Why do our intuitions lead us to condemn murder, rape or theft? The answers offered by these theories may be correct, but they are only partial and far from convincing. Nichols (2004), for example, argues that moral judgments are supported by "normative theory," reflecting the commonly accepted culture and values of any given society. According to Haidt (2000), moral development is primarily a matter of the maturation and cultural shaping of endogenous intuitions. These intuitions are gained primarily through participation in customs involving sensory, motor and other forms of implicit knowledge.

In Prinz's view (Prinz, 2007, p. 268), negative feelings about the harm done to another and positive feelings about helpfulness are the result of education and the values instilled by parents. Prinz thinks that it is a serious mistake to believe that we arrive at moral insights without much education. Parents spend much of their time with their children teaching them how to do the right thing. Prinz argues that if morality was innate, all this effort and time would be unnecessary.

Though social norms, parental education and peer group pressure have a huge influence on a person's moral values. This fact alone does not explain the existence of universally accepted moral cognitions. First, it is the case that education and social norms also apply to conventional demands such as "talk during a performance is not allowed." However, children regard moral rules as far more binding than rules relating to politeness (Smetana, 1985). Young children judge that intentional harm is worse than unintentional harm, and that actions that produce greater harm are worse than actions that produce less harm. Did they acquire this knowledge from their caregivers or do they have some natural capacity to understand something about intentions and harm?

What is it about moral failure, which even small children understand, that makes it more serious than violating a convention? It could be argued that this view of the gravity of moral failure, too, has its origins in social norms and education. But this explanation seems weak in light of the fact that the norms of every culture prohibit violence, murder and theft.

Moreover, fine distinctions are made in the process of reaching a moral judgment that depend on the particular nature of the actual event. It is hard to believe that we acquire these distinctions as the result of education. For example, we have very negative feelings about murder in the first degree. These differ from the feelings we have about manslaughter or the killing of another person in self-defense. Are these three very different responses to the taking of a person's life a consequence of social norms, education or peer group influence? Do we ever *learn* to make these distinctions from someone else, or do we make them on the basis of some norm or other? Is it not more plausible to think that a profounder, more basic mechanism is at play here, a mechanism that is generated in our minds, and which enables us to understand the moral differences between these three instances of homicide?

The abundant research showing that infants have basic moral capacities as early as in the first year of life (see Chapter 3) is not in line with the approach suggesting that moral values are based on emotions learned from parents or one's surroundings (Hamlin & Wynn, 2011; Hamlin et al., 2007, 2010, 2011; Kuhlmeier et al., 2003). If a 9-month-old infant shies away from a triangle that is blocking the path of a round object struggling to climb a hill, it is conceivable that basic moral capacities are in existence long before the parents verbally target the child's thinking skills and teach him or her the difference between right and wrong (Hamlin et al., 2007, 2010).

Moral judgments and aesthetic values:
the un-specificity of sentimentalist accounts

Perhaps the most serious problem with theories based on emotions and intuitions relates to there being no description of any feature that is specific to moral judgment. Kohlberg, at the other extreme, also considered moral development as closely related to cognitive development, and moral thinking to be no different from any other kind of thinking.

At this point, therefore, we can refine earlier observations and argue that approaches whose entire purpose is to persuade us that morality is a disjunctive question of either cognition or emotion share the following feature: they all remain highly generalized and have difficulty encapsulating the singularity of the field of morality and its unique components.

Theories emphasizing the importance of emotions and intuitions in establishing social norms are often domain-general and do not distinguish themselves from theories addressing other domains. Theories explaining how emotions determine moral judgment can, for example, similarly explain how emotions determine aesthetic judgment.

The equation between moral judgments and aesthetic judgments is so widespread in sentimentalists' accounts that it deserves a lengthy discussion. Indeed, it was David Hume, sentimentalism's most prominent advocate, who thought that sentiment is the sole source of values governing human activity.

Sentimentalists maintain that morality is a human construction driven by our passions, and that emotions are constituent parts of moral judgment because emotions are "token instances" of concepts such as right and wrong (Prinz, 2007). Moreover, they argue that an action is judged as morally right only in cases in which, given certain conditions, it triggers an emotion of acceptance in normal observers.

These claims could equally be applied to aesthetic judgment. One could argue that aesthetic judgment is a human construction driven by our passions, that emotions are constituent parts of aesthetic judgments because emotions constitute token instances of concepts such as beautiful, ugly and boring. It could also be argued that a work of art is praised only in cases in which, given certain conditions, it triggers an emotion of acceptance in normative observers.

Look at another version of sentimentalism according to which healthy moral judgment involves two components: a normative theory and a system of emotions (Nichols, 2004). The normative theory specifies rules, and the system of emotions alters their character and gives them motivational force. One can also think about art in the same way. Aesthetic judgment includes two important components: a normative theory and a system of emotions. The normative theory defines what can be regarded as "good art," and feelings shape the judgments and provide them with motivational power.

The theory of social intuitionism (Haidt, 2000) can also provide an explanation of aesthetic judgment. The central claim of the social intuitionist model is that moral judgment is the result of quick moral intuitions, and is followed (when needed) by slow, *ex post facto* moral reasoning. Haidt (2000) himself points to the similarity between moral and aesthetic judgment. Moral intuition, he writes, "is . . . a process akin to aesthetic judgment: one sees or hears about a social event and one instantly feels approval or disapproval" (p. 6).

It is true that moral judgment and the assessment of the aesthetic value of art (whether it be music, literature or painting) share a considerable number of general characteristics: individuals commonly have some knowledge of moral right/wrong, just as they can appreciate certain forms of artistic expression. Everyone acquires a certain intimacy with local variants of art and moral norms. Similar statements can be made regarding other human capacities, for example the capacity for social and cultural interaction (Jackendoff, 2007).

It is certainly the case that moral judgment and aesthetic values are firmly embedded in social and cultural interaction. However, that does not mean that the ability to reach moral judgments or admire a work of art is a mere subgroup of a capacity within an overall social or cultural context. Other factors, too, come into play.

The distinction between aesthetic and moral judgment has attracted much attention from philosophers, and seems to have been well established.

Came (2012) writes:

> Moral and aesthetic judgments are, as far as most of us are concerned, usually distinct. The zones of ambiguity and continuity are restricted and the respects in which they differ are numerous. If the attempt to separate them out is in tension without normal ways of thinking, then any theory which would have us assimilate them both to the same model also does violence to ordinary thought by compression.
>
> (p. 171)

Came (2012) mentions the different types of experience that mark the moral and aesthetic domains. Art experts classify works on the basis of their direct experience together with their rich, professional exposure. Direct experience does not count as a necessary component of moral judgment. So, we may condemn the behavior of people who lived long before us, and we have no difficulty forming a judgment about hypothetical moral situations. This is different with aesthetic judgment, which has to be based on an encounter with the artistic object. It would be hard to say that the *Birth of Venus* is a beautiful painting if all we had was a verbal description of it.

Still, Came adds that the differences between these two types of judgment are not always very clear, and their boundaries may be blurred and ambiguous.

In Walker's view (Walker, 1967, p. 27), moral judgment requires a certain commitment to action, a choice of objective or way of life. It may take the shape of taking a consistent position: if one supports abortion, then one advocates this right for all women. Aesthetic judgment, by contrast, does not essentially imply action: the person who makes such a judgment is thereby committed to neither action nor way of life. One cannot act on an aesthetic principle, though it is possible to follow it. A moral principle is a condensed expression of a general truth about what people may and may not do – an aesthetic principle is a general demand, usually aimed at objects, as to how they should appear or be experienced, and reflects the artistic appraisal these objects deserve. Aesthetic judgment is informed by a notion of observation and immersion that is distinctly unlike a notion of action, much like a consumer of art is not the same as an art dealer. We associate aesthetic principles with play – an activity without consequence, "not serious" – exactly in the sense that action is thought of as serious and consequential, while play is not.

None of these distinctions is set in stone. Action and productivity involve play, and games are made up of actions. Actions can moreover also be considered from an aesthetic perspective, while works of art may very well convey and instigate moral judgments. Moral judgment is commonly exhausted when the relevant principle is applied to a certain moral dilemma. These principles are general in order to protect us from fanaticism, hypocrisy and inhumanity. The same cannot be said of aesthetic judgment, which involves ideals as expressed in real objects. Again, the distinction is not sharp: we may call some of our human ideals aesthetic.

There are, nevertheless, aesthetic ideals that cannot function as personal values, just as there are practical/personal ideals that no one will think of calling aesthetic.

In most school systems, Walker notes, the study of art is not one of the core subjects. But it is considered of cardinal importance to study and acquire moral principles and to learn how to apply and protect them. No form of education fails to relate to moral issues. We are not similarly bound to engage in art, to look at or listen to it. That this is generally so is of course a contentious issue. Some would argue that aesthetic education should be part of moral education, or – at least – it should be considered, and used, to advance the process of moral development.

Walker (1967, p. 24) also mentions that moral evaluations will tend to include a discussion of the aims, desires and motives of the person in question. Thus, it is important to determine to what extent the person who was involved in the action at hand acted consciously and intentionally, and what was his or her state of mind at the time. There is some connection to one's psychological judgment of the artist when one considers aesthetic work, and some argue that we must know what the artist meant. But it would be curious were an aesthetic theory only to reflect the artist's perspective. It is unclear whether the artist's perspective is either important or relevant to the work.

Hampshire's (1954) argument is that moral problems are not invented to simply look at, to reflect on and enjoy. They are dictated by the world in which we live. From the moment we wake up and throughout the day, we face situations that demand action. We have to decide what is the right thing to do, what to avoid. We cannot but make these practical decisions – even if it is a decision to refrain – and this then exposes us to moral praise or censure. In the case of art, these are the artist's personal expressions or the problems he or she chooses to pose through his or her aesthetic decisions. The latter reflect the artist's personal approach to his or her work. While practical decisions made as the outcome of moral considerations are consequential and necessary, aesthetic decisions are, according to Hampshire, gratuitous.

In a moral discourse, Hampshire argues, we are obliged, when we object to a certain action, to suggest an alternative action. A choice has to be made between actions, each of which comes at a price. The right action is the best in the given circumstances, and one's comment will carry little weight if one does not offer an alternative. This is not the responsibility of the artistic audience. They may reject a certain work of art, says Hampshire, without articulating alternatives to the artist's approach. That responsibility lies with the artist, it is commonly agreed.

The criterion for judging a work of art does not refer to the optimal choice in the circumstances – these are determined by the artist him or herself. Also, the relevant conditions or circumstances of a work of art are always idiosyncratic and contingent; this is why the critic may examine it in isolation, looking for its singular beauty, without reference to other works. Moral judgments, for Hampshire, must be rationally grounded and the moral discourse must generate such judgment in terms of its own stipulations. Aesthetic judgment, as opposed to this, is shorn of methodical causality, and it is marked by a total absence of responsibility. In the moral domain, when one offers reasons, it means that one points at a general principle that is applicable in this case as in all similar ones.

No matter what its specific values, Hampshire argues that on a more general level, a moral theory will be useful as long as it fulfills certain goals that aim to make the world into a better place, where people suffer less. Morality is the struggle against suffering. The whole point about art, however, is that it does not serve any objective as such beyond the specific creation at hand. Though art may be valued as a contribution to humanity's general happiness, this contribution still has to be understood in the very singular terms of the specific work.

Santayana (1955) focuses on the emotional/psychological context of moral versus aesthetic judgments. Our enjoyment of beauty and its artistic expressions, he argues, depends on a claim on freedom: in order to find pleasure in art, we must be free of the burden of fear and anxiety. In the case of morality, we try to escape from horrible things we have encountered in reality. Moral judgment commonly takes the form of a negative evaluation of what was wrong, evil and offensive. There are negative aesthetic values, too, where ugliness is paradigmatic, but they are relatively rare, and they usually carry a moral resonance, such as when we are enraged to find they're planning a huge high-rise in the middle of our neighborhood.

Another factor I would like to add, regarding appreciating art, is that familiarity with it is often needed. Someone who has had no exposure to a certain type of music will find it hard to have a sense of its aesthetic value. Things are different when we make right/wrong judgments. We can judge moral situations that are completely novel for us, and in fact we do it on a daily basis by simply reading today's news.

Between those who appreciate a given work of art and those who don't, there usually will be agreement that one cannot argue about taste, and that individuals, societies and cultures each have their own ways of judging art. People do not kill each other because they disagree about the aesthetic quality of a piece of art. This is not the case when it comes to moral arguments. Disagreement in this domain may all too easily escalate into violence (for example, the attacks of pro-life extremists in the US on abortion clinics and their staff). Moral judgment has a non-negotiable quality; it seems objective and universal. Murder is murder is murder.

That said, these distinctions are not absolute. About art, too, there is heated, passionate debate; there are fashions, and experts who decide what's good art and what's bad. But the antagonism seems less emotionally intense and less concretely violent.

To be sure, museums have been ransacked, looted, destroyed on purpose; paintings have been slashed or destroyed or prevented from being shown. But this always happened because of some moral/ideological defect, not because their beauty was not appreciated. So, destroying a work of art or burning books is an aggressive art not toward the works of art as such, but against the human values they represent. It has nothing to do with art or literature as aesthetic objects.

The problem is that the terms "debate" and "dispute" are used in discussions about both moral issues as well as issues unconnected to morality such as art. Moral feelings and feelings of a different kind must be differentiated. The reply to the question "What distinguishes moral debates from other kinds of debate"? has to be part of every moral philosophy.

Often people who disagree on moral issues are engaged in an activity that cannot be described by the word "debate." The interlocutors are defending an individual or a group. They are responding to a sense of menace or imminent danger. Fleetingly, they revert to being members of an ancient tribe who sense that an enemy is threatening children or friends within the tribe. Changing the other side's mind is not their real objective. That is only a means of achieving a far more concrete purpose: obviating the threat. What is so frustrating for the attached person is that his or her opponent wants to deprive the individual or group with which they are identified of their rights, or, alternatively, expresses indifference as to their fate and does not share their feelings of anxiety, compassion and concern.

To sum up, while aesthetic values and moral values share a considerable number of general characteristics, many of these are domain-general.

Moreover, the fact that aesthetic values and moral values are both deeply subjective and are culture-specific has little to do with their formal structure.

Significantly, Jackendoff (2015) thinks that memory, processing, attention and learning function pretty much the same across all areas of the brain. He believes that structural features such as grouping, sequencing and even recursion are common to many different kinds of mental representations (Jackendoff, 1987, 2002, 2011; Lerdahl & Jackendoff, 1983; Pinker & Jackendoff, 2005). But that, Jackendoff (2015) notes, can't be the end of the story: "One must also specify what makes vision different from language, and language different from music, and music different from actions like washing dishes, and washing dishes different from morality" (p. 4). Jackendoff's working hypothesis is that these differences are a consequence of the character of the mental structures appropriate to each, and that the similarities that cut across these domains are rather like the similarities we find across domains in the body – for example, cell structures and metabolism, which are shared across muscle cells, stomach cells and even brain cells (on the conservatism of neural mechanisms, see Gallistel & King, 2009). But this hypothesis cannot be seriously tested without a fair amount of detailed information about what these different mental structures are like.

Paraphrasing Jackendoff (2007), I recognize that there is something right about all these approaches to the mind. We do use our emotions to make moral judgments; we do base abstract moral reasoning on moral intuitions; we do learn what is right and wrong on the basis of education and cultural norms; and detached reasoning is indeed important in the judgment of moral dilemmas. But something important is missing: a general theory of moral psychology that will clearly set out the specific characteristics of the process through which we reach right/ wrong judgments.

The crucial question is this: How is a moral rule instantiated in people's minds so that they can understand and reach various moral judgments, including situations of which they have little or no experience? How do people acquire this ability?

Structural theories of moral judgment

Two major theories addressing the specific characteristics of moral judgment are universal moral grammar (UMG) (Hauser, 2006; Mikhail,

2007, 2012) and the theory of dyadic morality (Gray et al., 2012b; Schein & Gray, 2017). These theories abandoned the emotion/cognition dichotomy in order to gain a deeper understanding of the ways in which moral situations are represented in the mind. While, as we will shortly see, these theories differ significantly, they do share one thing: both argue that moral situations are specific to the field of morality, and do not fit in with other fields of judgment such as those linked to aesthetics. Both are also formal theories of mental structures that can explain how moment-to-moment moral judgments processing takes place and how moral data are encoded.

As we shall see, the attachment approach to moral judgment is closer to the theory of dyadic morality than to the theory of universal moral grammar, but it also shares some important features with the latter.

In its explanation of the nature and origin of moral knowledge, universal moral grammar relies on ideas and paradigms similar to those used in Noam Chomsky's theory of generative grammar in the field of linguistics. Chomsky radically changed the field of linguistics and cognitive science by demonstrating that everyday language can be precisely and formally analyzed by reference to a universal grammar rooted in the human biological program. Universal moral grammar proposes that the same can be done with certain facets of everyday human moral cognition. This approach, it suggests, offers a productive way of investigating individuals' moral capacities, and thus their ability to reach moral judgments from computational, ontogenetic, behavioral, physiological and phylogenetic viewpoints (Mikhail, 2007).

Underpinning UMG are two fundamental lines of argumentation: the evident existence of a moral grammar and what has been termed the "poverty of the moral stimulus." The characteristics of moral judgment suggest that the human mind contains a multifaceted and perhaps domain-specific moral grammar. This grammar, it is argued, consists of a set of rules, ideas and principles that link a variety of representations. This system makes it possible, among others, for individuals to decide upon the rights and wrongs of a host of actions and omissions within a given moral situation (Mikhail, 2007).

The argument relating to the "poverty" of the moral stimulus suggests that some of the most significant qualities of our moral grammar are innate. "Innate" here is used in a dispositional sense to refer to cognitive systems whose fundamental characteristics are mostly determined by the intrinsic structure of the mind. However, the development of these characteristics in the course of maturation has to be activated and informed by relevant experiences, and can be inhibited if the learning environment is insufficient.

UMG theory posits that in order to identify the key constituent elements of a given action, the mental systems that underpin moral cognition have to produce a multifaceted representation of that action which transmits relevant information about its time-related, causal, ethical, deliberate and deontic properties.

Every naturally developed language seems to include words or phrases expressing basic deontic concepts, such as obligatory, permissible and forbidden. These concepts represent the essential features of most ethical, juridical and religious systems, and relate most naturally to moral agents' voluntary acts and omissions.

It is important to note that UMG lacks a clear theory of moral acquisition, and it also does not clarify how the innate moral syntax is triggered and functions. As we shall see, moral attachment theory can, in a certain way, be compared to UMG, as both assume that moral aptitudes are innate but need a certain stimulus to be activated. Both theories also discuss similar questions such as: What are the essential elements of moral knowledge? How do we acquire moral knowledge? How are we taught morality? What is it that activates moral knowledge in the brain?

Both theories hold that the properties of moral judgment imply the existence of an inherent moral grammar: a complex and possibly domain-specific set of rules, concepts and principles from which various types of mental representations derive and interact. One thing this system makes possible is for individuals to determine the deontic status of an infinite variety of acts and omissions (Mikhail, 2007). Where the theories diverge is on their radically disparate syntax.

Another theory that has a close affinity to moral attachment theory, and is one of its sources of inspiration, is Kurt Gray's theory of dyadic morality. Gray et al. (2012b) argue that the analysis of morally charged events always involves consideration of both the roles of an "agent" who performs the action that results in an outcome and a "patient" who is affected by that outcome.

Gray et al. (2012b) suggest the centrality of mind perception to moral judgment. Different people's perception of a person's mind varies tremendously (Gray et al., 2011).

These authors suggest a cognitive template of two perceived minds – a moral dyad of an intentional agent and a suffering moral patient – in which moral judgment is rooted. Dyadic morality is supported by different research approaches.

Gray conducted a large-scale survey that investigated specific links between mind, perception and morality. Respondents evaluated both the mental capacities of diverse targets (e.g. adult humans, babies, animals, God) and their moral standing (Gray et al., 2007). In particular, participants assessed whether target entities deserved moral rights, and whether they possessed moral responsibility. The mind survey revealed that people perceive minds along two independent dimensions. The first dimension, *experience*, is the perceived capacity for sensation and feelings (e.g. hunger, fear, pain, pleasure, consciousness). The second dimension, *agency*, is the perceived capacity to intend and to act (e.g. self-control, judgment, communication, thought, memory). An entity can be high on both dimensions (e.g. adult humans), low on experience and high on agency (e.g. God, Google), high on experience and low on agency (e.g. children, animals), or low on both (e.g. the deceased, inanimate objects). The mind survey demonstrates key connections between mind, perception and morality.

While agency qualifies subjects as moral agents who are capable of doing good or evil, experience qualifies them as moral patients who are capable of benefiting from good or suffering from evil. Adult humans usually possess both agency and patiency, and can therefore both be blamed for evil and suffer from it. A puppy, according to Gray, is a mere moral patient; we seek to protect it from harm but do not blame it for injustice.

A dyadic template of morality features people as either moral agents or moral patients – a phenomenon called *moral typecasting* (Gray & Wegner, 2009). Moral typecasting also influences our perception of the target person's mind. When someone categorizes another person as a moral agent, he or she thereby automatically infers agency. This means that any action that is morally relevant entails corresponding attributions of intention, especially evil intentions (Knobe, 2003; see also Gray & Wegner, 2009). Likewise, when someone is categorized as a moral patient, a capacity for experience and greater sensitivity to pain will be automatically attributed to him or her (Gray & Wegner, 2009).

From this model, many questions arise. We want to know why it is that people consistently make sense of moral and non-moral events in terms of agents and patients instead of thinking through some other set of roles? Why is the agent/patient relationship so fundamentally significant that it forms part of our core knowledge? How did it become part of our intuitions and common sense?

This is where the *attachment approach to moral judgments* becomes relevant, as it argues that the division between patient and agent is based on two prior categories: dependent and independent, or, as I will refer to it here, child and adult. These categories emerge during the first year of life as a result of the many interactions between the infant and its caregiver. Thus, moral competency is rooted in these very early interactions.

The next chapter will offer a survey of theories in a variety of disciplines, all of which support the claim that interaction with a caregiver in the first year of life is the most crucial in the process of moral development.

Chapter 2

Morality and early interactions

Main theories

That there is a connection between childhood experiences and morality is commonplace today. In virtually every criminal trial, the wretched childhood of the accused is at the center of the defense's argumentation. It is usually assumed that any individual involved in violence, theft, rape or other forms of criminality is likely to have had a tough start in life. These are not mere intuitions; they are backed up by empirical research.

Adolescents or adults who, as children, were mistreated or neglected, were found to be almost twice as likely to be involved in some form of violent crime than other participants in matched controls. People from such backgrounds were also found to be 53% more likely to have been arrested for criminal offenses in their youth (Ou & Reynolds, 2010).

In 2007, a longitudinal cohort study of young males considered to be at risk was published by Jennifer Lansford and her colleagues. Those whose background involved some form of abuse or abandonment were more prone in late adolescence to manifestly antisocial behavior and clashes with the police than those from backgrounds without abuse and neglect. Similar findings were reported in studies by Terence Thornberry and his colleagues (Ireland et al., 2002; Smith & Thornberry, 1995; Thornberry et al., 2001). Lansford et al. (2007) found that individuals who had been physically abused in the first five years of life were at greater risk of being arrested as juveniles for violent, nonviolent and status offenses.

But rather than being discussed in the studies of moral psychologists, the link between morality and the circumstances of a child's upbringing seems to have been left in the hands of criminologists. Moral psychology's central theories were advanced by Piaget and Kohlberg, who were cognitive developmental psychologists. Their theories focused on how children from a normal population *think* about and *analyze* moral situations. The cognitions that lead to moral judgment, as well as moral behavior itself, remained, until relatively recently, disconnected from the study of the developing mind of infants and/or children and their relations with their caregivers.

Five leading theories in modern psychology and neuroscience all subscribe to the view that the aptitude for moral judgment originates in an infant's initial interactions with the caregiver. I am referring to John Bowlby's *attachment theory*, Donald Winnicott's *object relations theory*, Carol Gilligan's *ethics of care*, Darcia Narvaez's *triune ethics theory* and Patricia S. Churchland's *neurobiological theory of care, trust and cooperation*. Anton Dijker's (2014) theory of vulnerability-based morality also belongs to this group of thinkers. His theory will be discussed in Chapter 5. Covering a variety of disciplines, these theories have one thing in common: the belief that the moral faculty originates in the infant/caregiver dyad. They agree that the caregiver's response to the infant's absolute dependency is the most crucial aspect in the development of the latter's moral skills.

The importance of early infant/caregiver interactions was clearly a latecomer to moral psychology. As we shall see, there are profound reasons as to why these theories were so neglected in moral psychological thought.

Let us first examine the principal lines of thought of the above-mentioned five theories.

John Bowlby: attachment theory and its moral applications

John Bowlby's attachment theory is considered by many to have been one of the most important developments in infant research. Bowlby, who was trained as a psychoanalyst, believed that psychoanalysts' typical preoccupation with the inner world prevented them from paying full attention to real-life experiences of children raised in their specific surroundings. He and his colleagues devoted decades of painstaking research in an attempt to understand the genesis and influence of the various patterns of attachment and their psychic representation.

In his search for ways of analyzing the individual's mental health, Bowlby devoted his career to advancing ideas about the critical importance of an infant's first few months of life and the crucial role of the caregiver/infant relationship in determining mental health.

Bowlby's ensuing attachment theory had a marked influence in a number of fields, including social work, psychotherapy, psychology and psychiatry. His theory described the huge impact of patterns of early attachment on adult life.

The relations between child and caregiver, Bowlby contended, are formed in the early months of life, with the caregiver ensuring the infant's survival by feeding, nurturing and protecting the young child from being harmed (Bowlby, 1958).

Bowlby regarded the dependency between caregiver and child as a unique structure of behavioral patterns that is in part pre-programmed. In normal surroundings, these patterns begin to emerge in the first few months of life. As a result, the child remains more or less in proximity to his or her mother figure (Bowlby, 1958). At the end of the first year of life, this pattern of behavior is active under certain conditions and ceases to be active in their absence. Thus, for example, the child's attachment behavior is activated especially when he or she is in pain, tired, facing anything that frightens him or her, or when the mother is not accessible, or is felt to be so. Attachment behavior has to be adapted to the infant's dependency needs. At a low level of activation, it is sufficient for the infant to merely be able to see his or her mother or hear her voice. Such reassurance is particularly effective in signaling the mother's recognition of the child's presence. At a higher level of activation of the child's dependency needs, attachment behavior is bound to require physical contact and proximity to the mother or caregiver. At the most extreme level of activation, when the child is frightened and highly distressed, nothing other than a prolonged hug will suffice. Bowlby assumed the biological role of this behavior was a form of protection, especially against predators.

Bowlby thought that parental behavior, like attachment behavior, was to a certain extent pre-programmed. In other words, in the course of a day's routine, the child's parents feel a strong pressure to behave in a certain typical way (e.g. placing the infant in a crib, comforting him or her when he or she cries, keeping him or her warm, feeding and protecting him or her).

In Bowlby's view, sensitive care of an infant is the foundation of a healthy psychic life. He believed that such distressing experiences as lack of emotion, loss, rejection, ambivalence, neglect and physical/sexual abuse are the origins of psychopathy.

Bowlby was not a moral psychologist. He was not interested in the question of ethical judgment, moral reasoning or in the different ways in which people respond to complex right/wrong situations. He was familiar with Piaget's theory, and accepted some of his conceptualizations (Pallini & Barcaccia, 2014). However, Bowlby didn't intend to offer an alternative to Piaget and Kohlberg's theories of moral psychology. Bowlby's focus was to explain clinical phenomena such as depression, the response to separation or attachment disorders. And yet Bowlby's was the first serious attempt to point to the link between the initial year of life and moral behavior. Bowlby made two significant contributions to moral psychology. The first was a lengthy article, "Forty-Four Juvenile Thieves: Their Character and Home-Life," which he published early in his career in 1944. In it, he traced the link between juvenile criminal behavior and early loss. His second influential contribution was to show how attachment patterns are stored as internal working models that shape the nature of the maturing individual. Although this contribution bears no direct connection to moral judgment, it supplies us with a basis for understanding how attachment patterns increasingly become the cognitive foundation that gives rise to our intuitive moral faculty.

Attachment theory and the etiology of delinquent behavior

Bowlby's interest in the early relations between parent and child arose from his clinical work with juvenile offenders. This interest spurred Bowlby into developing his attachment theory (Follan & Minnis, 2010). Bowlby was convinced that serious attachment failures with the mother figure and, in particular, early separation were responsible for delinquent behavioral patterns in adolescence. The research he undertook and the resultant monograph, "Forty-Four Juvenile Thieves," aimed at tracing the early patterns of attachment of adolescents who had been accused of theft.

The 44 cases cited by Bowlby in his 1944 monograph were all drawn from children attending a guidance clinic that he ran. Within the overall group of 44, there was a subgroup of 14 whom Bowlby characterized as "affectionless characters".

These children were suddenly removed from their known environment at an early stage of development, finding themselves in the custody of complete strangers. All familiar and loved people and places were taken away, replaced by unrecognizable and menacing surroundings. According to Bowlby, the juveniles in this group differed significantly from children who had to adjust to the early loss of their mother but were cared for by familiar close relatives. The sudden early loss of a mother would, more likely than not, involve an emotional shock even in the best of circumstances. There will normally be an aunt in the family, or a grandmother, or a sibling who will assume the maternal role and with whom there is an existing libidinal bond that can be enhanced relatively easily and naturally. Bowlby's juveniles had either had no such prior relationships or lived in circumstances that undermined any close attachments. They had difficulties in forming new relationships, and thus became affectionless and uncaring. Also significant in this context is that in most cases, these children had experienced multiple disruptions in their relations with a caregiver, and had to adjust to being in at least two or more foster homes or in some form of institutional care.

Since infancy, these 14 children appeared to be devoid of any sentiment or kindness for anyone. Members of this subgroup tended to be loners, showed no concern for others and were aloof. It seems from parents' or foster parents' comments that nothing either said or done, whether kind or harsh, appeared to make any difference. Apart from engaging in theft, these children often stayed away from school and roamed the streets. This aimless wandering was symptomatic of their lack of interest in social groups, whether in school or in the narrower frame of the family, a trait that characterized the group as a whole. Like all thieves, Bowlby observed, they were liars, but it seems that these particular children lied more often and that their lies were more blatant than those of the rest of the larger group.

The aloneness exhibited by these children needs some explanation. Most of them went about their business of stealing on their own. Though on occasion they would be seen with other children, these were mere acquaintances who were replaced in quick succession. Thus, no real friendships were established, and no close emotional ties were apparently formed.

In terms of general behavioral patterns, the group was far from homogeneous. Some appeared unapproachable and indifferent. But there were quite a few who were full of vim and vigor. It seems that the more active the child, the more prone he or she was to turn his or her hyperactivity into aggressive and intimidating behavior towards others.

Christopher Reeves (2005) argues that Bowlby's work has successfully demonstrated that emotionally underprivileged children are particularly prone to resort to petty criminality as opposed to some other psychopathological pattern of behavior. Bowlby's thesis was that this tendency was due to a powerful, mostly unconscious desire for "libidinal satisfaction," as well as the child's pressing need to express fury with authority. His further hypothesis was that because within the subgroup of 14 the emotional deprivation had occurred at a very early stage of life, they had never been able to develop a superego. For Bowlby, this explained: (1) the children's propensity to initially steal from their caregivers, and at a later stage continue that pattern of behavior whenever and wherever they wanted; (2) the children's lack of concern for their victims and for the value of other people's possessions; and (3) the low likelihood that these children could stop being delinquent (Bowlby, 1944, pp. 50–52).

Assessing the validity of Bowlby's findings: an ambiguous picture

A highly respected evaluation of Bowlby's findings can be found in the work of Michael Rutter (1972/1981). In Rutter's view, Bowlby was only partially right in his assessment of the impact of separation, and even where he was right, his reasoning was wrong. Rutter posits that Bowlby probably exaggerated the damage caused by sudden separation and underestimated the complexity of such breakups.

For example, Hinde's rhesus monkey studies (Hinde & McGinnis, 1977) provide evidence to support the view that the extent of the emotional pain caused by separation depends on the nature of the mother/child relationship prior to the event. The closer their attachment was, the more harmful the separation was likely to be. Findings of this kind indicate that the role and the nature of parent/child relations is a good deal more complex and variable than Bowlby's initial notion of separation would suggest. What is significant is not the event itself, but the context in which it occurs and the way the infant experiences it. A similar conclusion applies to the relationship between antisocial behavior and maternal deprivation.

In Rutter's (1971) view, antisocial behavior should not be exclusively linked to the sudden loss of the mother figure. Such behavior, he argues, rather than from the absence of the mother alone, stems from the family conflicts that come in the wake of, say, a parental divorce and the subsequent temporary separations between mother and child. A child whose mother dies is not particularly more likely to be delinquent later in life than any other child. Conflict in the family, on the other hand, especially where parents are openly feuding and show no warmth towards either each other or their children, significantly raises these odds. However, in such cases as well, Rutter argues, the outcome will be affected by: (a) the way in which the loss of the mother is handled by those who replace the mother; and (b) the child's own understanding of what happened. It is more likely that the event itself is only one factor affecting a child's later social behaviors (Brown & Harris, 1978). Rutter's research has shown that delinquency is the outcome of a complex amalgam of many difficult factors, including the way the social services or any other state authority intervenes, school quality and experience, and the quality of the housing in which they grow up. Notwithstanding the great significance of maternal deprivation in an infant's early life, for Rutter, the chances of delinquency being caused by this one factor alone are slim.

Thus, if we accept Rutter's critique, attachment theory may be less relevant to the lives of "juvenile thieves" than Bowlby and his followers originally supposed. This is how Rutter (1995) puts it: "the adverse environments that predispose to attachment insecurity usually include a wide range of risk features that may have nothing much to do with attachment as such" (p. 558).

If diagnosed today, Bowlby's juveniles may have been confirmed as suffering from reactive attachment disorder (RAD), a disturbance in a child's ability to form appropriate social relationships. The publication of case reports and various research studies has led to the establishment of a symptom profile of children who were taken into care at an early stage in their lives. Regardless of the observed disorder, the relevant manual calls for an RAD test (Goldfarb, 1945; Richters & Volkmar, 1994; Spitz, 1945; Tizard & Hodges, 1978). In most cases, this pathology stems from parental neglect, pathogenic care or serious mishandling in the early years. In all cases, the onset of these difficulties should be evident before the age of 5, and is subject to improvement if the child is subsequently cared for within a supportive family environment (Follan & Minnis, 2010).

Studies of a group of Romanian orphans adopted by families in the UK led to a number of conclusions (O'Connor et al., 1999, 2000; Rutter, 1998). The children had arrived in Western countries having experienced up to two years of extreme social deprivation and a variety of infectious diseases. Those children who arrived in the UK prior to the age of 6 months recovered in terms of both their physical growth and cognitive abilities by the age of 4. However, follow-up studies on orphans adopted after the age of 6 months revealed that the adopted children suffered from attachment disturbance, including indiscriminate friendliness (O'Connor et al., 2003). This implied the existence of some form of early biological programming of neural damage as a consequence of institutional deprivation during the first few months of life.

What clearly emerges from these studies is that age is a critical factor in terms of the harm caused to the child. Those children adopted prior to the age of 6 months developed in much the same way as (in this case) native non-adopted infants (Gunnar et al., 2001; MacLean, 2003). However, children adopted after experiencing years of deprivation suffered not only from attachment disturbances, but also from chronically elevated serum cortisol (Gunnar et al., 2001) and reduced activity in limbic system brain regions (Chugani et al., 2001). Moreover, such children ran a well-above-average risk of being diagnosed with autism at some later stage, or with post-traumatic stress disorder, as well as attention deficit disorder and hyperactivity (Hoksbergen et al., 2003, 2005; Kreppner et al., 2001; Rutter et al., 2001). Harry Chugani and his colleagues (Chugani et al., 2001) used PET imaging to examine the impact of adoption on a sample group of Romanian orphans whose average age was 9 and who had spent an average of three years in an orphanage. They found that the adopted orphans had "mild neurocognitive impairment, impulsivity, and attention and social deficits" and "significantly decreased metabolism bilaterally in the orbital frontal gyrus, the infralimbic prefrontal cortex, the medial temporal structures (amygdala and head of hippocampus), the lateral temporal cortex, and the brain stem" (Chugani et al., 2001, p. 1290). It is these regions of the brain that are usually activated in the making of moral judgments and in various other psychological functions (Damasio, 1994; Nelson et al., 2005; Raine & Yang, 2006). It can be assumed that changes in that circuitry would help explain the elevated risk of impulsivity disorders.

These studies suggest that Bowlby's understanding of the connection between criminal activity and the loss of a parent was somewhat simplistic. Apparently, Bowlby's intuition that serious attachment disturbances irreparably harm moral judgment was partially right, though not as unequivocally as Bowlby himself had supposed.

What we can say is that early loss of a parent in conjunction with frequent moves from one foster family to another, an acrimonious divorce and parental violence, are all factors that increase the chances of an individual acting impulsively, and hence also criminally. Despite its shortcomings, Bowlby's work plays an important role in understanding the link between a childhood spent in difficult circumstances and criminal activity later in life.

Internal working model

Bowlby assumed that early attachment to a caregiver installs an internal system that supports many of our decisions and judgments. The idea of internal models of attachment relations appears in a systematic form in the first volume of Bowlby's *Attachment and Loss* (1969). The idea of an internal model of the world owes its origins to Kenneth Craik's *The Nature of Explanation* (1943/2010). In Craik's view, living beings possess a "small scale model" of reality. This equips the brain with a range of potential actions and reactions to various hypothetical events, thus enabling the organism to deal more effectively with unexpectedly challenging and possibly hostile situations.

Bowlby suggested that internal working models reflect patterns of social interactions formed in early childhood through attachment relations. People continue to follow these patterns long past childhood, and possibly never quite abandon them (Bowlby, 1969, 1973, 1980, 1988). These patterns, Bowlby thought, resulted from the infant's gradual internalization of representations associated with attachment. He believed that such internal working models are formed in the first few years of life through children's ongoing assimilation of their own and others' attachment experiences, patterns of behavior, feelings and thoughts. In other words, the response of infants, toddlers and young children results from having internalized their experience and planning their behavior according to their internal working models.

According to Bowlby, people create their individual internal working models of attachment on the basis of their own experiences in their ongoing daily relations with their parents or caregivers. These models enable one to anticipate the conduct and strategies of the attachment figure, making it possible for future emotional bonds to be formed (Bowlby, 1973). Thus, in Bowlby's view, new emotional relationships can be linked to a previous affective attachment and be molded by stored representations of attachment.

Bowlby (1973) traced these relational dynamics (termed projection and transference in the psychoanalytic literature) back to Piaget's conceptualization of assimilation. Piaget's hypothesis, Bowlby argued, reflects our propensity to view any object in relation to a model, even though there may be variations between the model and the object we perceive. The newly perceived object is assimilated by our existing model (Bowlby, 1973, p. 204).

Thus, in the course of our daily lives, both as children and adults, the model's predictions can either be perceived to be accurate and endure or, alternatively, be altered and updated in the light of our real-world experience. There are times in life (marriage, the birth of a child, the death of someone close) when a far more significant modification of the model is required to take account of a radically altered environment.

Secure and insecure children naturally construct very differing models. A child from a stable home who is closely attached to a mother figure will build and store a model of a loving, accepting and dependable caregiver, and of a self that deserves the love, care and attention that is bestowed upon him or her. This mindset will be applied to any other relationship the child forms. A child from a conflicted background, by contrast, who has suffered from maternal deprivation may think of the world as a dangerous place and have a poor self-image as someone who is ineffectual and undeserving of love. These cognitively and emotionally based assumptions are comparatively invariant and enduring; this appears to be particularly true of assumptions developed in the very early years of a child's life.

Internal working model and moral judgment

Bowlby argues that patterns of attachment increasingly conform to the child's individual characteristics. In the first year of life, the child builds a number of working models – of his or her mother and the characteristics of her attachment and behavior towards him or her, of his or her father, and also of him or herself interacting with both these parental figures. These models become rapidly anchored as highly influential cognitive structures. Bowlby believed that models of parents and self-interacting tend to last and appear so self-evident as to function unconsciously. In effect, the models are intended to explain secure and insecure patterns of behavior in adult relations on the basis of the pre-adult model of parental behavior. At the same time, these models can be perceived through a broader lens as paradigms that can also influence moral judgment.

How does an internal model contribute to the understanding of good/ bad judgments? In Bowlby's view, "bad" is linked to danger and "good" is bound up with protection and security. Infants expect to be protected by their mothers. When his distance from the mother grows, he feels endangered.

Infants are born genetically biased to develop a close proximity to their caregiver. It serves to protect the infant from a number of dangers, among them the danger of being at the mercy of predators. The various forms of behavior that serve to maintain children in proximity to their mother could then conveniently be grouped together under the term "attachment behavior" (Bowlby, 1980, p. 245).

Thus, 8-month-old infants seem to expect a protected and secure environment. But infants also have representations of a dangerous and "bad" environment. Children's most palpable expression of their sense of a bad environment is his or her fear of strangers.

An experiment carried out by Spitz (1965) investigated what he labeled "stranger anxiety," which becomes evident in the eighth month of life. The infant's response to a stranger, in Spitz's findings, is a reaction to "something or somebody with whom he never had an unpleasurable experience before" (Spitz, 1965, p. 155).

Spitz conjectures that the manifestation of anxiety on the approach of a stranger in this phase of life is due to children having to assimilate a "unique object" hitherto never seen. Who the stranger actually is does not matter. Children are unable to match the new object's attributes with those of any other animate or inanimate object they ever come across. Thus, rather than wanting to know who this person is, infants are aware of who the stranger is not. They are certainly aware that it is not their mother, hence the anxiety. This response reflects children's gradual acquisition of the ability to distinguish between caregiver and non-caregiver, between a safe and an unsafe environment or between good and bad.

From their caregiver, the child expects protection, security, help in times of need and a generally compassionate approach. The stranger, however, is perceived not only as someone not to be trusted, but as potentially injurious. The infants understand that there is an environment which is responsive to their dependency and neediness, and one that might fail to provide those basic necessities or even harm them.

The fear of strangers suggests that our notion of moral failure may well be founded on feelings of existential threat. *Thus, what is perceived as*

good and bad stems from a perceived stance adopted in relation of the
environment to dependency, neediness and vulnerability.

Donald Winnicott: holding environment and the origins of morality

As with Bowlby, Winnicott's thinking about morality evolved from the relations he observed between mother and infant. Winnicott thought that human infants cannot start to *be* persons except under certain conditions. Infants come into *being* according to whether the conditions are supportive or unsupportive. At the same time, conditions do not predispose the infant's potential. The latter is innate, but it cannot evolve in an infant unless supported by maternal care. During his clinical work with children and their mothers, Winnicott developed the view that the way in which an infant was held both physically and emotionally by its mother was of critical importance to that child's future mental health.

Winnicott's work with young children together with their caregiver led him to formulate his idea of the "holding environment." In his view, "the foundations of health are laid down by the ordinary mother in her ordinary loving care of her own baby" (Winnicott, 1957, p. 44).

Ideally, the mother is able to fully identify with her child's needs and wishes. Thus, she will know almost precisely how the child wants to be held and the kind of environment it wants to be in. Winnicott believed that in the absence of such identification with the child, the mother would be incapable of providing a lively, immediate response to her baby's needs at birth, and in the early days and months thereafter.

Winnicott (1957) observed that the "mother's technique of holding, of bathing, of feeding, everything she did for the baby, added up to the child's first idea of the mother" (pp. 86–87). Moreover, the mother nurtured the infant to experience the physical body as a safe habitat.

At this first stage of development, the infant is unable to distinguish between "me" and "not me" objects. All the infant can do is react to something good or bad. When disappointed or surprised, the infant mentally records a "failure of reliability." He or she has achieved this concept of reliability as a result of the dependable way in which he or she has been cared for by mother or father. Thus, a failure of reliability constitutes a trauma since each time it occurs, continuity (Winnicott called this "going on being") for the child is rudely interrupted, and its sense of vitality is fractured.

Winnicott's areas of interest were broader than Bowlby's. Whereas Bowlby limited himself to researching attachment, Winnicott also took an interest in social and cultural matters and was involved in issues beyond the clinical scope. One of the subjects that interested him was how a capacity for having a moral sense, for experiencing guilt and concern, was formed in a child's mind.

Winnicott wrote numerous articles on the subject of moral development, which included "Psychoanalysis and the Sense of Guilt" (1958), "The Development of the Capacity for Concern" (1963) and "Morals and Education" (1963/1990). In this last article, he opposed certain religious thinkers' assumption that only religion – through education – was capable of making children act morally. Winnicott formulated a better alternative:

> This good alternative is not to be found in a more and more subtle teaching of religion. The good alternative has to do with the provision of those conditions for the infant and child that enable such things as trust and "belief in," and ideas of right and wrong, to develop out of the working of the individual child's inner processes. This could be called the evolution of a personal superego.
>
> (Winnicott, 1963/1990, p. 94)

Winnicott argued that religion or moral education first robbed the maturing individual child of "the good" that was within him or her, and then proceeded to establish a pathway through which that stolen good was returned to the child through what he labels "moral education." Winnicott's view is that what is known as moral education will not be effective unless the child has already developed an inner representation of what is good in the environment. This notion of goodness is a reflection of his or her real-life experiences in infancy.

A child nurtured in a reasonable holding environment comes to understand the idea of goodness and the notion of a reliable parent – or a personal God for that matter – in a very natural way. But a child who has experienced an unsupportive environment is incapable of accepting a personal God as a replacement for infant care. Moral education cannot be a substitute for love. Such love inheres in delicate, preverbal mother/infant communications; it is expressed in proper caring for the child and the provision of an environment that gives him or her the opportunity to grow and mature. The critical importance for Winnicott of this environment is that in time, it allows the parental figure to subtly introduce moral codes into the infant's life. This can be done by displaying expressions of acceptance and by the threat of a withdrawal of parental love if the child continues to behave badly.

According to Winnicott (1963/1990):

> There is *more to be gained from love than from education*. Love here means the totality of infant- and child-care, that which facilitates maturational processes. It includes hate. Education means sanctions and the implantation of parental or social values *apart from* the child's inner growth or maturation.
>
> (p. 100, original emphasis)

In Winnicott's opinion, just as the learning of arithmetic has to be postponed until a child understands the concept of "one," moral education has to be delayed by the natural developmental processes that good care facilitates. In Winnicott's thinking, when the child understands the phrase "I am," he or she becomes ready and eager to be taught a multiplicity of subjects, including morality.

On the face of it, Bowlby's and Winnicott's theories seem similar in that both emphasize the centrality of the real attachment to the mother. Yet there is a substantive difference between their approaches. As far as Bowlby was concerned, the main factor in relating to and dealing with the child's disorders, as well as his or her experience of his or her own self and his or her surroundings, was "the objective quality of the maternal care." Winnicott was not concerned with objectivity. On the contrary, what mattered most to him was the way in which the child interpreted and responded *from within* to the quality of his or her care. In other words, Winnicott focused on the subjective aspects of the experience of attachment.

Whereas Bowlby sees mental health as being simply and directly linked to a good and stable attachment, Winnicott's perception is more complex. Bowlby regards the infant as a passive "receiver" of the mother's love. For Winnicott, by contrast, a whole drama unfolds. This is linked to Melanie Klein's (1932) idea that the "primitive love impulse" is ultimately ruthlessly aggressive, and includes destructive notions that override any concern the children may have for their mother's welfare.

Infants love their mother and at the same time attack her. Mothers have to understand the child's aggressive actions and be prepared for them. They must not allow themselves to be vengeful or to be "destroyed" by their infants. They have to survive the hostility. If they don't infants will try to repair the damage they have inflicted on their mothers through their destructive fantasies. If the mother is adaptive enough, infants will have the time to assimilate the fact that they have been attacking the very person who cares for them.

By then, infants will have acquired a sense of being responsible for his or her actions, which, as Winnicott (1963/1990) puts it, is "at base . . . a sense of guilt" (p. 102). It is a sense of guilt that arises from this duality of destructive tendencies accompanied by feelings of love for the same object. This guilt pushes the child towards more constructive and affectionate patterns of behavior. In the event that the mother fails to be sufficiently adaptive, the child, according to Winnicott, will either be unable to find or completely lose the capacity to feel guilt, and simply continue to be anxious, an anxiety that is purposeless and wasteful.

Winnicott's theory provides us with an important view of moral judgment. Feelings of anger and hatred swell up within the infant towards an aggressive parental figure, and he or she experiences unconscious murderous feelings towards her. He or she might act in an aggressive way. However, the reasonable parent does not retaliate revengefully or even judge his or her infant harshly. As the infant is not a separate independent entity, intentionality and motive cannot be attributed to it. It is a needy and vulnerable creature utterly dependent on its parents for its physical and mental being. The infant's murderous intentions do not pose a real danger to the parent. Its power to destroy is limited. As we shall see, the principle that aggression by the weak side of the dyad is treated in a different way than similar behavior by the strong side is a significant factor of moral judgment.

The antisocial tendency

Reeves (2005), like Bowlby, Winnicott was interested in what led young adults into a life of crime. Winnicott thought that behind juvenile delinquent behavior, there was a "maladjusted environment" that failed to meet the needs of the child he once was. At first, this was a failure of nurture. To this could be added the failure of family and close relations to find a way of healing the wounds of these early failures of nurture, and beyond that the failure of society as it "takes the family's place" (Winnicott, 1963, cited in Reeves, 2005, p. 207).

Winnicott thought that a child in this predicament had had something that was good – maternal care – at some stage of childhood that was then taken away. At that point in time, Winnicott argues, the child registered this loss as a trauma. There is thus a degree of logic from the perspective of the antisocial child in the idea that he is "owed something by those around him" (Winnicott, 1965, p. 134).

Winnicott thought that the antisocial juvenile's compulsion to steal was an expression of a desire to compensate for the early loss of an object, demonstrating his belief that the object – the non-available mother – can indeed be retrieved. The juvenile's expectation, it would appear, is that society will understand their behavior as a "moment of hope" in their life and respond accordingly. However, more often than not, what is viewed by the delinquent as an opportunity to retrieve a loss is ignored. The adolescent discovers that society, staying indifferent to his or her fate, wishes only to remove them from its midst by putting them away in an institution. No appropriate treatment is provided, and thereby society loses this additional opportunity to offer the adolescent a sustaining and holding environment. As a result, the deprived individual is likely to become even more desperate, and the antisocial behavior more deeply entrenched. According to Winnicott (1956/1975), the "anti-social tendency compels the environment to be important" (p. 309). In this, he is not referring to the environment of family and friends, but rather to society as a whole. The young delinquent, Winnicott argues, "is merely looking a little further afield, looking to society instead of his own family or school to provide the stability he needs if he is to pass through the early and quite essential stages of his emotional growth" (Winnicott, 1946/2012, pp. 99–100). These young delinquents lay claim on people's time, concern and money. The delinquent's expectation, argues Winnicott, is that he or she will force the outside world to provide him or her with "that degree of structural strength, organization and 'comeback' that is essential if the child is to be able to rest, relax, disintegrate, feel secure (manifested by destruction which provokes strong management" (Winnicott, 1963/2012, p. 213).

According to Reeves (2005), Winnicott did not accept Bowlby's finding of antisocial behavior in the wake of maternal deprivation as being in any real sense a diagnosis. In his view, delinquency as such was not a clinical condition. Instead, he regarded delinquency as a tendency to defy accepted social norms. Winnicott sees this defiance as a sign of hope, and this is a basic and constant premise in his thinking.

Bowlby, Winnicott and moral psychology

The idea that the role of the caregiver in the first months of life was important to moral development had not yet found its place in the contemporary thinking on moral development. Though both Bowlby's and Winnicott's work was widely read and respected, it hardly had any influence on moral psychology during their lifetimes.

There are a number of reasons for this neglect. Ideas develop within a particular context. Bowlby's and Winnicott's theories, to begin with, were the work of psychoanalysts working within their specific discipline. From the outset, neither Bowlby nor Winnicott addressed the field of moral psychology. Their research focused on the etiology of mental health and, more specifically, adolescent delinquency, a phenomenon they sought to explain by using psychoanalytic tools.

The field of moral psychology at the time was preoccupied with entirely different issues. Piaget and Kohlberg were not interested in behavior, let alone pathological behavior. As I mentioned above, they studied how children from non-pathological populations understand and analyze moral situations through their cognitive skills. A further relevant difference is that while Bowlby and Winnicott researched non-conscious, preverbal processes, Piaget and Kohlberg concerned themselves with conscious and logical reasoning.

Piaget and Kohlberg thought that younger children were unable to make intention-based moral judgments. They had no interest in infants. Infants do not consciously ruminate about such weighty and abstract issues as "universal human rights." Rather than considering morality an emotional skill, they regarded it as a cognitive aptitude that developed in line with the child's increasing reasoning abilities.

These theories thrived in worlds of their own, detached from each other and leaving each other pretty much untouched.

Carol Gilligan: ethics of care

Carol Gilligan's ethics of care added a further dimension to early moral development. In *The Origins of Morality in Early Childhood Relationships* (Gilligan & Wiggins, 1987), she posits that relations with others, in particular the mother figure, are the cornerstone of moral judgment. In Gilligan's view, our moral judgment is based on feelings and caring, no less than it is based on intellectual reasoning.

As said, John Bowlby and Donald Winnicott were not moral psychologists. The ethics of care, on the other hand, originated from moral psychology itself. Gilligan had studied and worked with Lawrence Kohlberg. Her famous book *In a Different Voice* (1982) was written in response and as an alternative to Kohlberg's own theory.

Gilligan's book and lifetime endeavor were to redress the biases and errors of male psychologists in the field. Piaget, for example, thought that the legal sense "was . . . far less developed in little girls than in boys" (Piaget, 1932/1965, pp. 69, 75). When it came to moral development, Kohlberg's findings also displayed a sense of male bias in suggesting that boys demonstrated a higher level of moral reasoning than did girls when confronted with hypothetical events and moral dilemmas.

Initially, Kohlberg formulated his theory of the six stages in the development of moral judgment on the basis of interviews with male participants only. The first studies that included female participants revealed that women outscored men in stage 3. This is the stage in Kohlberg's theoretical model in which the competence to make moral judgments – specifically in the course of interactions with other individuals – is tested. In stage 3, young people conform to social standards. They are sensitive to approval or disapproval from others as it echoes society's norms. In stage 3, an individual may judge a moral situation by evaluating its consequences in terms of a person's relationships, which now begin to take into account respect, gratitude and the "golden rule" (the principle of treating others as one would wish to be treated). Males outscored female participants mostly in stage 4 of the model, where the focus was on such areas as preserving the rules and regulations of the society, maintaining social order and authority (Kohlberg & Kramer, 1969). Gilligan did not dispute the stages of development as such, but strongly contested the notion that stage 3 represented women's functionality as homemakers and mothers. In Gilligan's view, women were not somehow "stuck" at stage 3, but they attained their reasoning skills in a different way than men, namely through their engagement in care. Gilligan contended that what Kohlberg and Piaget perceived as "female developmental deficiencies" resulted from a biased research method. She pointed out that the models used and the way that moral "levels" were measured referred almost entirely to studies of male populations. "By implicitly adopting the male life as the norm," Gilligan (1982) notes, "psychologists have fallen into an observational trap . . . and have tried to fashion women out of a masculine cloth" (p. 6). Consequently, girls' moral development was left unexplored.

A less biased approach to moral reasoning, Gilligan argued, would bear out that though female moral thinking was different, it was no less developed and mature. Moral development, in Gilligan's view (Gilligan, 1977, 1982), is the outcome of an infant's experience of attachment to the mother and the sense of its dependency on her. An infant's moral abilities, Gilligan argued, were rooted in the structure of the family and the way in which boys and girls experienced different paths of moral development through their differing relations with their parents. Gilligan investigated the differences between women and men in their approach to moral dilemmas. Following Gilligan (1982), Gilligan and Wiggins (1987) argued that relationships with others, especially the mother, are the cornerstone of any person's moral judgment.

In their opinion, one's awareness of self in relation to others is best exemplified in terms of two dimensions, namely equality/inequality and attachment/detachment. The origin of observed gender differences in moral outlook, Gilligan contended, lies in the differing relations of boys and girls with their parents in terms of these two dimensions. Children of both sexes are aware of the equality/inequality dimension. However, according to Gilligan, a girl's identity is forged through her relationship with her mother and her need to sustain that relationship. That experience of attachment, of maintaining relations not only with the mother, but with others, is central to a girl's definition of self. Thus, girls grow up with an interdependent sense of self and a moral outlook that is focused on care and the maintenance of relationships. In contrast, a boy is initially attached to his mother but identifies with his father. A boy's identity develops in the context of detachment from the mother, while at the same time relating to the father's authority and power. The result is an individualistic sense of self and a moral orientation towards rationality, justice and abstract principles detached from emotions.

Ultimately, Gilligan (1982) argues, men and women claim different moral imperatives: women feel "a responsibility to discern and alleviate the 'real and recognizable trouble' of this world," whereas men's moral imperative "appears rather as an injunction to respect the rights of others" (p. 100). From this, we can see that moral judgment is a product of the different developmental paths that characterize men and women.

The theory of ethics of care represents an alternative and critique of traditional Kantian moral theory. According to Gilligan, the quest for impartiality and the "standpoint of detached fairness" propounded by liberal theories of justice ignore the moral role of attachment to those close to us. In the field of medical ethics, for example, it is evident that the outlook embedded in ethics of care inspires not only the parent, but also the physician, nurse, friend and whoever else is charged with looking after a patient: "In this field, the contextual response, attentiveness to subtle clues, and the dependency on the deepening of special relationships, are of greater significance morally than is impartial treatment" (Beauchamp & Childress, 2001, p. 372). Ethics of care focuses on the moral significance of looking after and meeting the needs of those who are close to us and require support.

Ethics of care is well recognized as a normative ethical theory – a theory about what makes actions right or wrong (Allmark, 1995). It occupies a prominent place among a cluster of normative ethical theories advanced by feminists in the second half of the twentieth century. It was successful in establishing a significant and timely alternative of Kant's moral philosophy, utilitarianism and virtue theory (Slote, 2006). By placing the emphasis on the way in which the work and practice of care originates in the private realm, it distinguishes itself from the character of the man of virtue, or the man of reason's exercise of universal rationality in the public realm (Held, 2006).

A theory will mostly be employed in the field in which it resolves a conceptual or empirical problem with which that particular discipline is preoccupied (Laudan, 1977). Nowadays, care ethics is considered to be a key concept in ethical debates linked to routine practices in social work and nursing – the allocation of resources, the preference given to certain populations or patients, and the way in which a patient or any other individual in need should be treated. That particular perspective has led to the development of important insights into the moral values involved in the caring practices relevant to family relations, relations between friends and individual caregiving.

Carol Gilligan's book *In a Different Voice* (1982) has been widely read and is one of the most influential works in the feminist discourse. Ethics of care gave to the world a new way of thinking about caring, nursing and social work.

And yet on contemporary moral psychology, ethics of care has only had a marginal impact. None of the key theories in moral psychology refer in any central way to the key concepts of ethics of care – compassion, concern, relations and dependence – not even those that significantly discuss the central role of emotions in moral judgment (Nichols, 2002; Prinz, 2007). Other than Carol Gilligan, the leading figures identified with ethics of care are active in the fields of education, philosophy and political science, not moral psychology.

Considering that ethics of care was originally developed as a sub-discipline of moral psychology, its lack of influence in that particular area requires further enquiry.

Five reasons for the marginality of ethics of care to moral psychology

The first reason for the irrelevancy of care ethics to moral psychology is the name of the theory itself: the word "ethics" emphasizes the philosophical rather than the psychological application of the theory. Thus, the latter merely serves as a backdrop to the ethical aspects, but is not researched in its own right.

The reason why care ethics triumphed over care psychology is directly related to the debate between Kohlberg and Gilligan.

The controversy is not only about the existence or nature of gender differences in moral thinking. It is a debate about values: what form of moral thinking is more developed, mature or advanced – in this case, the abstract versus the compassionate. Thus, the argument steered away from psychology and became part of the realm of philosophy.

The second reason for the irrelevancy of the ethics of care is that the theory itself showed little interest in the questions that preoccupy moral psychology, such as: What is the basis of morality (cognition, intuition or culture)? What are the sources of evil? How is one supposed to draw up the parameters of blame ascription? In fact, care ethics took a closer interest in the psychology of women than it did in moral judgment. The idea that women define themselves through a web of relationships of intimacy and care, rather than through a hierarchy based on separation and self-fulfillment, runs as a leitmotif through Gilligan's theory, giving it much of its structure and, indeed, attractiveness.

The developmental theory espoused by the ethics of care is also not exactly a theory of moral development. Indeed, it should rather be viewed as a theory of the development of gender identity, achieved through the child's relations with his or her mother.

The third reason for the irrelevancy of care ethics to moral psychology is linked to its close tie with feminist ideology. This tie was originally important because moral psychology had hitherto, as we have seen, excluded women as a research category. As critics pointed out, however, the problem was that this focus on women risks ignoring the larger social and historical context of which it was a part (Kerber, 1986), hence maintaining cultural exclusion. As a result, it trapped the important ideas linked to ethics of care in an ideological ghetto where everything entering that ghetto was automatically identified with the idea that women were different from, and usually superior to, men (Dubois et al., 1980).

The fourth reason for the irrelevancy of the ethics of care is linked to the difficulty that the theory had in substantiating its assumptions through empirical research. In 1984, Lawrence J. Walker published "Sex Differences in the Development of Moral Reasoning," a broad-based study that analyzed 61 research studies using Kohlberg's model to assess the level of moral reasoning achieved by both genders. This showed that, in general, there were no differences in judging moral situations between the sexes, either in childhood or adulthood. Moreover, it demonstrated that where disparities were identified, the men in question were more highly educated than the women surveyed, implying that education, not gender, was the explanation for women appearing to have achieved a lesser level of moral reasoning. There is no indication in Walker's comprehensive study that the two sexes follow separate paths in relation to their moral thinking about conceptual, theoretical issues.

Gilligan (1986) disagreed with the results of this research, insisting that other studies had in fact found gender differences in moral thinking. Gilligan claimed findings showed that men tend to define and resolve moral problems within the framework of the justice system, even though they do admittedly introduce considerations of care into their thinking.

The fifth reason for the irrelevancy of care ethics concerns the fact that the debate between Kohlberg and Gilligan was mainly about people's reasoning in relation to moral situations. This debate became outdated when moral psychologists found that reasoning played a negligible role in moral judgment.

It seems that the debate between Kohlberg and Gilligan was so central to the identity of care ethics that when Kohlberg's theory grew superannuated and lost its relevance in moral psychology, the same happened to ethics of care.

Narvaez's triune ethics theory

It was only recently that the relations between mother and child in the early months and years of life began to be taken seriously as a factor in determining moral skills.

Darcia Narvaez's triune ethics theory (TET) (Narvaez, 2008) offers an overarching hypothesis combining the results of numerous research studies. Narvaez (2008) argued that "the emotional circuitry established early in life underpins the brain's architecture for morality and ethical behavior, influencing moral personality and potential for moral functioning" (p. x).

According to triune ethics, a significant number of the brain's systems related to emotion are assimilated at an early stage in life as a consequence of a bottom-up learning process. Neuroscientist and psychologist Jaak Panksepp explains this as follows: "states constructed during early social development from more elemental units of visceral-autonomic experiences accompany certain behavior patterns" (Panksepp, 1998, pp. 44–45). A human being's distinctive emotional neural network is a product of early engagements with caregivers and other support systems in his or her immediate surroundings. Support from within the immediate environment, particularly the quality and levels of interaction between infant and caregiver, one or more, affects whether or not genes are activated and whether an infant's emotional response systems are healthily established. These factors also have an impact on whether or not mental development unfolds optimally. According to TET, the emotional network triggered in an individual's first months and years of life becomes the foundation of that person's brain schema for morality as a whole, and ethical behavior in particular. Thus, the emotional neural network determines both the individual's moral personality as well as his or her potential for moral functioning.

The theory suggests that morally motivated actions are underpinned by three fundamental and well-supported principles: security, engagement and imagination. The resulting different ethical approaches, it is argued, are determined by different brain regions that evolved over millions of years, and they are evident in both individual and group-based moral actions. Security is the primary motivational force, while engagement with others and imagination are viewed as more advanced levels of moral aptitude. The latter rely on the nature and extent of nurturing in the early months and years of life to achieve the optimal level of development.

These three ethical propensities can be described as "central motives" in guiding our emotions when we confront complex moral situations. As motivated cognition, when a particular ethic is active, it is presumed to influence perception, information processing and goal setting (Moll et al., 2002, 2005).

Each of these ethics changes and adjusts the norms to suit it. The individual's particular orientation becomes a normative imperative and has ethical significance. So, for example, the ethic of security centers around self-preservation through safety. When the security ethic is highly active, the individual will not allocate resources to attending to the needs of others because this ethic is active in brain and body systems that are self-focused. Actions that prioritize self and in-group safety over the well-being of other lives will be perceived as moral. When not attenuated by other ethics, the security ethic is prone to brutality and achieving a security goal at the expense of sensitivity to others, no matter what the consequences of such an act may be. For example, when a threat is serious, individuals will be more likely to favor military resolutions and tough policies against outsiders (Jost et al., 2003).

The ethic of engagement centers on direct contact and emotional affiliation with others, especially through caring relationships and social ties; when this ethic dominates, people will focus on the needs of others and empathic acts will be perceived as moral. According to Narvaez, physiologically, the security ethic and the engagement ethic are based on incompatible systems. The security ethic is related to an increase in levels of stress hormones (norepinephrine/adrenaline), which muster the organism's energy for fight or flight, while the engagement ethic is associated with calming hormones (e.g. oxytocin), which enable people to bond with others.

Emotional neural networks activate the imagination ethic, which can stem from either security or engagement. The ethic of imagination uses high-order cognitive processes such as reasoning capacities to cope with ongoing social pressures and to address forthcoming situations; it enables the individual to detach him or herself from immediate and concrete requirements, and includes modes of calculated and well-thought-out action.

According to Narvaez, people's moral orientation may shift between these three ethics, depending on what social pressures and threats are at play. The individual may also experience the activation of conflicting ethics – shifting between security (self-concern) and engagement.

Narvaez thinks that attachment is crucial to the development of all ethics. It is through attachment that trust evolves. The infant/caregiver dyad highly influences the structure and wiring of neural networks. These systems give rise to capacities for moral functioning. For example, stressful experiences early in life can lead to an enhanced orientation to self and a depressed empathic response to others (Henry & Wang, 1998).

Narvaez's theory thus links into an idea that, as we have seen, has enjoyed only a brief but significant history. It postulates that early relations with the caregiver play an important role in the individual's development of moral understanding.

Patricia Churchland: what neuroscience tells us about morality

The fundamental question raised by Patricia Churchland in her book *Brain Trust* (2011) is how the neurobiological perspective may contribute to the understanding of human moral values. Churchland posits that in terms of evolutionary theory, protecting the self against external dangers (including other persons, especially strangers) is a basic function of the mammalian nervous system. Fears of these dangers appear at the most basic level of existence, and are integrated and coordinated by subcortical structures such as the brainstem, amygdala and hypothalamus. These structures respond to potential threats by stimulating protective behaviors such as exercising foresight, being on guard, acting cautiously, and considering whether to stand one's ground and fight or flee the danger zone.

Although social emotions and behaviors appear to conflict with these elementary responses, Churchland (2011) points out that the former "are not the result of a wholly new engineering plan" (p. 46). She argues that social behaviors and values emerged through evolutionary modifications of the self-preservation mechanisms. The first step towards the effect of "caring about others" is, in Churchland's view, an expansion of the ingrained instinct of self-preservation to include vulnerable offspring.

In situations that are life-threatening, evolutionary adaptations in the emotional, endocrine, stress and reward/punishment systems expand the ambit of "others" being cared for. Thus, a mother rat cares for and protects her offspring in the same way as she cares for herself. She keeps them fed, clean, warm, and protects them from danger. In the event that her young face an external threat, she deals with it as though she herself was the target. It is as if the boundary encircling and protecting the "self," which the nervous system has evolved, has expanded to include its defenseless offspring.

In social animals, the nervous system has developed the ability to deal with threats to the well-being of other members of the society as well as to their own. When infant mammals are frightened by the absence of those to whom they are attached, they find a way of effectively signaling their distress. Since they are unable to feed or defend themselves, the ability to alert the parents becomes an essential tool. Mammalian mothers, and in some species fathers as well, become uneasy and distressed when they hear the signal informing them that their children are anxious. They know their newborns need them. As well as reacting to bodily pain, the insula and the anterior cingulate cortex (ACC) are also responsive to social distress brought about by such events as separation, rejection, harsh criticism and the hurt resulting from mistakes and unrealized expectations.

In Churchland's view, this expansion of the self's boundaries is an outcome of the "maternalization" of the brain, a process that relies on neuropeptides such as oxytocin (OXT) and arginine vasopressin (AVP), and a number of other related hormones.

Churchland's main thesis is that the neurochemistry of attachment and bonding in mammals provides us with the most significant explanation of the human pathway to morality. The critical steps that lead from caring just about the self to the numerous types of social interaction typical of mammals depend, according to Churchland, on the neural and other body mechanisms involved in processes of so-called maternalization in the female mammalian brain. These mechanisms were not at first intended to serve any broader social purposes, but merely to ensure that the female had the resources and motivation to nurture, protect and more generally to dedicate herself to the welfare of her vulnerable young. However, once established, the modification results in a ripple effect: caring for others who are not offspring, and whose welfare is perceived as having a significant impact on one's own welfare and that of one's dependent offspring.

The particular form the social life of a species takes is highly dependent on how that species sustains itself. Clearly, in such matters as hunting, foraging and protection against predators, in-group membership has its advantages. However, for many other non-human species, for example bears, such group membership has been unnecessary.

Churchland argues that the curbing of the infant's autonomic urge to fight or flee a perceived danger enabled social interactions with peer groups, neighbors and other affiliates by increasing the tolerance of in-group members for non-kin others.

The maternalization of the brain, that is to say the extension of caring for dependent infants to caring about relatives, friends, colleagues and other in-group members, is, according to Churchland, the critical adaptation that makes *Homo sapiens* social. Once strangers belonging to another tribe come to be seen as entitled to protection, a general human morality becomes possible.

Churchland assumes that our Middle Stone Age ancestors in Africa and Europe had nothing like the moral convictions of our contemporaries. The gradual move away from hunter-gatherer societies to an economy based on agriculture led to the formation of groups numbered in the thousands, and these inevitably included non-kin members and complete strangers. In such circumstances, clear advantages were to be gained from forming positive relations with strangers. This, Churchland posits, may well have led to the gradual evolution of morally based concepts such as fairness and trust in relation to non-kin individuals and groups. It is conceivable that the progression towards such bedrocks of contemporary morality as universal human rights or trial by jury may not have been the result of the evolution of the brain, but rather an outcome of the shift to an agrarian system of subsistence and the larger communities that it spawned.

Conclusions

In this chapter, we have seen that researchers from different disciplines, such as psychoanalysis, feminist thought, evolutionary psychology and philosophy, point to the link between attachment and mechanisms that enable us to reach moral judgments.

These are the first thinkers to put early infant/caregiver relations at the very center of the development of moral skills. If we were able to show that some kind of representation of the infant/caregiver dyad is embedded within every moral situation, this would significantly support this assumption. If we could demonstrate that moral judgment involves an entire system of cognitions that is linked to attachment, we might assume with a great deal of confidence that right/wrong judgments are, in effect, largely linked to attachment behavior. For that purpose, we would have to show that the main factors making moral judgments severe or mild, simple or sophisticated, and eliciting strong emotions such as fury or pity, must, as a rule, have some commensurability, some aspect in common, with the infant/caregiver dyad. We would have to show that attachment at the beginning of life leads to the development of a particular cognitive and affective mechanism that organizes the data of the moral situation and is capable not only of generating a judgment vis-à-vis that situation, but of turning that judgment into moral principle.

However, before doing this, we need to look at the world of infants. In order to assume that infants acquire the knowledge required to reach moral judgments, we have to also assume that in the first years of life, these infants already possess a highly developed social and learning capacities.

Chapter 3

The moral skills of infants

From a cognitive perspective, reaching a moral judgment is a highly complex matter. It requires the assessment of multifaceted social factors, taking into account a plurality of variables. Thus, a moral judgment requires many fine distinctions to be made in relation to what led to the act, what motivated it and the mental state of the participants.

For example, for a person to take responsibility for an outcome implies he or she has caused that outcome (Weiner, 2006). Moreover, the inference of responsibility requires that the agent has the freedom of choice and is acting voluntarily. Similarly, intentionality is also a crucial antecedent. It has been firmly established that one is held more responsible for an intentional than an accidental occurrence. The difference between the legal verdict for murder and manslaughter bears this out (see Malle & Knobe, 1997). Thus, no moral judgment can be reached in the absence of a proper evaluation of intentionality, motivation, circumstances and free will, and without taking the perspective of all of those involved in the moral situation. It also requires responding with empathy to another person's pain. This raises the question of whether infants are capable of making such very elemental attributions.

This chapter explores the developmental origins of our capacity to understand and judge the actions of others. In this chapter, I will cite extensive evidence according to which an infant possesses a minimal set of skills required for moral judgment already in the first 12 months of life.

According to Baillargeon et al. (2015), the turning point in the exploration of infants' ability to reason psychologically came when researchers began to use looking time methods as a way of investigating infants' physical world.

The violation of expectation (VOE) looking time method is based on the known innate inclination among infants to look longer at a situation that breaks their expectation in the context of their current understanding of the world. When encountered with a situation that contradicts their expectations, the infant can be observed to examine the event, taking their time to face the violation and change their expectations to adapt to what they have encountered. These investigations led to the insight that even before language acquisition, infants as young as 3 or 4 months have expectations about physical and social events that go well beyond what was formerly assumed (e.g. Baillargeon & DeVos, 1991; Powell & Spelke, 2013; Spelke et al., 1992; Wynn, 1992).

Such studies offer us an unparalleled opportunity of discovering humans' socio-moral anticipations at the very beginning of life. Thus, investigating infants' expectations about how individuals should behave towards one another is bound to clarify the structure of the human mind as it relates to intuitive socio-moral reasoning.

As we shall see in what follows, the model presented is largely based on an infant assessing what has occurred between two people and comparing it with their prior knowledge of dyads. Our expectations of others depend on the extent to which we have understood every aspect of the two parties' behaviors and relations.

Intentionality

According to Sodian et al. (2016), theory of mind and moral understanding are interconnected in cognitive development. That is, there is a strong link between the ability to know that other people have mental states different from their own and the ability to understand prescriptive rules such as fairness and equal treatment. Perceiving mental states is essential for moral judgment because children need to be able to infer an agent's intentions to morally weigh another's acts. Often a person's intentions can only be perceived when the beliefs of another are accurately represented. An understanding of intentionality has its origins in infancy. Infants in the first years of life interpret human action in terms of agents' goals and intentions rather than spatiotemporal surface properties of actions (Woodward, 2013). Furthermore, they can tell between intentional and accidental action outcomes, and they recreate intended actions when they observe a failed attempt (Meltzoff, 1995).

Early VOE investigations of infants' psychological experience focused on their responsiveness to the principle of consistency. Thus, for example, the research investigated whether infants attribute preferences to agents, and if so whether they expect those preferences to be consistently embraced. For example, an innovative two-object experiment was conducted by Amanda Woodward (1998, 1999) to establish whether, in their observation of an agent, infants are able to attribute a goal-oriented intentionality when that agent reaches for object A (a teddy bear) rather than object B (a ball). Also, having watched the agent pick up object A, infants would expect him or her to be consistent and choose object A whenever given a choice.

Woodward's experiments among 5- to 9-month-old infants were designed to address these questions. In the first instance, two objects, a ball and a teddy bear, were placed on an apparatus in front of a curtain. After between 6 and 14 habituation trials, the infants saw a woman's hand reaching out from behind the curtain on the right-hand side of the apparatus and clutch the teddy bear. Once the infants were seen to look away, the trial ended. In each repeat, the infants' looking time decreased. The trial continued until the looking time reached a predetermined target. The position of the toys was then switched. Having been given time to observe this change of position, the infants again saw a woman's hand grasping either the teddy bear, as had been the case in the habituation trials, or the ball. Every child in the test group gazed appreciably longer when the hand grasped the ball, signifying a violation of their expectation that the agent's hand would be consistent in its choice, even though the toys' positioning had changed.

From this, it became apparent that in the initial trials, the infants had understood the agent's actions to have been *intentionally directed*, leading them to infer that the agent had a preference for the teddy bear over the ball. The agent's choice of the ball in the subsequent test trials thus violated the infants' expectation of consistency, leading them to look at this event for a discernibly longer period of time – a well-known pattern among adults surprised when someone close to them behaves quite unlike expectations in the circumstances.

While there was recognition of *intentionality*, the agent's lack of choice in this situation meant that the infants could no longer infer whether the agent preferred that particular toy or was simply reaching for it because it was the only one available. When a second toy was introduced in the display and test trials, the infants had no basis for expecting the agent to reach for either the toy in the single-object test or the toy introduced in the second phase. Thus, they looked for an equal span of time at both events.

From this, we can conclude that the key to an attribution of preference as opposed to intentionality lies in an agent's consistent choice of object A over object B. The two object habituation trials and subsequent tests opened up new horizons in the exploration of infants' capacity for psychological reasoning.

Moral judgments in preverbal infants

What kind of evidence shows that infants possess basic moral understanding?

Let us begin with helping behavior and empathy, one of the key emotions in moral judgment.

From birth, infants show rudimentary emotional reactions to others' suffering (Martin & Clark, 1982; Sagi & Hoffman, 1976). As soon as they are physically able, infants begin to supplement these emotional responses with a variety of active prosocial behaviors, including comforting others in distress, helping others achieve goals, informing others of things they should know, and sharing their own resources (see Dunfield et al., 2011; Eisenberg et al., 2006; Warneken & Tomasello, 2006, 2009). Although active prosocial behaviors emerge after birth, they are unlikely to be entirely the result of mere socialization; they occur spontaneously, are present in our primate relatives, and are intrinsically motivated (see also Aknin et al., 2012; Hepach et al., 2012). Infants are able to point to an object being searched for by an agent who (in pre-test trials) was clearly not able to locate the object by him or herself. They were also able to retrieve an object for the agent when he or she was looking in completely the wrong place (e.g. Buttelmann et al., 2009; Knudsen & Liszkowski, 2012; Liszkowski et al., 2006, 2008).

Subsequent groundbreaking experiments further explored the circumstances in which infants participate in helping behavior (see Dunfield & Kuhlmeier, 2010; Warneken, 2013; Warneken & Tomasello, 2006, 2007, 2008; Warneken et al., 2007). One experiment consisted of 10 conditions grouped into the following four categories: (1) objects beyond reach of another individual; (2) obstacles preventing an individual reaching the object he or she wanted; (3) failure of an agent to place an object in a particular place; and (4) considered attempts to retrieve an object. Each scenario had an experimental and a control version. Thus, in the category of objects out of reach, 18-month-old infants saw a version in which the experimenter accidently dropped the object and tried, but failed, to reach it. In the control version, the individual was seen intentionally throwing the object on the floor but not attempting to retrieve it. The infants all viewed 10 scenarios, five in the experimental version and five in the control version. In six out of the 10 scenarios, the infants produced helpful (positive) responses, with reliably more infants helping the tester in the experimental than in the control version. Additionally, the majority of the tested group acted positively in at least one of the five experimental versions, and virtually all of the positive responses were spontaneous. Based on their results, Warneken and Tomasello (2009) concluded that infants' tendency to be helpful to others is evidence of an innate predilection to be generous and good-willed.

However, Over and Carpenter (2009) show evidence that infants might be less likely to help an experimenter they do not perceive as a member of their in-group. Dunfield and Kuhlmeier (2010) show that even in the earliest instances of helping behavior, infants are not unselective, but rather point their help on the basis of previous interactions with agents. It seems that often the intentions of people appear to clearly influence their subsequent helping behavior, more than the actual results of the interactions. In three experiments, they found that infants favored to help an individual who, in an earlier interaction, meant to provide a toy over one who did not, and that infants count this positive intention, even without a positive result. In another experiment, they demonstrate that infants do not merely keep away from reluctant individuals, but also selectively assist those who have demonstrated a motivation to support. These experiments show that helping behaviors among infants show qualities of the rich give-and-take relationships seen in adult helping behavior.

Overall, these tests suggested that: (1) infants do not instinctively assist an unknown adult; and (2) having been stimulated into adopting an in-group mindset, the children were significantly more likely to be socially helpful, mostly within their own social group.

Moral evaluation among infants

If infants have some capacity for making right/wrong judgments, they also need to be capable of moral *evaluation*: the ability to identify and dislike those who are uncooperative/unempathetic/unhelpful, or who are likely to be so in the future, requiring an ability to analyze others' social behaviors.

They must have some sort of expectations about the relationship of two individuals in terms of what may and may not happen between them.

This led investigators to explore the question of whether infants may possess expectations about the way in which two or more individuals *should* behave towards one another; in other words, whether the skeletal psychological reasoning system that enables us at an early age to anticipate *how* people will behave in a given set of circumstances is matched by a socio-moral reasoning system that includes a set of principles enabling infants as young as 12 months and even younger to make moral judgments.

The first question to arise in our exploration of the socio-moral expectations of infants in the first year is whether they have the capacity to differentiate between positive and negative actions, and, if so, what are the stages of development between birth and the end of the first year of life?

In a series of experiments, 12-month-old infants were at first habituated to four computer animations depicting helpful and hindering events (Premack & Premack, 1997). In the course of the habituation trials, infants' looking time at the helpful and hindering events hardly varied, suggesting that in general infants have no a priori expectations in relation to positive and negative actions. However, when infants habituated to helpful actions in the computer-animated display were exposed to an animated hindering action, their looking time was measurably longer than that of the infants who had been habituated to hindering events. This suggests that by the age of 1 year, *given a choice*, infants are capable of discriminating between positive and negative actions, and attribute a positive valence to helpful actions and a negative one to hindering actions.

Researchers attempted to discover whether in a scene involving two individuals – one acting positively and the other negatively – infants preferred – and expected others to prefer – the individual who acted in a helpful manner, that is, positively (e.g. Hamlin & Wynn, 2011; Hamlin et al., 2007, 2010, 2011; Kuhlmeier et al., 2003). In one such experiment, infants aged 6 and 10 months were offered a scene featuring a steep hill and three differing blocks with clearly identifiable human eyes depicting a "climber," a "helper" and a "hinderer." In alternating familiarization trials, the infants were exposed to scene (a), in which the climber was aided by the helper in his final determined effort to reach the summit of the hill, and scene (b), in which the climber was clearly hindered in his attempt to successfully reach the hilltop.

Following the familiarization phase of the experiment, the infants, having been shown the helper and the hinderer, were invited to choose one of them after being asked to "choose a toy." Both age groups were clearly inclined to choose the helper rather than the hinderer, suggesting a preference. Using images with humanlike features, as in the first experiment, children as young as 9, 5 and even 3 months old exhibited similar responses to a variety of positive and negative actions to those observed among 6- and 10-month-old infants (Hamlin & Wynn, 2011; Hamlin et al., 2010).

In the VOE test, the contours of the hill were changed, its steepness replaced by a shallow symmetrical mound, showing the climber standing on the top of the hill flanked by the helper and the hinderer. The climber then stood alternately either next to the helper or the hinderer. By the age of 10 months, infants looked measurably longer at the approach of the climber towards the hinderer. This suggested that by showing a preference for the hinderer, the climber had violated their expectation that he or she would show a preference for the helper – their own preference. In an experiment using an anticipatory looking measure, Fawcett and Liszkowski (2012) discovered that 12-month-old infants expected the climber to approach the helper, providing further evidence that by the end of the first year of life, infants expect others to prefer individuals whose actions are perceived as positive.

These tests added further scientific validity to the theory that in the first few months of life, infants are capable of distinguishing between positive and negative actions observed in others.

Affiliative preferences can also arise through what has been termed "evaluative contagion." Hamlin et al. (2013) conducted an experiment involving 9- and 14-month-old infants who were asked to choose between two snacks. At first, the participating infants watched as the puppets signified their preferences for one snack or another. The infants then saw a chain of events in which newly introduced actors behaved either positively or negatively towards the puppets (i.e. handed back an item the puppet had accidently dropped or alternatively stole the item from the puppet). Infants who identified with the puppet's choice of snack showed a clear preference for the new actor who returned the item rather than for the one who stole it. In the scene showing the newly introduced actor behaving positively towards the puppet who exhibited dissimilar snack preferences to theirs, the infants identified with the other puppet.

Research by Hamlin et al. (2011) demonstrated that preverbal infants as young as 5 months have a preference for individuals who harm hinderers over seemingly prosocial agents who help obstructive individuals. One has to assume that many of the infants had never witnessed others being punished. They certainly had never been given the task of positively or negatively evaluating such acts of punishment. In Hamlin's view (Hamlin et al., 2013), there could be two possible reasons why infants have a preference for individuals who harm obstructive agents. They might believe that such agents deserve to be punished, and therefore show a liking for those who administer punishment; alternatively, even at this early age, infants may be able to positively assess the behavior of individuals who hinder antisocial others by perceiving them to be the enemy of their own enemies. This latter line of reasoning can refer to any individual who may be harmful. This may not only apply to obstructive agents, but also to out-group members who are friendly to enemies. By extension, infants may also prefer those who hinder rather than help puppets who are different from them (Hamlin et al., 2013), implying that they view friends of friends as their friend and perceive the enemy of an enemy as a friend.

Understanding in-group principle

Baillargeon et al. (2015) posit that in the adult world, members of a social group, whether family, friends, co-workers or neighbors, adhere to the in-group principle. This principle suggests that individual members of the social net will act in ways that sustain the interests of the group as a whole. This expectation naturally leads to in-group and out-group situations where individuals will side with members of their own group and protect in-group individuals who are threatened by the possible actions of out-group assailants. Also, individuals tend to accord preferential treatment to in-group over out-group members when, say, distributing resources. Interactions within the group must be positive (helpful, supportive, sharing resources) and refrain from unprovoked negative behaviors, which is to say the impulse to retaliate in response to a negative action by an in-group individual must be restrained. Recent findings suggest that infants as young as 10 months prefer in-group individuals and make choices that are in line with those approved by their in-group.

Infants are perceptive to dissimilarities between languages (e.g. Hohle et al., 2009). An experiment devised by Kinzler et al. (2007) tested whether

10-month-old infants would show a clear preference for an individual who spoke their own native language over a foreign speaker. The preference would be exhibited by the infant preferring to receive a toy from the native speaker rather than accepting an identical toy from the foreign speaker. The infants were split into two groups, one from a monolingual English-speaking family and the other from a monolingual French-speaking family. The trials were divided into two phases, a speech phase and a toy-offering phase. The infants from the English-speaking family were discovered to be reliably more likely to pick up the toy below the image of the English woman, while the infants from the French-speaking family were more likely to opt for the toy below the image of the French-speaking woman. Results suggest that infants expected two people who spoke the same language to be more likely to affiliate than two people who spoke different languages. Infants perceive language as an important social marker and use language to make judgments about third-party social relationships (Liberman et al., 2017).

The results suggest that even before speech acquisition, infants assign unfamiliar individuals to social groups and loyally base their own choices in line with that of a speaker of their own language.

Infants and toddlers are capable of forming the concept of social groups so long as they have sufficient information about the significant aspects of the group – distinctively colored clothing, for example – and classify them accordingly. Once this is achieved, infants and toddlers have expectations regarding interactions within and between these two groups. On the basis of the tests previously discussed, we can say that one such expectation is the abstract concept of group loyalty. The tests detected a violation of expectation when an individual helped an out-group member who had harmed someone from within his or her own group. The expectation was, of course, that the in-group individual would take some form of retaliatory action against the individuals in the aggressor group. In analyzing infant sensitivity to the principle of reciprocity, we saw that infants understand retaliation: after E1 hinders E2, infants deem it unexpected if E2 helps E1, but not if E2 hinders E1 (He, 2012).

The studies also showed that while infants and toddlers have no particular expectation as to whether they should act positively or negatively towards out-group individuals, they do have expectations about how in-group individuals should behave towards each other. Infants then expect individuals from different groups to take aggressive retaliatory action if attacked.

Kyong-Sun and Baillargeon (2017) show that from an early age, an abstract expectation of in-group support contributes to in-group favoritism in human interactions.

Infants and authority

Are infants able to represent a social hierarchy? Can they hold differential expectations about the actions of more dominant and subordinate individuals within the hierarchy? As a first step in addressing these questions, researchers examine whether infants can represent a relationship of dominance between two individuals.

Thomsen et al. (2011) report five studies with 144 infant participants. The studies showed that 10- to 13-month-old, but not 8-month-old, infants recognize the existence of conflicting goals between two novel agents, and that they use the agents' relative size to predict the outcome of dominance contests between them from the very first such contest. Two differently sized blocks (each with an eye and a mouth) had the goal of moving to the opposite side of the platform from where they started. As anticipated, infants looked longer at the unanticipated outcome in which the larger agent yielded to the smaller one.

The infant/caregiver dyad

So far, we have reviewed research studies describing the impressive range of infants' cognitive abilities without reference to the social experiences they had with their caregivers. Most contemporary research on the subject somehow divorces the infant from their surroundings as if their mind was detached from their immediate environment and developing quite independently of it. According to Hamlin et al. (2007, 2010), an infant's ability to judge individuals based on their social interactions is an unlearned skill. Similarly, Hoffman (2000) posits that infants' emotional and societal faculties are not influenced by experience and develop naturally. According to Hamlin (2013), infants possess an "innate moral core" (p. 186) and infant research has discovered "surprisingly sophisticated and flexible moral behavior and evaluation in a preverbal population whose opportunity for moral learning is limited at best" (p. 186).

Even though infants' social and empathic abilities are a salient feature of any contemporary book on moral development, the role of the caregiver and the primary dyadic relations in moral development was not directly theorized or studied. This lacuna has a long history in moral psychology that stretches from Piaget and Kohlberg to the social domain approach (Nucci, 1982, 2001). And yet infant research conducted outside of moral psychology shows that of all the influences around them, the one that affects the newborn most is the primary care that infants receive.

Why is the centrality of the infant/caregiver bond so easy to miss, to forget about or to dismiss? As Mitchell (2000) points out, this tendency to ignore early ties must surely have something to do with a confusion about the respective ways in which the mind and the body develop. Even though infants rely for a significant period of time on adults to take care of their physical needs, our bodies seem to be more or less pre-programmed. This manifests itself in the way in which infants mature in an ordered sequence. From immobility, the infant progresses to being able to roll over, then to pull him or herself up, then to being able to crawl and finally to walk. Aside from those of us who suffer from a physical disability, we ultimately gain control over our bodies and become physically functional almost totally through our own efforts. It is tempting to believe that our minds develop in a similar way.

As we shall see, there are many reasons to think that alongside the innate moral faculties, a significant degree of learning, too, plays an important role in the development of moral faculties in the first year of life. Three, six or nine months is plenty of time for learning. It is plausible to assume that moral skills are not learned directly, but are rather "activated" by the thousands of daily interactions between infant and caregiver.

Infant researchers with psychoanalytic orientation show warm interest in the origins of relatedness. Rather than investigating infants' cognitive ability in isolation, they examine how participation in the dyadic interaction reorganizes intrapsychic and relational processes. Studies of this type focus on how the unique configuration of organizing principles that emerges from the mother/child dyad constitutes the initial organization of the individual's domain of relational knowledge. Several terms and conceptual approaches have been proposed, each accounting for somewhat different relational phenomena. These include, among others, Bowlby's "internal working models" of attachment (1973), Stern's "proto-narrative envelopes" and "schemas of being with" (1995), Sander's "themes of organization" (1977) and Trevarthen's "relational scripts" (1993). The models are complementary, and they are all appropriate to describe the organizing principles that govern the child/parent dyad. Beebe and Lachmann's research offers one of the most cohesive models for understanding how the infant's mind is organized through interactions with the mother. According to Beebe and Lachmann (2002), for the first years of life, the infant is involved in a reciprocal, split-second, mutually adjusting system with a caregiver.

Based on an impressive number of studies, Beebe and Lachmann (2002) suggest three organizing principles that determine the salience of events for the infant and organize what the infant expects from interactive encounters. These three principles are *ongoing regulation, disruption and repair of ongoing regulation,* and *heightened affective moments.* These principles provide a hierarchical definition of interaction patterns. Ongoing regulation (the broad pattern) is the overarching principle based on the expected and characteristic ways in which an interaction unfolds. Disruption and repair (sequence) captures a specific sequence broken out of the broad pattern. In heightened affective moments (a moment), one dramatic instance stands out in time. These principles determine what becomes salient for the infant. For example, it is the infant's awareness that something changes or disrupts their interactions or violates his or her expectancies, along with the subsequent effort to repair the disruption, that organizes their expectancies (Beebe and Lachmann, 2002, p. 145).

Here, I describe the three principles and show the astonishing resemblance between them and our response to moral failure.

In ongoing regulation, patterns of experience are initially organized as what Beebe and Lachmann (2002) term "expectations of sequences of reciprocal exchanges, and associated self-regulatory style" (p. 13). They term this reciprocal or bidirectional influence, in which each partner contributes to the ongoing exchange, "co-construction." In this process, partners come to expect patterns of response where each affects and is affected by the other (p. 13).

The principle of ongoing regulation centers on the characteristic, predictable and expected ways in which an interaction unfolds (Beebe & Lachmann, 2002). A shared system of rules for the regulation of the two partners' behaviors develops. The principle of ongoing regulation derives from a regulatory system perspective (Beebe et al., 1992; Sander, 1977, 1983).

In his study of early ties Sander (1977; 1983) suggests that the organization of the infant's behavior should be perceived mainly in dyadic terms rather than as a belonging to the individual. The dyad, rather than the infant, is regarded as the system. From this perspective, mother and infant are no longer perceived as two isolated beings. Rather, they are seen as a practice of "shared organizational forms", such as shared patterns, or shared affective tracks. Numerous studies found that there are many such shared systems for the regulation of joint action in the first year of life, well before language develops (Bakeman & Brown, 1977; Beebe et al., 1985; Bruner, 1977, 1983; Cohn & Tronick, 1989; Field, 1981; Stern, 1977, 1985; Tronick, 1989). According to Beebe and Lachmann (2002), "That expectancies operate so pervasively, so early, accounts for the enormous influence they have in organizing experience. Neurophysiological evidence also suggests that familiarity, repetition, and expectancy underlie the most powerful organizing principle of neural functioning" (p. 151).

The *interactive regulation model* is central to the principle of ongoing regulation (Beebe & Lachmann, 2002). It has emerged over the past two decades in reaction to much previous work that focused on one-way influences on the child/caregiver interaction. As recognition of infants' social abilities evolves, studies have been shifting their interest to patterns of interactive regulation. There is a consensus among infant researchers that:

> Although each partner does not influence the other in equal measure or necessarily in like manner, both actively contribute to the regulation of the exchange. The mother obviously has greater range of flexibility in this process. By mutual regulation we mean that each partner's behavioral stream can be predicted from the other's.
>
> (Beebe & Lachmann, 2002, p. 152)

Infant research studies (Beebe, 1985; Beebe & Lachmann, 1988a, 1988b; Beebe & Stern, 1977) found a central role for early interaction patterns in the organization of infant experience. The dynamic interplay between the actions of the two partners, as each influences the other, creates a variety of mutual regulatory patterns. The infant learns to recognize, remember, expect, generalize and represent characteristic interaction patterns.

In *disruption and repair*, repair of ongoing regulations following disruption is the "infant's recognition that something changes or disrupts his interactions or violates his expectancies, along with the subsequent effort to repair the disruption that organizes his experience" (Beebe & Lachmann, 2002, p. 145).

If the principle of ongoing regulation emphasizes what is expectable in the interaction, within the principle of disruption and repair, interaction patterns are organized by violations of expectancies and ensuing efforts to resolve these breaches (Beebe & Lachmann, 2002). The metaphor of disruption and repair covers a broad array of phenomena, from mild to severe. DeCasper and Carstens (1980) have demonstrated that confirmation of an infant's expectancies is associated with positive affect and that violation of an infant's expectancies is associated with negative affect. Mother/infant interactions can be described as continuously shifting back and forth between greater and lesser degrees of coordination, matches and disjunctions, with a flexibility to span the range. As Beebe and Lachmann (2002) put it, "Data show that, when less coordinated states occur, there is a powerful tendency to right the interaction by returning to a more coordinated state within two seconds. Thus, repairing disjunctions is a pervasive interactive skill for infants" (p. 163).

Cohn and Tronick (1989) found that when the two partners entered an unmatched state, 70% of the unmatched states returned to a match within two seconds. They found that both mothers and infants were responsible for the repair, and that both influence the repair sequence.

Tronick (1989) and Tronick and Gianino (1986) suggest that the infant's reparation abilities increase his or her self-efficacy, elaborate his or her coping capacities and contribute to an expectation of being able to repair. Beebe and Lachmann (2002) suggest that "an interaction where the mother does not also contribute to the repair might interfere with the infant's experience of righting" (p. 164). Experimental disruptions of infant social expectancies have been examined in many studies (Gianino & Tronick, 1988; Tronick, 1989; Weinberg, 1991). In the "still face" experiment, the mother presented a completely motionless, unsmiling face to the infant (Tronick et al., 1978), a situation that can be seen as dramatically violating the infant's expectations of a contingently responsive partner. It therefore fits the usual definition of disruption as violation of expectancy (Beebe & Lachmann, 2002). The infant first attempted to elicit the normal interaction by greeting the mother with smiles. As the mother's face remained unchanged, the infant repeated a sequence of looking at the mother with an animated face, then looking away. After a number of failed attempts to "elicit" the mother's response, the infant withdrew, often slumping. These persistent efforts to repair, demonstrated so early in development, gives the concept of repair more firmly grounded developmental status (Beebe & Lachmann, 2002, p. 165).

In the principle of *heightened affective moments*, interaction patterns are organized through intensified affective moments in which the infant experiences a powerful state transformation. These supercharged moments become important to the organization of a range of percepts and memories, and are seminal in their effect far out of proportion to their mere temporal dimension.

Rather than being viewed as operating separately, these principles need to be integrated. For example, an ongoing pattern of regulation must first emerge before a disruption can be perceived. The particular quality and progression of disruption may itself become an expected interaction pattern. A heightened affective moment may work either as disruption or as repair. The three principles operate like different angles of the camera. In specific situations, one principle may dominate the others.

These three principles become even more important when the infant is in distress. Much ongoing regulation concerns the infant's physical needs and survival: feeding him or her, keeping his or her body warm, enabling him or her to rest and sleep, shielding him or her from noise, protecting him or her against strangers or other types of danger, providing for regular medical care, monitoring his or her growth, nursing him or her through illnesses. This regular, everyday care for the infant's mental and physical well-being envelops him or her in security. But this envelope is not perfect, so that the infant has to express distress every so often, usually through crying. There is, in this crying, an expectation of parental response – which will repair and restore the infant to his or her secure state.

The process of ongoing regulation and disruption and repair can be seen as the basic code with which our psyche works whenever it encounters a person in distress.

Let us for a moment return to the infants who observed "moral failure" where a triangle prevents a circle from ascending a steep hill, or were surprised to see a square awarding a prize to the "bad" triangle. These situations can be described, respectively, as violating expectations. The hindering act caused disruption, and one can also perhaps assume that it led to a heightened affective moment in the form of distress or anger (just like an adult would feel witnessing a similar event with real people). Is it possible that these expectations were the outcome of a learning process due to the thousands of interactions the infant had experienced with his or her caregiver, or at least that these expectations were reinforced by such interactions? Would it not also be reasonable to assume that infants based their evaluations regarding the helpful and hindering figures as a result of having learned from their repeated personal experience to anticipate the likely relation between the helper and the one asking for help?

So, we might posit that an infant and a caregiver engage in an ongoing process of mutual interplay that co-creates a systematic higher-level dimension. These processes might be innate in the same sense that our ability to use language is innate. But they are practiced and reinforced within the infant/caregiver dyad. This perspective offers a way to see right/wrong judgments as stemming from a co-created and reciprocal interplay of two asymmetric participants in a process that has high-level coordination and direction in spite of being messy, fluid, nonlinear and context-dependent (Stolorow, 1997, p. 341). After the first year, representations become increasingly symbolic and are translated to a verbal form.

In the case of moral failure, we may feel, in terms of disruption and repair, that "this is not how things should be" or that "something has gone wrong." We describe what has happened in terms of a violated expectation.

Conclusion

Much of the contemporary research reviewed in this chapter claims that by the end of the first year, infants possess a range of basic moral skills (e.g. Hamlin & Wynn, 2011; Hamlin et al., 2007, 2010, 2011, 2013; Kuhlmeier et al., 2003). In addition, infants in that age range also have the essential cognitive skills to make moral judgments. They are able to attribute causality, know others' intentions and identify with in-group members. They have the capacity to understand what others want and they even have expectations about how people should behave towards one another in certain situations. We have assumed that this rich, multisensory set of experiences is the source of the infant's knowledge as to what to expect from other people in various situations. However, in contrast to other researchers who thought that these social skills are developed in a vacuum and in isolation from the infant's early ties, I have shown evidence from infant research that makes it plausible to assume that participation in the dyadic interaction reorganizes intrapsychic and relational processes. These processes become the foundations of understanding and experiencing regularities behavioral patterns in other dyadic relations.

In the three foregoing chapters, I have been developing the theoretical foundations for the attachment approach to moral judgment. To begin with, I showed that psychologists adopted, for a long time, moral philosophy's central dilemma, namely whether morality originated in the emotions or in high-order cognitions. This prevented them from looking for the specific nature of moral judgments. Subsequently, I reviewed the key theories linking moral competence and the infant's early relations with his or her caregiver. Most of this type of work did not emerge from the field of moral psychology; rather, it was produced by disciplines such as psychoanalysis, evolutionary theories and attachment theory. In this present chapter, finally, I presented the rich literature that shows that infants up to 1 year old have developed emotional and cognitive abilities that are highly relevant to moral judgment, and I argued that these abilities must have evolved through the interactions between infants and caregivers.

It is now time to deal with right/wrong judgments as such, to shed light on their deep structures and consider how the moral situations we face are broken down in our minds into asymmetric dyads, and how this structure becomes the foundation of our moral skills.

Part 2

The attachment approach to moral judgment

Chapter 4

The building blocks of moral judgment

My central thesis is that our ability to recognize, understand and judge moral situations relies on our possessing knowledge of a special kind.

I will define moral judgment as the evaluations (right/wrong, good/bad) an observer makes with respect to events involving conflict between two or more parties. I will look particularly closely at the way in which observers judge an event that causes harm to one or more of the parties concerned.

The word "observer" is, in a sense, misleading because often, for many reasons, the distinction between observer and participant is far from clear-cut. First, people make moral judgments as both observers and participants. Every harm people inflict on others in their daily lives has a moral implication, and no doubt people make moral judgments about their own actions and intentions. An action that is being judged as morally wrong might elicit both self-blame as well as blame directed at others. Some actions by others that arouse our anger may also make us feel guilty (Prinz, 2007), and in both cases we make similar moral judgments. Second, observers may be external to the situation on some parameters, while being part of it in others. They can, for example, be relatives or close friends of one of the parties, or they can belong to the same ethnic or social group. They might favor or care for one of the parties for reasons unrelated to the moral situation itself. The observer I am referring to is in no way an impartial, disinterested onlooker who can put aside preferences imparted by culture. Every observer judges a moral situation with respect to a set of values regarded as unquestionable by a culture or subculture.

Even though "observer" therefore seems rather a fuzzy term, it does have the advantage of referring to an agent judging events that are somewhat external to him or her. The observer I am referring to has no direct personal involvement in the moral situation he or she is judging.

At this stage, I am interested to understand what leads us to judge theft or medical negligence as a wrongful act, rather than to consider the perspective of either the thief or his or her victim. Of course, both thief and victim make moral judgments concerning the event, but because the two are physically and emotionally involved their judgments are heavily influenced by their self-interests. I will argue that in judging harm and violations, we use a constant set of rules, rules that are cross-cultural and universal. These rules are more apparent when we judge others than they are when we judge ourselves.

Of course, the moral domain extends far beyond harm norm violations and encompasses many other types of cases – for example, cases in which people judge situations as morally wrong even though no harm is involved. Consider Murphy et al.'s (2000) scenario in which a brother and his sister have protected consensual sex. They do it only once, they enjoy it, and they don't share their secret with anyone. People tend to think of their act as morally wrong even though no one is harmed. Murphy et al. (2000) found similar responses when they asked their subjects to relate to a case involving cannibalism. A woman working alone late one night in a medical pathology lab decides to cook and eat a discarded piece of human cadaver that was donated to the lab for medical research. Once again, subjects who were asked for their judgment deemed this act to be wrong.

In my view, the ways in which such cases are judged is closely related to the aversion some people feel towards same-sex relations or towards certain foods. They make an appeal to conventional, religious and cultural norms. But these are not harm norms, and eating a corpse is not like hurting other people. Violating cultural or religious norms may be judged as wrong and give rise to feelings of disgust. But harm norms are of a different class, with separate cognitive and affective mechanisms. Murphy et al.'s subjects thought that incest is revolting and gross, but they did not say that they either pitied the siblings or empathized with them, emotions that people usually mention when relating to victims of rape or murder.

It seems, then, that the word "moral" is applied in different domains. Hence, we are dealing with different "wrongs." For example, Shweder et al. (1997) refer to moral systems that emphasize purity – Shweder calls them "ethics of divinity" – in which immoral acts contaminate the soul. Ideals of purity are central to the moral system in such communities. There are moral rules pertaining to what you can eat, who you can talk to, what you can wear in temples and so on. In these cases, violators are regarded as pollutants. In collectivist cultures, Shweder et al. (1997) identify "ethics of community," which includes rules governing rank, respect for the family and the handling of communal resources. I will limit my model to moral judgments about the violation of harm norms, which I believe has a unique cognitive system.

Norms against harm play an important role in all societies. As Nichols (2004) aptly puts it, "even though the moral domain is hardly exhausted by harm-based violations, it is plausible that judgments about harm-based violations constitute an important core of moral judgment" (p. 7). Nichols argues that an understanding of the significance of harm-based violations emerges at an early stage of human development and appears to be universally applicable across cultures. In most societies, behaviors that cause harm are construed as crimes against the person and are likely to be the subject of moral censure.

How are moral situations represented in our mind?

The world we live in consists of a huge assemblage of objects and happenings that can be infinitely partitioned, generalized and simplified. Consequently, a vital element in any description of human knowledge representation is the account of the human ability to embrace a certain specific partitioning within the bunched mass of information that it has to deal with (Hahn & Ramscar, 2001).

The questions this book seeks to address relate to the partitioning of moral or right/wrong situations: What characteristics do different moral situations have in common? How do people recognize moral situations and identify regularities within them? What are these regularities?

My assumption is that we deal with moral situations in the same way we deal with other objects or events. We categorize the situation as moral and then judge it according to which *pre-existing representation* it most closely resembles (Hahn & Ramscar, 2001).

What kind of categorization do we use when processing a moral judgment?

Knowledge representation and its processing in the social field are subjects that have been investigated by cognitive psychologists. Their focus has been on how information is encoded and stored so that it can be retrieved later on.

Where, then, should we start?

The main area of interest to us in the inquiry of how we organize information about moral issues is the *act of recognizing a social situation as moral and the act of the judgment itself.*

In moral situations, the observer's mind is presented with a wealth of information on issues such as the harm done, the victim's and the perpetrator's states of mind, the motive, the narrative's detail and so on.

Above all else, there are two things we want to know:

1   Within all this wealth of information, how does the observer recognize that it is a moral situation? What are the defining components of moral situations for any given observer?
2   Once the observer recognizes that he or she is facing a moral situation, what is it that influences that observer's judgment?

Because I believe that ideally psychological investigation should begin with no prior assumptions, I will simply identify some of the features that are intrinsic to moral situations. The answers I am looking for should be internally coherent and fully consistent with these features.

It will quickly become apparent that, paradoxically, because they are so very basic, simple and intuitive, these features go virtually unnoticed most of the time, and we hardly give them much thought.

In *Philosophical Investigations* Wittgenstein (1953/2001) wrote:

> The aspects of things that are most important for us are hidden because of their simplicity and familiarity. (One is unable to notice something – because it is always before one's eyes.) The real foundation of his inquiry does not strike a person at all. And this means: we fail to be struck by what, once seen, is most striking and most powerful.
>
> (p. 129)

I will show that even though we tend to think that factors such as justice, fairness or individual rights play a major role in moral judgment, moral situations are in reality defined by more basic units. These are not merely emotional components of moral situations that, as sentimentalists would have it, form our moral judgments (Prinz, 2007). Nor is it a matter of conscious mental activity that involves intentional effortful and controllable processes. We will soon see that the process is made up of basic units that both cognitions and emotions take part in their construal.

The dyad-dominance effect of moral situations

What, then, are the most invisible and yet the most salient characteristics of a moral situation?

First, *the fundamental unit of moral situations is the dyad*. I call this phenomenon the *dyad-dominance effect* of moral situations. Essentially, this means that *moral situations are mentally represented as two parties in conflict*.

As noted in Chapter 1, this assumption was validated by Gray et al. (2012a) in their theory of dyadic morality. The dyadic structure is a global feature of the narrative of moral situations. It is also the most general component of moral situations: a dyad is always present in these situations, regardless of whether it involves many parties or a group (several individuals, large groups or even nation-states).

I suggest that this clustering of social data into dyads can be explained in terms of a far more general theory about how people make sense of events. My claim is that people show a quite general tendency to construe events in terms of dyads. This hypothesis should of course be tested in the laboratory. However, to illustrate the dyad-dominance effect of events, think, for example, of World War II. Encyclopaedias on World War II contain thousands of entries. Thousands of books have been written on various topics related to that war. Some 50 nations actively took part, and in effect it was a conflict that engulfed the whole world. On the side of the Allies, the main partners were the British Empire, France, the Soviet Union (from 1941), the US (again from 1941) and China. The main Axis powers ranged against them were Nazi Germany, Fascist Italy and the Empire of Japan. World War II changed the world, and hence everyone's lives, and those affected were not only the millions of widows, widowers and orphans, but also succeeding generations. The life of every orphaned child, as well as every child who had lost just one parent, brother or sister, was damaged. World War II involved a multitude of war crimes, innumerable people who were to blame and human suffering on a massive scale. Now, what is the first thing that comes to mind when one thinks of this war? Despite the numerous and complex historical events and constellations, moral failures and human suffering that occurred in the course of this worldwide conflict, the first thing that might well come to mind is a dyad: Nazi Germany against the Allies. In a sense, the dyad Nazi Germany/Allies represents a kind of global feature of World War II. The dyad Nazi Germany/Allies is a super-category that enables the mind to pack a wealth of information about World War II into a single unit. Of course, how you group the information is culturally dependent. A holocaust survivor might choose the Nazis/Jews dyad and a survivor from Hiroshima, if asked, would perhaps group World War II into a Japan/US dyad. But all will probably use the dyad as an organizing schema.

Following Gray et al. (2012a), I suggest that a dyad is present in the background of every moral situation, regardless of whether it involves many parties or a group (several individuals, large groups or even nation-states).

Second, *most moral situations include an observer who evaluates the dyad*. In most moral situations, three sides are involved: two conflicting parties (a dyad) and an observer.

We can represent all moral situations with the following abstraction:

O relates to the following dyad: A → C

O – observer

A – perceived wrongdoer

C – perceived victim

→ relations, what happened between the two, harm done

Now I will demonstrate these first two essential features that experientially define any moral situation. I will show how moral situations remain constant in their dyadic structure across a wide range of moral dilemmas of entirely different content and associations.

(1) Capital punishment
    Does the state have a right to sentence convicted murderers to death?
    Observer (O) relates to the following dyad:

    (A) state → (C) convicted murderer

(2) Abortion
    Does a woman have a right to abort her fetus?
    Observer (O) relates to the following dyad:

    (A) pregnant woman → (C) fetus

(3) Totalitarian regime

Do rulers have the right to censor free speech, arrest their opponents and elect themselves?

Observer (O) relates to the following dyad:

(A) totalitarian ruler(s) → (C) the people

(4) Bombing civilians in self-defense

Does a state have the right to bomb civilian, non-military targets in a non-friendly neighboring state from which militants have launched rockets into its territory, killing civilians?

Observer (O) relates to the following dyad:

(A) state's army → (C) civilians of neighboring state

(5) Murder/manslaughter case

Did John kill David in cold blood, or did David provoke him prior to the killing?

Observer (O) relates to the following dyad:

(A) David → (C) John

(6) Medical negligence case

Were the medical complications suffered by the patient after surgery caused by the physician's negligence?

Observer (O) relates to the following dyad:

(A) physician → (C) sick patient

It hardly needs mentioning that the questions above relate to different issues. Some, such as those relating to the case of murder/manslaughter or medical negligence cases, are questions about facts. Others, such as those connected to abortion and capital punishment, are questions about personal beliefs and values. The moral situation of the totalitarian regime seems to already incorporate the judgment itself – the question posed resembling in some way the enquiry as to whether stealing is wrong. The bombing of civilians in populated areas from which missiles were fired illustrates the differences between a simple moral situation and a complex one. As is the case with many other moral dilemmas, the observer has to judge between two C's, two victims – civilians of the state into which the missiles were fired and civilians of the state from which the missiles were fired. In fact, in such situations, the observer has to grapple with two dyads:

(A) state army → (C) civilians of neighboring state

(C) militias → (A) civilians of state

Thus, in this case, the process of reaching a judgment involves deciding on the C you side with: the civilians of the neighboring state or those of the attacking state. In order for a judgment to be made, one of the dyads has to succeed in capturing the observer's mind while the other is discarded.

The important thing is that the A → C structure is the fundamental unit by which all moral situations are represented in our minds, regardless of content and outward manifestations.

Whether it is a tort law case, a war between nations or a petition against an unjust government act, the mind integrates the enormous amount of information available to construct one dyad in conflict. The dyad provides a cognitive framework within which we can relatively easily integrate and organize information relating to a particular moral situation. Without a dyadic structure, moral situations make little sense. In the absence of such a framework, we would be unable to extract meaning from the information we possess about the parties.

I suggest that the process of construing a dyad out of social information about conflict probably occurs at a very early stage in information processing, that several pieces of information relating to each party can be evaluated simultaneously, and that the basic process is fast, unintentional, efficient and occurs outside awareness.

Of course, one can think of many examples of moral situations that, strictly speaking, involve more than two parties. The above example of civilians being bombed demonstrates that military/civilian can also be paired so that despite each of the two groups consisting of thousands of people, the moral judgment is passed on a single dyad. But what of situations in which a number of crimes are committed against one victim by a single individual or a group of people?

Let us suppose that 10 thieves break into the houses of two neighbouring women. First, they break into one house, and then they go into the other. After the robberies, the group makes its getaway in two vehicles. Thief 1 drives off in the leading car and, in flight, collides with a pedestrian, who is killed. Subsequently, thief 1 joins up with thief 2 so as to rob thieves 3, 4 and 5 of the booty. A battle ensues between the two groups of thieves, in the course of which thieves 3, 4 and 5 are wounded by shots fired by thief 1. Meanwhile, the second vehicle carrying thieves 6, 7, 8, 9 and 10 continues its getaway, during which the thieves decide to stop and rob a supermarket. In the event, not only do they rob the store, but they also use their weapons to force four customers who happen to be there to hand over their personal cash.

How are we to judge this messy moral situation?

We will be unable to make a judgment unless we split up the narrative into its dyadic components, one thief and one victim. We will have to take a look at each thief individually to determine whom he harmed. Each incident in which a thief harmed a victim will be thought of as a moral situation that will have to be judged.

For example, thief 1 was a participant in the following six dyads:

thief 1 → woman 1

robbery

thief 1 → woman 2

robbery

thief 1 → pedestrian

accidental killing

thief 1 → thief 3

shooting and wounding

thief 1 → thief 4

shooting and wounding

thief 1 → thief 5

shooting and wounding

Thief 6 (like thieves 7, 8, 9 and 10) was involved in the following seven dyads:

thief 6 → woman 1

robbery

thief 6 → woman 2

robbery

thief 6 → supermarket owner 1

robbery

thief 6 → customer 1

robbery

thief 6 → customer 2

robbery

thief 6 → customer 3

robbery

thief 6 → customer 4

robbery

Of course, if one of the thieves commits more than 100 offences in the course of the same incident, we will at some point tire of judging each of the offenses separately. But the example nevertheless serves to demonstrate that when confronted with a mass of information, we split it up into dyads, and that judgment is made by clarifying what happened in each of the dyads separately.

So, the A → C format serves as an intrinsic unifier of the class of things that are moral situations. I suggest that *even though the structure A → C may take a variety of forms, it has one constant component: "someone did something that caused, or might have caused, harm to someone else."* The structure points to a strong causal link between A's act and the effect it had or might have had on C. Causality between A's act and the impact it had or might have had on C is a central component. Thomas Reid, the eighteenth-century philosopher who founded the Scottish School of Common Sense, argued that the only beings that can be truly regarded as causes and/or agents are those who are able to effect a change either in themselves or in another being solely by means of their own active power (Reid, 1788, p. 1). Besides, irrespective of the impact of that power, a claim of causality requires that there be something that is contingent and dependent on the power and will of its cause. The ability to generate a particular result implies an ability *not* to generate it. If this were not the case, the eventual outcome is not described in terms of cause and effect, but rather as an inevitability – a contradiction of the concept of power in the strict sense of that term. I suggest therefore that the categorization of moral situations in fact relies on our understanding of a particular causal relation between two people in the sense that Reid described it (the effect of active power that is contingent, dependent upon the will of its cause), and not on overall similarities between situations at the level of content.

But there is another point. Why is "might have caused harm" important? Is actual harm not necessary?

There are cases in which a wrong has no victim. Consider a case in which Smith points a gun at John but by chance misses his target. John sustains no physical harm at all, not a scratch. As Smith did not actually injure him, it would seem that this should not be considered a moral situation at all. We might think that John was harmed by being scared to death when Smith attempted to murder him. However, even if John had somehow remained totally unaware about Smith's attempt to murder him, we would still conclude that what Smith did was morally wrong. Even the attempt to harm someone is a wrongful act. A victimless act of wrongdoing is nonetheless an act that constitutes a moral situation. Even where there is no victim, the attempted infliction of harm signals a collapse of dyadic relations. As we will see in the next chapter, *it is the violation of expectation more than the harm itself to which we most respond.*

What can we say about a situation in which there is a victim who has suffered no intended harm? Consider a case in which Smith was pushed by another person and fell on John. As a result, John fell out of the window and broke his legs. At first sight, this example seems to clearly match the A → C format because Smith did something that caused harm to Jones, and yet it is hardly likely that we would condemn Smith and accuse him of breaking John's legs.

This case does not fall under wrongdoing because it lacks the causality factor. We understand that John was not wounded as a result of something Smith *intended* to do. We have no problem in recognizing that the chain of events that caused John's broken legs did not start with Smith, but rather with Smith being pushed by another person. Smith's mindset prior to and during the unfortunate act appears to be of interest to us, since such factors as intention and free will form a part of Smith's thought or mindset rather than being part of the observable facts. *Intention is part of the mindset the alleged perpetrator has towards his victim, and this mindset (or, more accurately, as we shall soon see, attitude towards the dependent aspects of the victim) is what we most focus on.*

What do moral situations have in common?

The common dyadic feature of moral situations leaves open many questions about the nature of moral situations.

Let us first consider the fact already established that situations in which right/wrong judgments are applied come in a variety of types. By what glue are situations such as stealing, rape, murder and medical negligence bound together? Does not this hypothesis go against the powerful intuition that "good, coherent categories group together things that are similar" (Pothos & Chater, 2001, p. 51)? Surely, if all of these cases evoke a right/wrong, good/bad judgment, then obviously they belong to the same category.

There is evidence that children begin to recognize moral situations and to differentiate between them and moral conventions quite early in life. Smetana (1981), Turiel (1983) and Nucci (2001) have demonstrated that children distinguish between moral and conventional rules. For example, children from nursery school age draw a distinction between rules prohibiting hitting and stealing, on the one hand, and rules prohibiting speaking without raising your hand in class or rules related to dress codes, on the other. They treat moral rule violations as more serious and less dependent on authority. Hitting would be wrong no matter what the teacher says, but talking in class would be appropriate if the teacher allows it. Children tend to justify moral rules by an appeal to harm inflicted by others, whereas they justify conventional rules by appealing to conventions. So, how do they recognize the common denominator of or similarity between moral situations?

We need to be quite clear about what we mean by similarity. Whether similarity is a sufficiently well-defined notion for it to be used as an instrument of classification is a question that has been raised by several leading theorists (Hampton, 2001). Nelson Goodman (1972) took the view that because any two objects can be alternatively regarded as being similar or dissimilar, depending on the aspects that one chooses to describe, similarity in and of itself may not be an effective tool of classification. Hahn and Ramscar (2001) argued that unless the similarities between two things are clearly specified, merely saying that they are similar has no significance in this context. All this comes to explain why categorization in general, and the categorization of moral situations more specifically, cannot be grounded in similarity alone. One option for categorizing moral situations is on the basis of the mental operation they require. Since all moral situations seem to require that the observer is required to make a right/wrong judgment, we can conclude that moral situations are all based on the similarity of the mental decision required by the observer. However, this would appear to be a circular argument since moral situations *are* right/wrong judgments. It's part of their definition.

So, we are looking for a system of categorization that allows affiliation to the group of many members who, if one were to go by appearance, are in many respects dissimilar.

If the A → C format is common to all moral situations regardless of their outward appearance, then moral situations demonstrate a dissociation between categorization and perceived similarity, or between surface features and deeply ingrained characteristics. The question whether categorization is based on perceived similarity or deeply embedded features has generated a wealth of research among cognitive psychologists. Medin and Ortony's *Psychological Essentialism* (1989) suggests that adults "act as if their concepts contain essence placeholders" (p. 186). The essence of something – its fundamental nature – is generally regarded as a property hidden from view that makes it what it is. It is thought to be the cause of the object's observable surface characteristics. According to psychological essentialism, therefore, what is common to all within the same category is the fundamental cause that has produced the immediately recognizable surface features. Psychological essentialism is therefore the tendency to view entities as if they have an underlying, often invisible, essence that makes them what they are (Medin & Ortony, 1989).

Much research has produced outcomes that are consistent with psychological essentialism. For example, the fact that natural kinds are categorized together based on internal, deeper features, despite differences in surface features (Ahn, 1998; Gelman & Wellman, 1991; Keil, 1989), supports the importance of essences/essential features. Essentialism has been credited with explaining why people will endorse an object as a piece of art regardless of its appearance, as long as the artist's intention was to create art, calling upon a deeper underlying feature of the category of art (Gelman & Bloom, 2000). Furthermore, inferences that would follow from belief in the existence of essences (e.g. biological bases, immutability, inductive potency) have been documented in domains as varied as social categories and mental disorder categories (e.g. Haslam et al., 2000; for review, see

Dar-Nimrod & Heine, 2011). Causal essentialism is restricted to kinds – to collections of individuals that fit with people's intuitive notions of natural and non-arbitrary categories (Ahn et al., 2013). This variety of evidence has been used to support the claim that psychological essentialism is a pervasive cognitive belief (but for evidence against psychological essentialism, see also Kalish, 2002; Strevens, 2000).

Given these results, it is plausible to suggest that we recognize a moral situation not on the basis of formal similarity, but on the basis of the nature of its cause and consequence. By revealing the deep commonalities among the diverse moral situations that fall under its scope, the current account is able to generate new insights into these phenomena, as well as new empirical predictions.

A reservation may be that it takes a high degree of abstraction to figure out that both rape and medical negligence entail right/wrong judgments. But note that to our purposes, people do not need to be consciously aware of the deeper nature of moral judgments. Even if they lack the conscious knowledge that both medical negligence and rape involve harm, they can still easily tell that it is wrong to rape, just as it is wrong for a surgeon to abandon his or her patient in the middle of surgery.

Moral situations in context

More problems with the current thesis regarding harm involve situations that completely fall under the A → C format and yet are not judged as moral, or are judged as moral by one observer and not by another. Consider the following situations:

A man throwing stones at a brick wall.

Two wrestlers competing in a wrestling match.

The sport of fox hunting, in the course of which the fox is tracked, chased and sometimes killed.

Note that the three examples, though very different in content, share many superficial features of the A → C format. In fact, although each of them triggers different meanings and associative networks, their one common feature actually seems to be the A → C structure. However, even though all include harm and two parties, it does not automatically follow that the mind interprets these dyads as A → C, as in "John killed David."

In the first case, there are two objects (a man and a brick wall) and what appears to be an aggressive act (throwing stones). Yet most people will probably not interpret the situation as an A → C structure, and the facts are not likely to be read in terms of moral conflict. Later, we will see that in order for a situation to be structured as A → C, the observer has to have a specific relation to the distressed party, a relation that does not exist between an observer and a brick wall. Here, too, there is a violation of expectations because we don't expect a man to throw stones at a brick wall. However, as I will show, in moral violations, the violation of expectation is of a specific kind, and entails two human beings or groups (and some animals with human features).

In the second case, two people are locked in a violent fight. If one of them overpowers the other, the wrestling match in which they are engaged may seem to have the structure of A → C. However, wrestling, even in its most aggressive forms, is not usually considered as a moral situation. This does not mean that wrestling is morally justified, and some people might indeed think it is not. But the question that concerns us here is not whether observers are right or wrong in their judgments, but the process of judgment itself. The participants, both strong adults, volunteered of their own free will to partake in the wrestling match, and wrestling is generally considered to be a sport. These facts will lead at least some people to conclude that from the point of view of both the participants and the spectators, wrestling does not constitute a moral situation.

The case of fox hunting demonstrates the relativity of what is perceived as a moral dyad. Note that victims need not be humans. They can be other living creatures. People in modern societies tend to judge cruelty against animals as morally wrong. But the important thing about this example is the relativity of the judgment. David might be appalled by the sport of fox hunting, but Sue is completely indifferent to the suffering of foxes. David forms a hunters/foxes dyad, but Sue does not place hunters and foxes into the A → C structure. Indeed, until the previous century, fox hunting was not generally considered an immoral practice. Had David lived in the nineteenth century, he, too, would probably have felt morally indifferent to this sport. Thus, recognizing a dyad in moral conflict depends on culture, context and other differences between individuals. Note that even though Sue does not condemn fox hunting, she is certainly able to understand what offends David. In this sense, though Sue is able to form a hunters/foxes dyad, one could say that while the dyad exists for her, it is turned off. I will leave the discussion on turned-off dyads to Chapter 7. Here, I will just note that we construe a *turned-off dyad* when we easily construe an A → C dyad but it does not trigger our emotions or engage us in any meaningful way. The construed dyad simply does not charge us with the emotions and cognitions in which we would favor A or condemn C. However, we can understand someone who thinks otherwise. Even though Sue has no feelings for foxes, she can understand David's position. In contrast, Sue will not understand David if he insists that a man throwing stones at a brick wall – or any other insensate object – constitutes a moral situation.

Thus, certain dyads simply do not make any sense, while other dyads can be so construed, even though the observer's reaction may be one of indifference or disagreement. Alternatively, there are dyads about whom observers hold contradictory views as to who is the perpetrator (A) and who is the victim (C).

The conditions necessary for construing a social situation as moral will emerge as we proceed. At this point, I am merely calling attention to the fact that many situations which appear to have the structure of a moral dyad do not, in fact, trigger a moral question in the minds of many observers.

Following the dispute between David and Sue regarding fox hunting, we are now ready to define another important feature of moral situations.

Moral judgments are observer-relative and constrained by our cognitions

The form of A → C is observer-relative. It is a configuration that depends on our mind, not on objective reality.

The recognition of a social situation as moral, and the subsequent judgment, are matters that are never just based on the external properties of social data, but are assigned by the observer's mind. The observer never simply reacts to some objective property of the moral situation "out there."

Hume (1739/2000) tells us:

> It lies in yourself, not in the object . . . when you pronounce any action or character to be vicious, you mean nothing, but that from the constitution of your nature you have a feeling or sentiment of blame from the contemplation of it.

> (III. i.i)

At first glance, this may appear to undermine the objective foundations of morality. Yet that is not the issue here. Remember that our question is not how things should be in the moral domain, but rather how we presuppose things to be. We want to tease out the observer's psychological suppositions without necessarily agreeing with these assumptions ourselves.

Our next step is to show that moral judgments, unlike our aesthetic tastes, are not arbitrary.

In the process of forming moral judgments, the observer will have contrasting cognitions and emotions towards the respective conflicted parties. A mental representation of A → C gives clear direction to our cognitions and emotions. When the moral judgment is unambiguous and the harm is judged serious, the observer will sense negative feelings such as blame and rage towards A, and positive feelings such as compassion, empathy and pity towards C. The affective response matches a set of cognitive convictions related to the questions of which party is wrong, needs help, deserves punishment and so on. Observers might react with different levels of emotional intensity because individuals differ in their sensitivity to these vital cues of wrongdoing. However, both affect and cognition will follow one fixed, particular direction.

Once we construe the dyad as A → C, the dyad takes over. It runs us. Our expectations from A run us. The fact that we can think about the dyad gives the false impression that we are running it, that we control moral judgment, whereas actually the dyad as we constructed it controls our judgment.

Suppose the observer is presented with the following information: "A burglar stole money from a poor, elderly woman." The observer construes the situation as:

burglar → elderly woman

    stealing

The implication of construing the moral situation in this manner is that the observer responds by pitying the elderly woman and/or by condemning the burglar. Some observers might respond with sorrow or extreme rage, others will be completely indifferent, and most will react somewhere between these extremes. Of course, numerous personal, social, contextual and cultural elements determine the observer's response and its intensity.

How the information is presented to the observer is also important (as text, film or real-life witnessing). For the moment, however, I want to concentrate on the fact that though people differ in the intensity of their affective response, the *direction* of both the affective and the cognitive reaction is similar once the observer has construed the situation as A → C.

Once people construe the burglar and the old woman as A → C, the pattern of moral judgment becomes fixed and constant. People will not condemn the elderly woman and empathize with the burglar; they will not think that the elderly woman was wrong or that she is the one who should be put on trial. The negative and positive feelings, as well as the feelings of those who remain relatively indifferent, follow a specific direction to the exclusion of others.

Our moral judgments are not arbitrary and are not just a matter of taste. Even when they lead to contradictory conclusions, they are not entirely flexible. Though it can be said that the construing of moral judgment is relative, and allows for diverse cultural and personal projections, it is not the case that each and every projection will be perceived by observers as sensible and/or acceptable. While some observers might think that because of Anthony's harsh childhood he should not be sentenced to death for killing Mark, it is hard to believe that anyone will think Anthony should be praised by the court. *The dyad constrains our cognitive apparatus. A dyad will allow certain projections and block others if, and only if, it is construed as A → C.* Thus, there is a sense in which a moral dyad can be viewed as being decisively intolerant when it comes to certain possible projections.

Moral judgment is intuitive and unconscious

Often the observer judges right/wrong situations intuitively, and with little effort. Often our intuitions about right and wrong are based on nonconscious processing.

As Bless and Forgas (2000) indicate, cognitive psychologists have repeatedly demonstrated that only a small fraction of the things we observe, think or do is dealt with by conscious experiences. The searchlight of consciousness can only ever illuminate a tiny circle of the phenomenological field. In the background, there is always a continuous ebb and flow of feelings, associations, somatic cues, implicit memories and dispositions – subjective experiences – that seem to play a key role in guiding us through

social situations and help us to understand and respond to the many challenges of social life (Bless & Forgas, 2000, pp. 372–373).

In *Strangers to Ourselves* (2002), Timothy D. Wilson presents the concept
of the adaptive unconscious. Wilson thinks that the mind is a wonderfully
sophisticated and efficient tool, more so than the most powerful computer
ever built. An important source of its tremendous power is its ability to perform quick, non-conscious analyses of a great deal of incoming information
and react to that information in effective ways (Wilson, 2002, p. 16).

Think of how our mind processes murder. Our emotional and cognitive
response to a murder occurs simply and directly, with little need for complex processing of information. The intensity of our response, however,
depends on the type of exposure. Thus, we will be much more shocked by
a murder we ourselves have witnessed than by one about which we read
in the paper. But the type of exposure will not affect the direction and the
very formation of the dyad, nor will it influence the intuition that something terrible occurred.

We just know that if A killed C, A did something entirely wrong and
appalling. Our intuitions steer the way to specific cognitions and judgments. The part that is processed non-consciously is the judgment itself –
the equation between cold-blooded murder and wrongful act – with a
matching negative emotional response. Of course, in some cases, understanding the nature of an A → C dyad might be a relatively complex task.
The analysis of the input of an A → C dyad with all its details (who did
what to whom and under what circumstances) requires a concerted effort
and full awareness, and might entail a high level of cognitive processing.

Moral judgments are therefore automatic, especially in serious harm
norm violations. Cognitive psychologists traditionally refer to "automatic
behavior" in relation to motor behaviors such as driving a car or playing
the piano. The mind processes a serious harm norm violation in a rapid,
non-conscious, involuntary way, as though on automatic pilot. In fact,
both emotional and cognitive responses to serious harm norm violations
meet most of the five defining features of automatic thinking: it is done
with little conscious thought; it is quick and effortless, in the sense that it
takes only a few milliseconds to judge murder as wrongful; it is unintentional, in that we unconsciously condemn the murderer and feel pity for
the victim; it is uncontrollable, given that we have little to say about the
operation of our non-conscious filtering mechanism, and we can neither
stop nor change it (we cannot condemn the victim and pity the murderer,

nor can we decide to feel nothing at all); and our response to serious crimes is something that happens to us without us having brought it about or agreeing to be part of it.

While in some important respects, moral judgments are comparable to other automatic processes such as riding a bicycle or driving a car, they differ strikingly in two ways: we had to learn how to drive a car, but we knew murder was wrong before anybody taught us that particular lesson. As we have seen, there is a great deal of evidence from developmental psychology to the effect that from an early age, children possess a basic capacity for making core moral judgments. The other difference between moral judgment and automatic behaviors is that moral judgments are affectively charged.

What can we learn from these commonalities and differences?

In such automatic behaviors as driving a car, the period of learning can be pinpointed (driving instruction). Our acquisition of moral knowledge is a different matter. How exactly is it that we took "moral lessons"? What are the innate or acquired mechanisms that enabled us to learn, and at which point in our development did we "take" such "lessons"?

All these are things that need to be explained. The fact that emotional response accompanies moral judgment means that affective mechanisms shape moral acquisition.

When making the judgment that murder is a wrongful act, or in making a judgment about any other harm norm violation, we do not need to look for evidence or weigh up a set of arguments for and against the proposition. Our judgment is not deduced or inferred from another. In and of itself, that judgment possesses a sense of truth that does not rely on any other source.

I do not want to underestimate the importance of the conscious and rational processes that are actually involved in the making of a moral judgment – those that occur more slowly, with intent, control and effort. Driving a car is a relatively simple operation, whereas the evaluation of moral problems is influenced by many types of information, contexts and experiences. The process of weighing *all* the relevant facts is conscious and non-automatic. Some moral dilemmas are extremely complex and consume huge intellectual resources. However, we must differentiate between deciding on the facts (see Chapter 6) and the act of judgment itself, which is achieved (in many cases) rapidly and smoothly.

According to Haidt (2000), we engage in moral judgment every day in a rapid, easy and holistic manner: "It is primarily when intuitions conflict, or when the social situation demands thorough examination of all facets of a scenario that the reasoning process is called upon" (p. 10). However, as I will show in the following chapters, conflicting intuitions and facts are driven by a mental process of which we are unaware. Even our conscious processes are grounded in unconscious thinking.

The dyad as a whole

How can we judge so easily and effortlessly in so many different dyads when every dyad is embedded in different contexts and circumstances? Indeed, at first glance, dyads appear to host infinite variables. A and C can be anyone, there are countless forms of harm one can inflict on the other, not to mention the array of psychological components such as criminal intent, motive and responsibility that are also part of the dyads. Look at the morning newspaper and you will read about a plethora of moral dyads: a hit-and-run accident on the highway, an armed robbery, a case of fraud, a suicide attack. Regardless of the staggering diversity of dyads, we feel that even though the parties in these dyads entertain various relations, and even if circumstances and outcomes differ, they are all part of a single phenomenon. Thus, quickly, automatically and with determination, we arrive at a general judgment. Although the range of possible dyads is very large, I will show that the number of principles by which we judge them is limited.

Given the enormous amount of data there exist in relation to any given moral dyad, how do we organize the information for a particular perceived dyad? Is there a specific component of the moral situation to which we respond? How do we extract a judgment from the basic features of A, C and →?

Let's return to the burglar/elderly woman dyad. Suppose one is presented with the following information:

A burglar broke into an old woman's house and stole her money.

burglar → elderly woman

stealing

Do we break the dyad down into its basic component parts – the wrongdoing of the burglar (A), the violent act itself (→), the fact that the woman is old and poor (C)? Or do we organize the individual elements into a global and holistic totality? What social data are (most) relevant and informative in assisting our moral judgment?

We might hope to find the essential component by first making a list of the different variables in each of the constituent parts of the moral situation, A, C and →.

Holding each of the critical parts constant while varying the others enables us to decide which provides a sufficient basis for making a judgment. If a particular moral component is sufficient, then even if we vary the other components it will not lead to a radical change in the moral judgment we make. Before we begin our experiment, we need to establish a set of standards by which we will judge the importance of the different elements such as intent, damage and so on.

One way to do this is to look at how the judicial system relates to different dyads. My assumption is that the law's attitude towards different dyads often mirrors our natural and intuitive response to these constructs. Therefore, facts about motive, intent and harm are crucial in penal law because we use them to define the essential features of the moral dyad. In fact, the law is designed to conform to our instinctive outlook (although this is not an obvious assumption, and it has fueled much philosophical debate). Thus, in order to further clarify the inner process involved in reaching a moral judgment, I resort to legal terms.

When we judge moral situations, we take into account information that corresponds to the basic structure of moral situations A → C.

(1) When weighing relevant facts concerning the *perceived perpetrator's (A)* state of mind, we will take into account the following considerations:

The degree of intent, deliberation, premeditation and malice. Did A intend to harm, or did he or she cause the harm accidentally? Was the killing intentional but without deliberation, premeditation and malice? In a case in which a life has been taken, we want to know if it was the result of a car accident (no intent) or armed robbery (deliberate, premeditated and with malice).

Motive. Why did A harm? In the case of a murder, we want to know if A killed for money, in self-defense or because C provoked him or her.

Mental health. Did A have the mental capacity to behave in conformity with the law?

(2) When weighing relevant facts concerning the *perceived victim (C)*, our interest will be focused on:

Degree of suffering. How much did he or she suffer? How severe was the damage, both physically and emotionally?

Responsibility. Was C responsible in any way for A's behavior? Could it be argued that he or she deserved to be dealt with in that way? In the case of a murder, we may want to know whether C provoked A, or alternatively had no contact with A before the killing.

(3) When weighing relevant facts concerning *the act itself*, we will want to know:

The nature of the harming action. Did A push C, kick C, stab C or shoot C? In mitigation, it may perhaps be argued that prior to the killing, C may have neglected A or failed to keep a promise to him or her.

The results of an "experiment" of this type strikingly bear out that though each of the essential elements is decisive for the moral judgment, it appears that no single element is sufficient for the observer to reach such a judgment. Suppose A killed C deliberately without C having in any way provoked him or her, but that A suffers from paranoid schizophrenia and killed C in the course of a psychotic episode. In such circumstances, A cannot be held accountable for his or her act because at the time of the killing he or she was insane, and therefore unable to tell the difference between right and wrong. Thus, as insanity may prevent a subject to comprehend the wrongfulness of his or her conduct, the finding of premeditation is not by itself a sufficient basis for making a moral judgment. Suppose that A shot C and was determined to kill him or her during an armed robbery, but that the bullet missed, and therefore C was not harmed in any way. A cannot be accused of murder in the first degree because he or she did not actually commit murder. He or she can only be accused of having attempted to murder C. It was only by accident that C was not murdered by A, and it would be reasonable to assume that had C in fact succeeded in committing murder, his or her sentence would be rather different. Thus, in addition to intent and insanity, the extent of the harm inflicted also matters. In going through the remaining components one by one, the reader will see that no single component is sufficient for reaching a moral judgment. Indeed, change to any one of these components will alter the entire judgment.

It seems that no one part of the dyad (A, C and →) can be separately judged. Only the dyad as a whole is subject to judgment. Each part captures certain essential features of the nature of the dyad, and we judge its role within the entire dyadic relation in which it is embedded. Thus, if A was *forced at gunpoint* to inflict harm on C, then the degree of C's suffering is not relevant to A's responsibility because, even in a case of extreme injury, A will not be held responsible for C's suffering. *The separate components are important – and can be understood – only insofar as they are part of the whole.* Moral judgment is an interactive process combining information gathered from multiple levels of processing, such as intent, motive, victim's suffering and so on. Judgments are established when one reaches a full gestalt of the dyad. The dyad's gestalt conveys a meaning that differs from each separate component. That is why when it comes to cases of murder, manslaughter and killing in self-defense, we form three different judgments, despite the fact that all three dyads resulted in a person's death.

Harman et al. (2010) have compared moral judgment with the actions of the Necker cube, an optical illusion in which the observer cannot decide whether he or she is seeing the cube from below or from above. This is so because there is a tension between the apexes in the representation of the cube such that when a certain intersection point between lines creates the perception of a certain apex, this changes the perception of the entire cube. Others described the multiplicity of factors taken into account in a single moral judgment as gestalt shifts (Churchland, 1996; DesAutels, 1996). According to Churchland (1996), moral perception will be subject to the same ambiguities that characterize perception generally. Moral perception will be subject to the same modulation, shaping and occasional "prejudice" that recurrent pathways make possible. By the same token, moral perception will occasionally be capable of the same cognitive "reversals" that we see in such examples as the old/young woman (a case of an ambiguous figure that can be perceived both as a young and old lady). It can display cases where one's first reactions to a novel social situation is simply moral confusion, but where a little background knowledge or collateral information suddenly resolves that confusion from "an example of something familiar, into an unexpected instance of some familiar moral prototype" (p. 102). For Churchland, moral disagreement takes place when the discussants try to reduce overstated components of the situation, and to increase the salience of certain other components in order to change which exemplar gets triggered.

My aim in this chapter has been to show the inner structure of moral situations: an observer evaluating a conflicted dyad (A → C). I have argued that much of the judgment process is rapid, intuitive, non-conscious and based on gut feeling. However, there is some order within our judgments. They are not arbitrary, and they involve cognitive processes as well. First, we have to construe a dyad. Second, we have to decide who is A and who is C, and what A did to C. The observer consolidates relevant facts concerning A, C and → in order to create a unified version or gestalt of the dyad. Once the observer constitutes the parties in an A → C structure, both affect and cognition follow in one fixed, particular direction. Armed with this knowledge, we can now attempt to gain an understanding of how the brute facts of the moral dyad (e.g. intent, motive, degree of suffering) translate into a psychic language of which we are mostly unaware, and which is rather unlike the one we encounter commonly in studies on moral psychology.

Chapter 5

Decoding moral situations

The structural analysis of moral situations reveals that we tend to constitute them as a conflicted dyad. Somehow, we appear to know a great deal about dyads. Our judgment of dyads seems to be fairly flexible, encompassing an astonishing range of situations. It is as if we use a single conceptual framework to judge a wide variety of conflicted dyads. What, then, can we say a about the characteristics of our conceptual framework to moral judgment? What is it that we do when we construe a dyad?

It is probably the case that in the process of forming a moral judgment, the moral dyad that arises in our minds is evaluated against some prior knowledge we possess about dyads. We cross-reference the situation facing us with a "memory bank of dyads," which stores all the knowledge and information we possess about them.

My main thesis is that the various components of a moral situation, such as intent, motive or degree of suffering (all of which, as we have seen, are crucial to the process of reaching a moral judgment), represent something beyond themselves. In other words, the particular components of a moral situation, the way they can be represented as A, C and →, suggest that there is yet a further property that plays an even more profound and instructive role in our quest for a moral judgment.

In the process of making the judgment, we use a fixed set of rules and apply it in order to decipher the components of a given moral situation. This is a profound property of right/wrong judgments that moral psychology tends to overlook.

What, then, is this code?

My key thesis here is that we represent each of the parties, in ways that are comparable to our representation of children (or infants) and adults. All our efforts are geared to construct the reality of the moral situation in terms of a child/adult dyad.

Our knowledge concerning children and adults and their interrelations is presented in the form of schemas.[1] Sternberg (1999) defined it as follows: "A schema is a mental framework for organizing relevant knowledge, creating a meaningful structure of related concepts and based on prior experiences" (p. x).

In Rumelhart's classic 1980 paper, he defined a schema as "a data structure for representing the generic concepts stored in memory" (Rumelhart, 1980, p. 34). He went on to state that "there are schemata representing our knowledge about all concepts: those underlying objects, situations, events, sequences of events, actions and sequences of actions" (p. 34).

Schemas have a number of characteristics that permit wide flexibility in their use. For instance, schemas cover typical, broad facts that may, in some instances, possess slightly different individual characteristics. Moreover, the degree of abstraction of any given schema may vary (Rumelhart & Ortony, 1977). For example, a schema that refers to the notion of responsibility is bound to be far more abstract than one referring to a child. Information about relationships can also be included within the framework of a schema (Komatsu, 1992).

On the whole, schemas are used by cognitive psychologists in their attempt to understand concepts. It is an organizational framework that might also contribute to understanding our use of information in the making of moral judgments.

Construing the two conflicting parties as a child/adult dyad probably activates a universal schema. It is sufficiently general to be applicable to a broad variety of moral situations.

Now we can understand the representation of a moral situation as an A → C dyad in a more complete way.

In this representation, I term the party identified with the adult position A, and the party associated with the role of the child C. Therefore, the basic structure of moral situations is represented in our minds as:

O relates to:

A → C

We judge a conflicted dyad by:

(a) Evaluating the child-related characteristics and the adult-related characteristics of each party, and deciding, if we can, which of the parties matches an adult schema and which a child schema. As we will see, the feature that most saliently differentiates between child and adult is dependency. Therefore, we tend to perceive parties conforming to the child schema as dependent and adult-schema parties as independent.

(b) Evaluating the relationship between the adult-schema and child-schema parties in terms of →, where → is the symbol for the harm done within the dyadic relations, and denotes the mode of wrongdoing of the adult vis-à-vis the dependent. That is to say, we do not only have schemas for children and adults. We also possess a schema for the dyadic relation, centered on our knowledge of adults' obligations to children.

Evaluating the child-related characteristics and the adult-related characteristics of each party

Let us begin with the first component of judgment – the identification of the child-schema and adult-schema characteristics of each party.

Our evaluation of a moral situation rests on our inner schemas of children and adults and their relationships. According to Dijker's (2014) evolutionary theory of vulnerability-based morality, an exceptionally strong care system may have become installed in humans, which is easily activated by the slightest evidence of vulnerability and immaturity. Complementarily, humans may be said to have evolved a rich variety of ways to signal vulnerability and immaturity in order to trigger a care system in others, thereby ensuring aggression reduction, diverse prosocial behaviors and various moral emotions. Dijker (2014) posits that our evolutionary reasons for our strong sensitivity to vulnerability may possibly be explained by the fact that human infants are *altricial* (i.e. initially dependent on adults) and have an exceptionally long childhood; a further element in this evolutionary development may have been due to the existence of a cooperative breeding system in which participants responded in non-aggressive ways to immature individuals and were often involved in offering care to non-descendent infants (Hrdy, 2009).

Dijker (2014) posits that a care mechanism produces different motivational states or moral emotions (e.g. tenderness, sympathy, guilt, moral anger) in response to individuals perceived as vulnerable. Basically, the mechanism consists of a care system that is automatically triggered by vulnerability cues, a system for defense and aggression, and a process of causally attributing changes in the vulnerable object's well-being.

According to Dijker (2014), a positive emotion of tenderness can also be aroused while observing others in acute need and suffering; it can co-occur with distress and fear. One explanation of this phenomenon would be that harm and suffering can be experienced as evidence of vulnerability. When the perceiver observes cues associated with a threat to, or actual reduction in, the object's well-being, it will be the perceiver's general goal to prevent (further) reduction in the object's well-being or to restore reduced well-being. When the care object is under threat or actually harmed, the perceiver may use aggression in order to help the object by arousing the necessary moral emotions. Indeed, aggressive or angry responses at a causally responsible agent seem to be involved in both guilt and moral anger.

Child- and adult-related schemes

We have different schemas for children and adults. These schemas include expectations, feelings, cognitions and mental images in relation to children and adults, respectively.

Our schemas for children imply that children or infants:

- cannot discriminate between right and wrong;
- are not responsible for their actions, even when those actions are harmful;
- are not fully aware of the consequences of their behavior;
- do not intend to harm (in the way adults do);
- cannot take care of someone else who is in need;
- are helpless to the extent that their basic needs have to be supplied by a caregiver in order for them to survive; and
- usually evoke in adults positive feelings of tenderness, caring and empathy when they are distressed.

According to our schemas for adults, the very opposite set of propositions applies. We think that, unlike children, *adults do discriminate between right and wrong, and are responsible for their actions.*

In the process of moral judgment, the more someone matches a child schema (C), the *less likely* it is that the observer will:

- hold him or her responsible for his or her actions; and
- respond to him or her negatively.

And the *more likely* it is that the observer will:

- understand his or her behavior and forgive his or her wrongdoing; and
- be more sensitive to his or her suffering.

Alternatively, the more someone in a moral situation matches an adultlike schema (A), the *more likely* it is that the observer will:

- hold him or her responsible for his or her actions;
- consider him or her to have acted with intent, deliberation, premeditation and malice;
- not forgive or understand his or her wrongdoing; and
- be less sympathetic to his or her suffering.

The two schemas, adult and child, are not discrete, and maintain an interactive relation. They always go together – one does not exist without the other. They represent one continuum that can encompass a large variety of situations. The schemas are fixed around defining features of adults and children such as big/small, weak/strong, helpless/powerful, dependent/independent, intentional/unintentional, knowingly/unknowingly and responsible/irresponsible. The schemas are broad enough to cover endless variations on these themes. When facing a moral situation, the mind uses the two schemas of child/adult to select and organize the information that will most effectively support the judgment process.

The schemas we use for these judgments are not related to what children and adults *really are like and how they actually behave*. Parents, teachers and anyone who simply remembers what it was like to be a child realizes that children can at times be cruel, aggressive and hostile towards others. Numerous studies have demonstrated that from an early age, children behave aggressively in all sorts of ways. Boys, when angry, generally harm others with physical or verbal aggression such as hitting, pushing, kicking, throwing objects or threatening to perform these acts. Girls' aggression includes a range of behaviors such as excluding another child from a play group as a form of retaliation, intentionally withdrawing friendship as a way of hurting or controlling a child, and spreading rumors about a child to persuade peers to reject him or her (Crick & Grotpeter 1995, p. 711). Patterns of relational aggression are seen in children as young as 3 to 5 years of age (Crick et al., 1997, p. 585) and appear to be relatively stable over time (Crick, 1996, p. 2326; Crick et al., 1997; Lagerspetz et al., 1988). Children can at times be malicious and cause premeditated harm.

Rather than basing our schemas on real and accurate representations of children and adults, we base our moral judgment on one *specific quality* possessed by infants and children: dependency, reliance on others. Even if children can at times be aggressive or malicious, they are still perceived as dependents.

Adultlike or childlike dimensions are not necessarily related to specific age, but to the quality of a person or interaction. To put it more accurately, we are looking for cues of dependency and independency. For example, people unconsciously associate disability with childlike features (Robey et al., 2006). College students spoke to others who they believed to be adults with disabilities much as they did to the 12-year-old child (Liesener & Mills, 1999).

In attributing childlike features, age is not important per se, but is a sign of dependency/independency. Parents who become angry with a 3-year-old child who is pulling at their baby sister's hair, and who threaten to punish them, believe that the child is sufficiently independent to be capable of restraining them, show sensitivity towards their sister and stop harassing her. They regard them as responsible and able to exercise self-control and free will. Under these circumstances, a 3-year-old is recognized as A.

Figure 5.1 demonstrates some of the features we take into account when construing a dyad. There are at least three possible ways by which we decide who is the dependent and who is the independent: role (diagram 1), personal characteristics (diagram 2) and harmful act (diagram 3).

The "detection" of childlike and adultlike characteristics is not entirely rational and not always relevant. For example, a number of experiments (Berry & Zebrowitz-McArthur, 1985) indicate that baby-faced people are less likely to lose their case than people considered to have a mature face (Berry & Zebrowitz-McArthur, 1988; Zebrowitz & McDonald, 1991).

However, this influence also appears to depend on the nature of the offence. A baby-faced defendant will be considered less likely to have committed an offence intentionally, and more likely to have committed an offence by negligence, than a defendant with a mature face.

The evaluation of child-schema and adult-schema characteristics in a particular moral situation is observer-relative. The same person in a particular dyad might be construed as A by one person and as C by another. In fact, construing a party as A or C is the act of moral judgment itself. If party X matches an adult schema (A) and party Y matches a child schema (C), it means that we think X has done harm to Y and that we sympathize with Y and condemn X. But this is only true for an observer who perceives X as

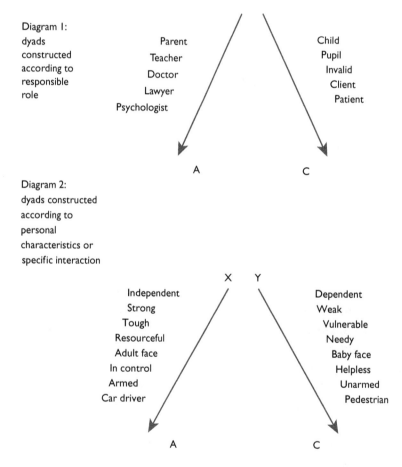

Diagram 1:
dyads
constructed
according to
responsible
role

Parent
Teacher
Doctor
Lawyer
Psychologist

Child
Pupil
Invalid
Client
Patient

A   C

Diagram 2:
dyads constructed
according to
personal
characteristics or
specific interaction

X   Y

Independent
Strong
Tough
Resourceful
Adult face
In control
Armed
Car driver

Dependent
Weak
Vulnerable
Needy
Baby face
Helpless
Unarmed
Pedestrian

A   C

Diagram 3:
dyads
constructed
according to
harm done

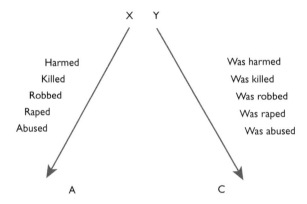

Figure 5.1 Constructing dyads. The sudden appearance in consciousness of a moral
judgment first involves construing two asymmetric parties as childlike
(dependent) and adultlike (independent). We construct these categories
according to particular cues, such as the responsible role of one party
towards the other (diagram 1), personal characteristics of each party or
according to a particular interaction (diagram 2) and the harmful act itself
(diagram 3).

associated with an adult schema and Y with a child schema. This construction happens largely outside awareness. So, child and adult schemas are not
just cognitive assessment of traits. They *are* our emotions, judgments and
actions towards the parties. Consider, for example, capital punishment.
To oppose the enforcement of capital punishment for humane reasons means
to construe the moral situation as:

state A → C convicted murderer

death penalty

It might seem strange that someone would construe a convicted murderer to
fit with a child schema. However, the asymmetry of power between prisoner

and state authorities establishes a strong link between prisoner and child schema and state and adult schema. The prisoner suffers, is defenseless, lacks freedom and depends on the prison authorities for basic needs; the authorities are armed, powerful and committed to supply all the prisoner's needs. But this asymmetry alone is not enough for associating the convicted murderer with the child schema; after all, the prisoner is guilty of serious crimes against people, who in their turn may be construed as dependent in relation to the prisoner (before his imprisonment). For some people, once the murderer is imprisoned and is sentenced to death, this is enough to construe an asymmetric dyad by which the convicted murderer matches a child-like schema and the state an adultlike schema. However, when the dominant factor in an observer's judgment is the prisoner's cruelty to his or her victim prior to his or her conviction, then this might prevent construing the convicted murderer as C, and may lead to support for him or her being sentenced to death. As we shall see, the decision whether a party in a conflicted dyad matches A or C is often personal, contextual and highly subjective. How we judge dyads thus depends on the perspective in which we place them (for a detailed discussion of the death penalty see Chapter 6).

In the case of the death penalty, for example, our support for it might be influenced by factors such as political values or religious beliefs.

Whereas the decision as to which party is A or C is highly subjective, *the general traits that are associated with children and those associated with adults are constant and universal.*

As we shall see in the next chapter, the fact that the judgment process is observer-relative and at the same time constant and universal is the basis of the fundamentally dual nature of moral judgment. Therefore, the judgment process seems at times to be based on self-evident universal truths, and at other times contextual and relative.

Evaluating the relationships between conflicting parties (→)

The second component of judgment is evaluating the relationship (→) between the adult-schema party and the child-schema party. Even if we match each party to adult and child schemas, the judgment remains incomplete. We do not simply compare the two parties and decide which one is more helpless, needier or more powerful. Our judgment depends on something more profound, namely the *nature of dyadic relations as such.*

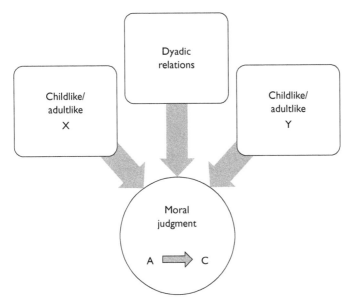

Figure 5.2 The attachment model of moral judgment. In generating a non-conscious moral judgment, we perform two mental operations: we impose a dyadic structure of child/adult and agent/patient (Gray et al., 2012a) on two parties in conflict, and we compare the behavior of A towards C with our prior expectations of what adults should and should not do to children. Acts that violate our expectations are judged as morally wrong. While the decision as to which party is C or A is highly subjective, the general traits that are associated with children and those associated with adults are constant and universal.

Just as we have different schemas for adults and children, we have a schema for the dyad as a whole (see Figure 5.2).

This consists of our expectations of what adults should and should not do in regard to children. Adults have obligations towards children, and we seem to know these obligations intuitively. To put it more accurately, adults have obligations towards others who are in the position of children (or dependents). But the word "obligation" fails to do justice to the speedy evaluation of a relation, which occurs outside awareness, nonverbally.

The question that lies at the heart of every moral judgment is this: *How did the perceived adult-related party relate to the dependency of the perceived child-related party during their interaction?* This criterion only concerns the perceived adult-schema party (A) since we infer from our schema for the child/adult dyad that children are not expected to take care of anyone. That is why the moral situation is construed as A → C, and not A ↔ C or C → A (see Figure 5.3). The one-way direction reflects the asymmetry between A and C. Thus, in the course of evaluating each party's characteristics under these rubrics, much weight is given to the evaluation of A's actions and his or her awareness of the dependency of the other side.

Let us turn again to another one of our earlier examples – medical negligence. Was the physician's negligence responsible for the medical complications suffered by the patient after surgery?

A quick and effortless analysis reveals that the physician matches the adult schema and the patient the child schema because the sick patient is dependent on the physician, and not the other way around. The dyad therefore consists of a physician mentally construed as A and a patient mentally construed as C.

However, the judgment process is not complete without the evaluation of →. We also compare the physician's acts to our schema of dyadic relations. In other words, we evaluate the behavior and attitude of the perceived A in the light of our expectations of an adult's obligations towards children. Only if the physician's actions failed to meet what we expect of those conforming to the adult schema in the presence of individuals matching the child schema will we judge the case as one of negligence.

Note that → has a substantial weight in the judgment, and that it often defines which of the parties matches the adult or child schemas. If A murdered B, this will lead to X being construed as A and Y as C, even though X can be physically weaker than Y, poorer than Y or younger than Y. In many cases, as noted in Figure 5.1, the mere act of harm and the suffering and injury it causes determines the asymmetry between the parties. So, the

Logical   burglar (A) ⟶ (C) old woman

Illogical   burglar (A) ◄⟶ (C) old woman

Illogical   burglar (A) ◄— woman (C)

Figure 5.3 The mental representation of A → C constrains our cognitions and emotions. Once people construe the parties as A → C, the pattern of moral judgment follows a specific direction to the exclusion of all others.

effect of → extends beyond the harm itself, and sometimes carries more weight than the individual characteristics of each of the parties.

Once the observer has matched each party to schemas for adult and child, and has evaluated the extent to which the "adult" has fulfilled or violated his or her obligations towards the "child," the moral judgment has been accomplished.

The attribution of child-schema and adult-schema characteristics does not take the form of an all-or-none decision, but is part of a complex process in which the salient features of each of the parties are weighed up in isolation, as well as together in terms of the dyadic relations between A and C. Often there will be a dynamic negotiation between these qualities as more and more information is gathered regarding each party, more affect is generated, and the features of the conflicted situation are calculated. The more serious the harm norm violation, the more polarized the parties become on the childlike and adultlike continuum. The more the perceived adult-schema party has failed to fulfill an obligation towards the child-schema party, the more negative the judgment of him or her will tend to be. However, the more either one of the parties, or both, are viewed as possessing a mixture of child- and adult-schema characteristics, the less clear-cut will be the judgment. An example is Danny, a 10-year-old boy who stole a purse from Ruth, an elderly woman. The information posits the following dyad:

A (Danny, 10 years old) → C (Ruth, elderly woman)

Note that even though Danny is just 10 years old, he is still construed as A because of the act of stealing. As I mentioned earlier, often the dyadic relation (→) is more significant than the child- or adult-schema characteristics of the respective parties. If Danny stole the elderly woman's purse, that makes her helpless and dependent (child schema) and him stronger and in control (adult schema).

However, for some observers, and for most legal systems, Danny's age is still relevant to the judgment, even though he is construed as A. The observer is confronted with two pieces of information: the theft (→) and the fact that the thief is a child. The observer might judge a 10-year-old thief differently than he or she would judge an adult thief. If the observer decides to take the thief's age into account, it would be because a 10-year-old still has many of the characteristics of a child schema. Danny's young age would, however, cause the observer's negative judgment to be milder: his or her recommendations concerning punishment would take the thief's young age into account. Therefore, the affective and cognitive response will be proportionally influenced by a cognitive judgment of the child-schema characteristics of the offender. In each moral judgment, we compute the child-schema and adult-schema characteristics of A and C, or, more accurately, we evaluate the dependency of each party, and → has a substantial weight in the evaluation process. Note that in the above example, the child-schema trait of the perpetrator is his youth. However, there are many other traits that match our inner schemas for children – such as unintentional, no control, no choice, weak, sick and so on. The more the information we have in relation to the parties tends to confuse categories, the more painstaking will the process of moral deliberation have to be (see Figure 5.4).

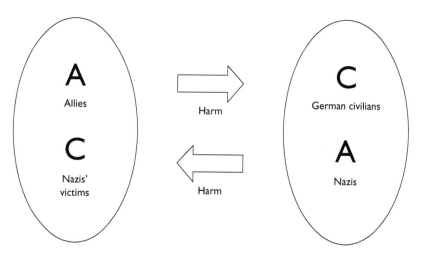

Figure 5.4 Representation of difficult moral judgment. In many difficult moral judgments, such as the bombing of German civilians in Dresden in World War II or the use of harsh methods of interrogation against terrorists, the victims are associated with the perpetrators and the perpetrators are associated with the victims. This induces a strong competition between perpetrator/victim category nodes, making it difficult for observers to reach a final judgment.

If we understand this point, we are well on the way to understanding how we process facts concerning A, C and →, and how these are translated into a psychic language that we are unaware of.

The imposition of child-schema and adult-schema characteristics on facts concerning the dyad

It seems that dependency and independency are universal expressive qualities that inform all our social understanding. Facts concerning the two parties such as motive, responsibility, intention and so on are important because they provide information that helps us evaluate the child-schema and adult-schema features of each of the parties and the nature of the dyadic relations. Facts about A, C and → possibly trigger a further data stream outside awareness. It is likely that an associative, non-conscious system tags on the new consciously acquired information to already stored schemas for children, adults and child/adult dyads. The observer's mind weighs and translates each fact into a meaningful representation on an inner child/adult continuum stored in memory. The evaluation is not just of technical facts concerning the wrongdoing. Every aspect of the person is used to evaluate where he or she is situated on the dependency/independency continuum – including physical appearance, words used, emotional tone and so on.Even data that appear irrelevant to rational judgment may color our final judgments. We have already seen how Berry and Zebrowitz-McArthur (1986) showed considerable evidence to suggest that baby-faced adults are perceived to be more naive and honest than those with mature features. If my theory is right, then persons who have baby faces match a child schema, and as a result are perceived to be less responsible, and less guilty, than other subjects.

To conclude, *what creates moral situations is a computational process by which we assign a dyadic structure of dependent/independent (child/ adult) to two parties in conflict.* We take the complex moral situation and we convert it to an A → C unit. Then we use our relational knowledge to detect a gross or mild mismatch, a violation of expectation, generated by the adult-related party towards the child-related party.

How can it be that a simple unit such as the dyad covers most types of moral situations? To answer this, think of the dyad as a sort of digestive

Table 5.1 How judgments change in relation to different dyads in the moral situation "John killed David"

The moral situation as presented to the mind	John's child-schema features	The dyadic relations → (How did A treat C?)	John's adult-schema features	David's adult-schema features	David's child-schema features	Possible emotional and cognitive response and judgment
John killed David while John was committing an armed robbery.	Does not match a child schema.	Recognizes a defenseless person prior to the killing.	Matches an adult schema: powerful, responsible, able to judge between right and wrong, intended to kill.	Does not match an adult schema.	Matches a childlike schema: had no control, was helpless, could not defend himself.	Strong condemnation of John, pity for David, severe sentence.
John killed David; John is 34 and developmentally disabled.	Strongly matches a child schema: cannot differentiate between right and wrong, is not able to take account of the consequences of his behavior.	John lacks characteristics of adult-like; he cannot be represented as A.	John is an adult; John was strong enough to kill David.	Does not match an adult schema.	Matches a child schema: had no control, was helpless, could not defend himself.	Mild condemnation of John, sadness for David, John is not accountable.

John killed David in a car accident while he was crossing a red light.	Unintentional.	Was careless about the results of his behavior towards others (child schema).	Adult, responsible; took an unreasonable and high-risk action.	Does not match an adult schema.	Matches a child schema: had no control, was helpless.	Mild condemnation (compared to premeditated murder), John accountable, mild sentence (compared to murder of first degree).
John killed David in self-defense after David violently attacked him. John used force that is reasonably calculated to prevent harm to himself. The killing saved John's life.	Before killing, was helpless and in danger.	David almost murdered John, but he does not match a child schema.	Adult, responsible, can judge between right and wrong, understands the consequences of his behavior.	Powerful, responsible, can judge between right and wrong, meant to kill a defenseless person.	The outcome of John and David's confrontation is that David was killed. Therefore, just prior to the killing, David was weak and could not protect himself.	John is not condemned, John is not guilty, John might be released.

system of the mind. In the digestive process, all kinds of food and drink – such as bread, meat and vegetables – are broken down into their smallest component parts (carbohydrates, proteins, fats, vitamins, water and salt) so the body can use them to build and nourish cells and provide energy. In much the same way, the mind breaks down complex moral situation into the simple unit of $A \rightarrow C$.

Table 5.1 demonstrates how the observer constructs a judgment of a given moral situation by referring to the child/adult continuum and dyadic relations. I hope this bears out how all cognitive and affective processes in moral situations are merely variations on a central theme, reflecting an underlying knowledge of infant/adult dyads.

The moral situations portrayed involve a situation by which John killed David in various circumstances:

John $\rightarrow$ David

    killed

It is clear from the above that the observer treats the dyad as if it represents a single unit. As the table illustrates, a moral judgment is meaningful only if we take into account a cognitive and emotional way of representing the conflict by using schemas for children, adults and their dyadic relations. How we perceive murderer and victim is not "out there" in the same way that trees, human bodies and planets are "out there." If we do not apply an inner representation of children, adults and their dyadic relations, what we will see are objects doing things to other objects rather than people harming other people. We will see a person holding a knife and plunging it into another person rather than a murderer and his victim. Without comparing the moral dyad to an inner representation of a dyad stored in our memory, words such as "malice" and "oppression" are meaningless, as are words such as "justice," "rights" or the "categorical imperative." The word "harm" presumes an $A \rightarrow C$ structure, as do the words "cruel," "bad," "theft," "murder," "totalitarian," "vicious military leaders," "rapists" and so on.

For meaning to arise, there must be a vehicle for interpreting dyads, some inner representation that the current dyad is compared with. The inner representation should be broad enough to cover endless variations of dyads.

Note

1 Over the years, psychologists have described a host of categorization models that are based on representational ideas such as schemas, central prototypes, stored exemplars and variable rules, and on processing principles such as similarity, that have considerable explanatory power and experimental support (see Komatsu, 1992; Rehder & Hoffman, 2005). While I think the schema theory might be useful as a simple model for understanding moral judgments, cognitive theory offers other possibilities to explain how we construe moral situations across the children/ adult spectrum.

Chapter 6

Variance and consistency in moral judgment

This chapter shows how beside the vastly different ways people have of making moral choices, there is also uniformity and consistency in how moral conclusions are reached. My central claim is that the way our cognitive apparatus organizes moral situations is constant and universal. We encode vectors of features corresponding to the childlike/adultlike properties of the parties and judge if, and to what extent, the adult party violated our expectations. However, the content, meaning and emotions differ from one culture to another.

The existence of remarkable variations in right/wrong situations has led many to argue that such judgments fall far short of being universal (Harman, 1975). Moreover, with the passage of time, the criteria used to make moral judgments alter even within cultures. Those who subscribe to the theory of moral relativism contend that there is no universal, definitive rule that distinguishes between right and wrong actions. The dialogue between Plato and Thrasymachus in Plato's *Republic* (2004) is an early illustration of a relativist view of justice in the history of philosophy. In Thrasymachus's view, what is considered "just" reflects the interests of, and is dictated by, society's rulers. To do the right thing, an individual must do what he or she is told to do by those in power. Thus, the judgment reached as to the rightness or wrongness of any given act is relative to principles pronounced by an acknowledged authority. In some cases, such principles will have been codified as law and enforced by the society's rulers. Other rules of conduct, related to morality, may be less strictly enforced, but will nonetheless derive from principles that serve the interests of the stronger forces in society. Following this line of thought, people's moral stance relies on an authority they accept, which could be a government, a religious creed, or perhaps even a member of their own family or tribe whose primacy is widely accepted.

Rai and Fiske (2011) argue that the "a priori categorization of a social-relational context as separate from bases for moral judgment is ironic given the rich history in social psychology of demonstrating the influence of context in nearly every aspect of social behavior and cognition" (p. 59).

These writers are, of course, ostensibly right. However, their analysis is concerned with the final outcome of a moral judgment, whereas we need to address the cognitive processes that lead to it. That is, we need to differentiate between *contents* – the moral judgment that results from an act of reasoning – and *process* – the mode of reasoning and the non-conscious psychological processes involved. In this chapter, I will show that once we make this distinction, we will see a huge variance with respect to outcomes and a high level of uniformity and universality with respect to processes. From this, we may conclude that the universality of these processes of reasoning is not based on moral objectivity or on some kind of rational test, but rather on our nature and the way the human brain is wired (see Churchland, 2011).

People across cultures break down moral situations into the exact same basic constituent parts: they detect the dyadic structure, identify the weak and strong parties in the dyad, and then attempt to assess the extent to which the strong side violated their expectations of how it should act towards the weak party. The moral situation triggers a moral computational system identifying the components of childlike and adultlike features in each of the parties to the dyad. However, the moral event itself, its contents and outcomes, are all subjectively assessed and influenced by personal and cultural factors. Thus, though the computation is universally conducted via the same parameters, the outcome differs from person to person and from one society to another.

The fact that the components of the computational task are unvarying helps people to understand one another when discussing a moral situation. Different sides will agree on the way in which the computation is to be formulated based on the dyadic rules, but disagree about the data on which the computation is to be based. Because of these disagreements, we frequently overlook the broad consensus there is between people in relation to the assumptions that underpin moral judgments. For example, it is universally agreed that if X is identified as A (i.e. the adult) and Y is perceived as C (i.e. the child), expectations must be directed at the side identified as A and not at C.

This assumption is indisputable. It is shared by Republicans and Democrats alike, by two lawyers confronting each other at a trial, by those who support honor killings and those who oppose such rituals. In effect, every person with an opinion, regardless of his or her political persuasion, his or her moral values, or his or her ethnic and cultural affiliations, will accept that if A, the adult, harms C, the child, the morally responsible agent is A.

All humans speak the same moral language, the language of the dyadic relations between a weak party that has suffered harm and a strong side that has violated the observer's expectations. Everyone will identify moral failure in the same way; they will present the victim as helpless and vulnerable, will point to the asymmetry between victim and aggressor, and the way in which he or she has demonstrably violated their expectations of him or her. Thus, the degree of agreement between people in relation to moral situations could hardly be broader. However, precisely because agreement in relation to dyads is so clear and universal, it is often taken for granted and barely noticed.

In his book *Common Morality* (2004), Bernard Gert argues that questions such as whether it is morally acceptable to hurt someone simply because you dislike him or her are not controversial at all. However, because they generate no discussion, they tend to be forgotten. To Gert's insight on shared agreement, we can add an even more radical assumption: even conflicting sides locked in fierce debate will find they have many points of agreement.

Take, for example, the disagreement between supporters and opponents of legalized abortion over the status of the fetus. The pro-life camp contends that the fetus is a vulnerable, defenseless human being, and is therefore entitled to live. Abortion, they claim, is murder. The supporters of legal abortion, on the other hand, put the pregnant woman and her rights at the center of the debate. They argue that the "right to life" doesn't imply the right of an embryo to live at the expense of the mother's rights. From this, we see that despite the disagreement between the two sides about the status of the fetus, they both in fact invest a great deal of effort in trying to understand the dyadic relations consistent with their worldview. Thus, while the pro-life side define the dyad as pregnant woman (abortion) → fetus, the supporters of legalized abortion portray the dyad as the state (laws against abortion) → pregnant woman.

Even though the moral judgments the two sides reach are polar opposites, their fundamental assumptions are the same. Both engage in the exact same mental exercise: in a given a moral situation revolving around the issue of the rights and wrongs of abortion, the two opposing camps identify the weak and the strong sides, and anticipate that the side identified as strong will act in line with their particular set of expectations. They demand that the strong side correct the perceived moral failure. The controversy between the two camps is *never about the rules of the dyad*. They are in complete agreement in relation to the building blocks of the moral judgment. They completely agree with each other that our expectations must be directed not at the weak side, but at the side perceived as strong.

Let us imagine another debate, this time between two individuals, one a supporter of harsh interrogation methods of suspected terrorists and the other an opponent of such techniques. It seems that the parties fully understand each other: neither thinks the other is talking nonsense. The two can communicate freely since they share the critically important assumption that any kind of object recognized as C is entitled to protection and compassion. They can also both accept the fact that the suspected terrorist may be perceived as C by some while others may perceive him or her as A. The two sides can understand each other because they have something in common: acceptance of the dyadic rules. These rules enable participants in the dispute to communicate within a similar linguistic framework and be capable of adequately performing the tasks of speaker/listener. As long as people talk morality, they understand each other, even though they might fundamentally disagree.

In the same vein, consider the extent to which there actually is agreement between the opposing sides arguing their positions in a court of law. All sides accept the rules of the dyad. In dispute is whether the accused matches an adult schema and the harmed party matches that of a child. The sides agree that if this is not the relation between the parties in the dyad, then the accused cannot be blamed. If it is proved that between the accused and the party harmed by him or her the relation is indeed $A \rightarrow C$, the two sides will begin the computational phase of assessing the childlike and the adultlike components of each of the parties.

Let us examine the case of Mark, who is accused of stealing a sum of money from Robert. (a) The sides agree that only if the link between them is one of Mark $\rightarrow$ Robert can Mark be accused. In other words, only if Mark stole money from Robert can he be charged, and only if that is the case can it be assumed that a violation of expectations may have occurred. (b) They also agree that the link has to be one-directional: Robert $\rightarrow$ Mark, and not Mark $\rightarrow$ Robert or Robert $\leftrightarrow$ Mark. In the event that Mark stole money from Robert, expectations will be directed at Mark and not Robert. (c) If there is agreement that Mark stole money from Robert, the dispute will turn to the computation of the childlike and adultlike components of each of the parties to the dyad. Now the tug of war will be over the specific dyad that is formed in the mind of the judge or members of the jury. The judge, the advocates, even the plaintiff have no way of understanding the moral situation other than subjecting it to the processes determined by the dyadic rules. The defense will try to depict Mark's childlike components as significant and Robert's adultlike components as notable. The prosecution will attempt to prove that the opposite is the case. The verdict will, to a large extent, be determined by the judge and jury's respective assessments and judgments of these components. If, say, it was the case that Mark had stolen Robert's social security payment and Robert is an elderly person who is dependent on these funds for his living, the violation of expectations will be viewed as severe, and it is highly probable that the sentence imposed by the court will reflect this. In terms of moral computation, Robert will be ranked as having a significant level of childlike components and a minor level of adultlike components, while Mark's ranking will be the reverse. On the other hand, if Mark stole a nominal sum and Robert is an affluent individual, the dyad will be viewed differently; the asymmetry between the two will be seen as less extreme, and this will be reflected in the sentence imposed. All sides accept these considerations. In other words, despite the appearance of a confrontation and disagreement, the dyadic rules make it possible, from the very outset, for an agreement to be reached as to how the legal debate is to be conducted and the way in which the distinctions between different moral judgments are to be formulated. The dyadic rules are unchallengeable so that they themselves are not in dispute. Yet it is our obligation to explain why, despite the simple computational basis that is universally accepted, moral judgment is also both culture- and context-dependent and is accompanied by much disagreement.

The two types of dispute relating to moral dilemmas

The fact that two sides holding differing moral views can communicate with each other doesn't mean that they can resolve their moral dispute. Indeed, the majority of such debates ends without agreement, and at times also ends up in an angry exchange.

According to A. J. Ayer (1936) and C. L. Stevenson's (1994) theory of emotivism, the inability to convince an opponent by rational argument to change his or her stance on moral situations proves that moral judgment is no more than an expression of feelings. This is why some have called emotivism theory hurrah/boo theory. Emotivism is the most extreme of the so-called non-cognitive ethical theories. Its followers argue that the notion of good is meaningless, that there is no such subject as ethics, that moral disputes involve nothing that can be said to be either true or false, nothing that can be known or believed. It reduces all moral issues to matters of inclination or personal preference.

Ayer considered the fact that moral values are not up for rational debate a proof that such values lack factual and epistemological significance. In Ayer's view, the only thing that moral judgments express is the feelings of the speaker at that particular moment in time. Since, according to the emotivist view, moral judgments reflect moral emotions rather than fact-based propositions, they cannot be scientifically debated. According to Ayer (1936/1946), there is no moral argument that "does not reduce itself to an argument about a question of logic or about an empirical matter of fact" (p. 167). In all moral debates:

> We do not attempt to show by our arguments that he has the "wrong" ethical feeling toward a situation whose nature he has correctly apprehended. What we attempt to show is that he is mistaken about the facts of the case.
>
> (p. 165)

Ayer (1936/1946) further maintains that:

> If our opponent happens to have undergone a different process of moral "conditioning" from ourselves, so that, even when he acknowledges all the facts he still disagrees with us about the moral values of the actions under discussion, then we abandon the attempt to convince him by argument. We say that it is impossible to argue with him because he has a distorted or undeveloped moral sense; which signifies merely that he employs a different set of values from our own . . . We cannot bring forward any arguments to show that our system is superior. For our judgment that it is so is itself a judgment of value, and accordingly outside the scope of the argument. It is because argument fails us when we come to deal with pure questions of value, as distinct from questions of fact that we finally resort to mere abuse.
>
> (p. 166)

Ayer thus distinguishes between two kinds of disagreement related to moral questions: disputes over *facts* and disputes concerning *values*. Let us for a moment dwell on Ayer's assertions and see how the model suggested here explains these two types of disagreement.

Any moral psychology needs to be held up against the criterion of its ability to provide a coherent account of moral reasoning and moral judgments (Arrington, 1989).

Moral judgment must be such as to be defensible by the type of moral arguments we describe, and, vice versa, these moral arguments must be functions of the type of moral judgments we formulate.

Consider the following examples:

Group A

- Stacy lives in a state where abortion is forbidden by law. The authorities claim that she has illegally aborted her fetus. Stacy denies this.
- Hari is accused of committing a murder in the first degree. The prosecutor has decided to ask for a death penalty. Hari denies he committed the crime.

Group B

- An abortion can result in medical complications later in life; the risk of ectopic pregnancies doubles and the chance of a miscarriage and pelvic inflammatory disease also increases (Lowen, 2017).
- The states that have the death penalty should be free of murder, but those states have the most murders, and the states that abolished the death penalty have less (Ornellas, n.d.).

Group C

- Everyone has an inalienable human right to life, even those who commit murder; sentencing a person to death and executing him or her violates that right.
- Since life begins at conception, abortion is akin to murder as it is the act of taking human life.

An analysis of the factual content of the three groups suggests that such disagreements involve three types of disputes:

1 Disputes over facts about relations between two individuals that answer the question "What happened?"
2 Disputes concerning facts that can change the perceived dyad.
3 Disputes concerning values.

However, as I shall show, moral debates are a messy affair. They are a complex mixture of verifiable facts, interpretable facts and expressions of feelings. Some objective facts concerning "What happened?" overlap facts concerning the childlike and adultlike components of the dyad. For example, Peter shoots Anthony. He claims to have done this in self-defense because Anthony was pointing a pistol at him. The prosecution maintains that Anthony was unarmed. Ostensibly, this is solely a question of fact. Was Anthony armed, and did he threaten Peter? But that question, in the observer's mind, is part of the calculation being made as to Anthony's childlike and adultlike components. If indeed Anthony was armed, the rapid calculation made by the observer will reduce Anthony's childlike components and will alter the moral judgment. Thus, facts about what happened become entangled with calculations made about an individual's childlike and adultlike components.

I. Group A: disputes concerning facts about the actual occurrence of a moral failure

An argument about facts must relate to an empirically verifiable event, in this case one in which two people involved. When referring to a factual basis, the debate stands a better chance of being more to the point and less emotional. The disputed facts concern the nature of the relations between the two people: What happened between A and C? The sides to the dispute can share the same set of values and there need not be a moral disagreement between them. In a situation in which Gill is accused of stealing from Carol, the fact in dispute may be whether Gill did indeed steal from Carol. Gill can deny the charge, and therefore argue that in her relations with Carol she violated no expectations.

2. Group B: facts linked to calculative assessments of childlike and adultlike components

Rather than relating to the question of "What happened?" the facts in dispute may in certain cases be facts of a completely different kind, namely the components of dependency/independency of each of the sides.

If abortion can result in medical complications later in life, then women who want to abort should be protected from this procedure.

If the state permits abortions, it endangers women's physical health. Therefore, protecting the fetus prevents an additional victim from being hurt. Here, the pregnant woman creates a new dyad in which a woman undergoing an abortion is regarded as possessing childlike components.

If, in a country in which the death penalty is extant, the number of victims nonetheless rises, the death penalty must be abolished because it is endangering the lives of the citizenry of those countries. Here, too, the attention drawn to the victims is aimed at changing attitudes to capital punishment.

In effect, the most common form of argumentation in moral disputes is heavily based on such facts. They are used in an attempt to alter the perceived dyad, and thus influence the moral judgment reached.

If David is accused of killing Bob, he may, for example, argue in court that Bob hit him or threatened to kill him, which forced him (David) to act in self-defense and kill Bob. The prosecution can argue that Bob did in no way provoke David's attack. Both sides agree that a murder case in which the accused was provoked results in a very different dyad. Different in the sense that from being the perpetrator only, now David turns out also to be a victim. David $\rightarrow$ Bob turns out to be preceded by Bob $\rightarrow$ David. This will entail a different computation than where there was no provocation or threat prior to the killing. Because such cases are based on empirically verifiable events, we can say whether the statements made by either side are true or false.

It is important to note the difference between the kinds of argument put forward by group A and group B. There is a big difference between a suspect claiming that he or she had no hand in the crime and one who admits the facts but argues that he or she is not to be convicted. For example, a person who took the life of another person might argue that he or she shot at the victim but contend that the victim had attacked him or her before he or she fired. In both instances, facts are clarified. However, in the first instance, there were no relations between the two sides, and if it is established that the suspect wasn't in the area at all there is no need for the observer to reach a judgment about their relations. Therefore, brute facts are more important than computing childlike and adultlike components. In the second instance, however, there is a clear dyad, and the observer has to decide on the nature of relations between the two sides. Though the issue of provocation is a factual question, it may influence the computation in the formation of the dyad of childlike and adultlike components.

Sometimes the component child/adult is not linked to the actual relations between the sides, but to the features of just one of the sides prior to their relations.

For example, an individual accused of murder alleges temporary insanity at the time. There is no dispute about what happened. By pleading temporary insanity, the defense tries to readdress the original computational bias of the dyad to the extent that A is presented as so dependent and vulnerable that it is doubtful whether he or she can be accused of premeditated murder. If Susan cannot differentiate between good and bad, she will have to be viewed as matching the child schema more than the adult schema, and thus she cannot be held responsible for her actions. More examples: Heinz stole medicines from the pharmacist but he did this in order to save his wife's life; a soldier killed an unarmed captive but did so because he or she had been ordered by his or her commanding officer to shoot the prisoner. Such disputes include a factual component. For example, in a case of murder in which the accused suffers from a mental disorder that renders him or her unable to tell the difference between right and wrong, the court will call an expert witness to confirm the defendant's plea.

However, in many cases, facts concerning childlike and adultlike components are more difficult to prove and are open to interpretation. These arguments include a considerable component, which Ayer calls "expressions of emotion." Thus, childlike and adultlike components may simply not be convincing, even if they are proven. The judge may remain indifferent when told of Jon's childhood of hardships, may conclude that Heinz shouldn't have stolen the medicines, irrespective of the circumstances, and that the soldier should have considered his or her officer's unlawful command and not obeyed.

In many cases, the attempt to change the dyad's computation is done by manipulating the likeness between the observer and the victim.

For example, in the US, over the past two decades or so, laws relating to Women's Right to Know have been approved in the legislatures of 26 states. Any woman requesting an abortion has to have an ultrasound of the fetus and has to be offered an opportunity to look at the image. There are states where the law calls for the monitor to face the pregnant woman and the attending doctor is required to inform her in detail as to what she is actually seeing.

This is, of course, all intended to make it more difficult for the woman to go through with the abortion. The assumption is that if in the photo she sees a small living creature, she will find it hard to kill that creature.

In conclusion, any attempt to change a moral judgment through a rational argument must focus on the perception of the childlike and adultlike features. Sometimes these features are influenced by the relations themselves, while in other instances it is the personality of each of the sides that changes it without there being any link to the relations. Extensive feedback loops and robust top-down constraints operate in a way that any information about these features influences the entire gestalt and may change the perceived dyad.

Also, since, as I will show in the next chapter, one of the most important factors is the emotional engagement between the observer and each of the sides, it isn't easy to separate fact from emotion and personal preferences. "Facts" in cases of moral judgment turn out to be very bendable, and can be bent to fit in with other dyadic components so as to engage the emotions of the observer/judge.

3. Group C: disputes over values

When we believe that every human has a right to life, including the most heinous murderer, we can then be said to believe in a "value."

Beliefs in values involve a more generalized type of principles than those employed in concrete verifiable cases of disagreement between two people. When Bernard is put on trial for stealing from Paul, we establish a dyad of Bernard → Paul by activating the calculation mechanism to assess the components of childlike and adultlike components of each side. But dyads do not necessarily refer to only two individuals. They can also be linked to entire groups as well as refer to abstract issues. They can relate to parties such as a state, a law, government ministers, a giant corporation, women, men, blacks, gays, children, people sentenced to death, fetuses and so on. Insofar as the action of the psychological mechanism is concerned, it makes no difference whether the dyad formed is connected solely and specifically to Bernard and Paul, or whether we are conducting an abstract debate about the morality of capital punishment. In both cases, the dyad will be based on the same principles: there are two parties, and it is for us to assess the nature of their relations. In both instances, the mechanism that computes the childlike and adultlike components of each side will be activated. However, in debates over general abstract principles, the discussion is always about values, and not about a specific real-life incident involving two particular individuals. Disputes over principles do not require us to provide clear factual proof explaining what happened between the two sides. In dyads concerning concrete individuals, in addition to being influenced by the values we believe in, we are strongly affected, both consciously and unconsciously, by the personal characteristics of each side: the extent of their credibility, their appearance, the narrative each presents, the nature of their argumentation, even the shape of their faces (Berry & Zebrowitz-McArthur, 1988). Dyads concerning disputes over principles almost solely make appeal on our values, and these, as said, are determined by religion, education and the society in which we live. When Ayer talks about the two sides disagreeing over values, he is referring to this category of disputes.

What I wish to show is that this category is not that distinct from the previous group of facts related to childlike and adultlike components. In most cases, observers' descriptions of an individual's childlike and adultlike components already express their moral judgment.

For example, if we were to ask someone to describe features of fetuses or of people sentenced to death without telling us what his or her stand on these moral dilemmas is, we would be very likely to form a fairly accurate idea of his or her views.

If the person in question would say that the fetus is a "human creature very much like a baby," one might conclude that he or she opposes abortion. But if he or she was to say that the fetus is "part of a woman's body and not yet a distinct human being," we would be entitled to infer that he or she is in favor of a woman's right to abortion.

Alternatively, think, for example, about the moral and political controversy over the welfare state. The dyad that triggers disagreement is:

state (welfare system) → (not supporting the) disabled, unemployed, etc.

The dispute revolves around two issues. First, there is the extent to which a state is required to provide welfare payments to the disabled, unemployed or single mothers. Second, there is the question of the extent to which the state is entitled to deny welfare support where the applicant is deemed not to have done enough to find work and improve his or her situation ("payment by results"). Two entirely different worldviews come into play here. One emphasizes the state's responsibility towards the weak in society, while the second emphasizes the responsibility of the country's citizens, including those who are evidently weak, to support themselves and their families and join the workforce. Each worldview formulates differing expectations from the state in dealing with weak populations and its citizens.

According to the first worldview, recipients of welfare benefits can be identified as C – they are needy and their chances to find work limited. The state has a responsibility to support this population so that they can live in dignity and can assume a social role that matches an adult schema. But according to the second worldview, the same population can also be depicted as fundamentally A, and therefore undeserving of forms of support that aim for child-schema individuals or groups; those who think of them in these terms describe them as people who exploit the state welfare system to get money without having to work for it. People of this persuasion think that welfare recipients refuse to behave like responsible adults and find work. The important point so far as we are concerned is that the description of the childlike and adultlike components of this population already includes the moral judgment. One can see this, for example, in the way in which the former British Prime Minister Gordon Brown justified the 2008 reform of welfare policy that drastically cut income support and disability benefits:

> Quite simply, we want everyone who can work to work – and that means more help with gaining skills alongside a requirement to take up these opportunities. It means medical support alongside an expectation that when treatment is successfully completed people will return to work. It means treatment for drug misusers coupled with clear consequences for those who fail to take it up. And it means channelling savings from all these measures towards real help for disabled people – supporting them to do the work that they are able to and not writing them off as unemployable.
>
> (Department for Work and Pensions, 2008)

This worldview expects from welfare recipients that they invest a great deal of effort in finding work (in the case of the unemployed), wean themselves off any drug habits (in the case of addicts) and rejoin the workforce immediately on recovery (in the case of ill health). Proponents of this approach argue that these expectations stem from perceiving those in receipt of unemployment benefit as strong, adult and responsible.

On the other hand, critics of this view present benefit recipients in an absolutely different light and focus on the violation of expectations by the state in its handling of this population:

> This system is supposed to care for us at a time of greatest need. That's why the welfare state was created, to recognize that any of us could fall victim to circumstances beyond our control. Yet the shame heaped on benefit claimants now shouts loudly in our collective faces that poverty is somehow a "lifestyle choice." That need and illness and disability and circumstance are all something to be ashamed of . . . Three years ago, a survey of GPs warned that many of their disabled patients were contemplating or actually committing suicide. The government didn't listen then and it isn't listening still . . . All of us who know and love someone who needs the safety net of social security have been left utterly hopeless by the weaponizing of the benefits system – a weapon the government deploys against its own people.
>
> (Clark, 2016)

The distress suffered by claimants can be heart-wrenching, clamoring for justice. Below is one such story reported in the British newspaper *The Sun*:

> A man who lost both legs, an eye and his spleen in the 7/7 terror outrage is being made to prove that he is still entitled to claim benefits.
>
> Mr. B., 36, was the worst injured survivor of the London suicide attacks, which killed 52. He was next to ringleader Mohammad Sidique Khan as he killed himself and six others on a Tube train at Edgware Road on July 7, 2005. But the wheelchair-bound post-traumatic stress disorder sufferer now has to answer questions on a form about how long he can stand and how many steps he can take. He may also have to undergo a face-to-face test to carry on receiving his £416 monthly Employment and Support Allowance.
>
> Last night Mr. B., of Abergavenny, South Wales, said: "It is a betrayal. To be asked questions like 'How long can you stand for?' How insensitive is that? If this isn't re-affirming how bad my life is going to be because of my injuries, I don't know what is."
>
> (Sales, 2016)

Such stories offer us an insight into the deep structures of moral situations. Often the moment the decision about the childlike and adultlike components of the situation is taken, moral judgment is reached.

Arguments about childlike and adultlike components are confusing and frustrating. At first, the sides to the argument will be engaged in a supposedly rational discussion. But the debate ends with the participants expressing their emotional preferences. In this sense, Ayer was right. If argumentation would be stripped down to its essence, it might have sounded more like this:

> The artificial termination of pregnancies killing the fetus breaks my heart.

> The fate of fetuses doesn't disturb me in the slightest. What bothers me much more is that forcing women to give birth against their will tramples their agency and removes their control over their own lives.

> Poverty-stricken pregnant women don't make my heart bleed.

> They do mine.

> Well, I remain unmoved.

> And so the argument continues.

And behind these differences are two emotional outlooks, not facts: (a) I feel closely identified with fetuses, not with women who are forced to give birth against their will. (b) I feel closely identified with women who give birth against their will, and not with the unborn fetus. So, Ayer was right in the sense that ordinary factual statements are not the main type of statement deployed in such a debate, and that insofar as they are not factual, they are simply expressions of emotions that can be neither true nor false.

However, does that mean we must accept that agreement in debates about values can never be reached? I maintain that on occasion, the possibility of reaching agreement exists, but that it won't happen by rational arguments alone. The supporter of the right to abortion will have to be convinced that fetuses resemble small and vulnerable human beings who deserve to be protected. The anti-abortionist will need to be convinced that women's right to decide about their own body should be protected. This debate was best illustrated by Charles L. Stevenson (1944). As an example,

Stevenson offers a discussion between two people about state benefit payments to the poor. According to Stevenson, the two positions each side adopts do not stem from a reasoned argument but rather from the starkly differing temperaments of the two individuals. A, according to Stevenson (1944), is compassionate, and B is cold-hearted:

> When ethical disagreement is not rooted in disagreement about belief, is there any method by which it may be settled? If one means by "method" a rational method, then there is no method. But in any case there is a "way." Let's consider the above example again, when disagreement was due to A's sympathy and B's coldness. Must they end up by saying, "Well it's just a matter of our having different temperaments?" Not necessarily. A, for instance, may try to change the temperament of his opponent. He may pour out his enthusiasms in such a moving way – present the sufferings of the poor with such appeal – that he will lead his opponents to see life through different eyes. He may build up, by the contagion of his feelings, an influence which will modify B's temperament, and create in him a sympathy for the poor which didn't previously exist. This is often the only way to obtain ethical agreement, if there is any way at all. It is persuasive, not empirical or rational; but there is no reason for neglecting it.
>
> (p. 29)

Since the moral choice is first and foremost an outcome of the way in which communication about the issue at hand is conducted, convincing the other side can only be achieved by adjusting the mode of communication, and not in finding new sophisticated arguments. The only way of transforming the discussion is by changing the way the mind computes the childlike and adultlike components of the parties. Thus, a new dyad has to be formed, backed up by both reasoned arguments and an emotional valence.

Dyad-based intuitions take precedence over moral principles

According to Kagan (2001), intuitions that build on experience play an extremely important role in the formulation of moral principles. He posits that whether or not we are convinced by the validity of a certain moral principle will greatly depend on concrete moral situations. If we replace

Kagan's "real cases" with the notion of the dyad, it transpires that we consider the logic of a moral principle by the application of concrete dyads, and that we judge these dyads intuitively. Here, Kagan's argument fits in very well: when we want to refine an existing moral principle, we examine the change by reference to carefully chosen and formulated dyads, ones that are marked by subtle differences. Moreover, in opposing a certain moral principle, we will tend to buttress our disagreement with dyads that show the unreasonableness of this moral principle intuitively. Even where we don't have any immediate intuitive feeling about a certain dyad, the most common form of deliberation is by comparing it with other dyads and putting different cases or experiences side by side. We turn to other dyads, about which we feel more confident and clear, in order to better understand the dyad being questioned. This is how important the role of the dyad is in our moral thinking.

So, we all rely hugely on our dyadic intuitions, and that includes philosophers and jurists. These intuitions are like the fuel of our moral judgments. This still leaves us with the question as to the extent to which and in what way our reference to them is justifiable.

The impact of these intuitions overrides moral principles whenever conflict between them arises. According to Kagan (2001), this raises the question whether it might simply be the case that we always prefer to rely on our moral intuitions. But even a moral principle that is supported by a powerful intuition may still clash with another intuition. Here, we will tend to favor the intuition that is associated with the concrete dyad over the one that accompanies the principle. This is illustrated by the case of the trolley we mentioned before. Here, an intuitively probable principle clashes with an intuition about a specific case. Even though the pragmatic principle by which the maximum number of lives must be saved looks so simple and right, not many people are likely to be willing to push one person onto the track in order to save five.

Philosophers will have a hard time understanding this unless they grasp the source of intuitions. Kagan (2001) noted, "While it is obvious that we constantly appeal to our intuitions about cases, it is far from clear what, if anything, makes it legitimate for us to give these intuitions the kind of priority we typically give them" (p. 46). Kagan compares our reliance on moral intuitions to the way in which we refer to observations in empirical research. Observations weigh heavily in considering the pros and cons of an empirical theory. It is easy to ascertain that the mass of some material is 2.1 kg or that paper is inflammable. An empirical theory must take such observations into account. We turn to these observations in order to shore up a theory – and when they clash with the theory, however correct it might appear to be intuitively, we reject the theory out of hand. Nobody would suggest that we set aside empirical findings as we decide on a theory's validity, but we do question the quality and motivation of the observation, the conditions in which it was made and so on.

And – again as with moral intuitions – in our judgments, we prefer empirical observation to general empirical theories.

So, perhaps when dealing with a moral principle, we turn to specific instances in order to check how applicable the principle is, in much the same way as we examine the specific observations supporting an empirical theory. Having said that, Kagan (2001) rightly argues that there are differences between these modes of deliberation. First, they rely on very different types of sources. As regards to empirical observations, we base ourselves on our senses – our eyes in the case of visual observations, our ears in auditory settings and so on. Only provided that the relevant senses operate properly can we use empirical observations. But as Kagan (2001) puts it:

> In the moral case, it is not at all obvious how it is that the corresponding "observations" – the moral intuitions – are produced. Is there a corresponding organ, a "moral sense," that is at work here? If so, it must be admitted that we know precious little about it.
>
> (p. 48)

Kagan believes that the problem does not inhere in the fact that we don't know anything about such an organ or "moral sense." People throughout history knew very little about their senses, but this never caused them not to rely on them. The real issue with a presumed moral organ that produces moral intuitions is that its actual existence is open to question, which casts a doubt over the validity of our appeal to such intuitions. However, even if there is no moral organ, something does generate these intuitions. Kagan (2001) writes:

> Presumably, something generates the intuitions – they do not arise out of thin air! – and if we want to talk of the mechanism responsible for generating them as a "moral sense" or a "moral faculty" it is not clear what objection there can be in doing so.
>
> (p. 48)

The important question for Kagan, therefore, is whether we have reason to rely on our moral intuitions as much and as unquestioningly as we do. We assume that it is safe to trust our senses because we assume that they convey something trustworthy about reality. Our senses tell us something exact and truthful about the world, and this is why we fall back onto them. What is it, however, that we fall back on when we give our moral intuitions such weight?

Kagan argues that because people's moral intuitions are so variable, there is no good reason why we should rely on them. We tend to be shocked when we encounter someone whose moral intuitions differ from ours; we expect that every rational human being thinks as we do. But in fact, there is a lot of disagreement about moral intuitions, and this seriously erodes our ability to rely on them.

With a degree of irony, Kagan toys with the idea that we might appoint people who we trust to have the right intuitions, and identify those who suffer some deficit in their moral judgment to represent intuitions that are unacceptable. He compares the latter to people who suffer from color-blindness. Perhaps just as there are people who cannot properly perceive colors because their vision is impaired, there are also people whose moral intuition is impaired, thus interfering with their ability to reach right/ wrong moral judgments. It will, however, be very hard to identify those with such an impairment. Unlike people who are color-blind, where the physical problem is not difficult to diagnose, moral impairment may eventually only be observed where intuitions are simply not the same as our own.

Attachment approach to moral judgment may point at a possible direction for further discussion. It suggests the very different origins of our concrete dyad-based intuitions as compared to those that come into play in empirical observations. The truth of moral intuitions, based as they are on our sense of justice, is not the same as the truth generated from reality-matching sense perceptions. In trusting our senses, we trust our sense of reality. We look at a tree and we believe it exists simply because our senses tell us so. Should someone argue that we're wrong, the tree isn't there, we'll be surprised and rub our eyes. But if what we next see is the very same tree, we'll be absolutely sure that we were right. The source of trust, in the case of moral intuitions, is something else. When we witness how someone intentionally causes a blind person to stumble, to mock him, just for fun, we confidently experience our moral intuition that what we have just seen is a moral failure. We don't get this confidence from observing something that corresponds with reality. Our confidence is based on our observation that the victim's physical or mental integrity is under threat. What we have here are two types of sources that may inform our confidence in judgment. The first of these is cognitive confidence. We will be sure that we have witnessed a moral failure simply because our intuitions are based on the law of the dyad. The law of the dyad is a form of knowledge we acquire early in life, and we place trust in it for the simple reason that we ourselves have been in the position of the blind man (helpless and vulnerable) – a position in which we needed the help of a competent adult to maintain ourselves both physically and mentally. Even if tripping up the blind man does not arouse us emotionally, then we are still bound to sense moral failure because the situation concerns a type of embodied truth that is beyond justification or explanation. The second source of confidence lies in the motivational/emotional domain. The moral failure in the situation with the blind man will also arouse our rage and anger with the aggressor – extending ourselves, as it were, to the blind man, who thus turns somehow into one of us, his physical and mental wholeness under threat from a dangerous enemy. This response can be of different intensities. If the blind person is a child of ours, our own flesh and blood, we will be more shocked and outraged than if the victim is a stranger. But underlying this whole range of reactions, there is one common denominator: the impulse to survive and to protect the integrity of our body and mind and of those we are close to, those who belong to our group, or with whom we identify.

This is why the confidence we have in our moral intuitions is unlike our confidence in our senses. It is not a matter of a color or a shape of whose perceived reality we are convinced. Confidence in our moral intuitions reflects an epistemic confidence that implies our impulse to survive. Not just our own life, but also our offspring, and any extensions based on them. We are simply sure that we (and those whom we include by extension) want to live, keep our bodies whole, and avoid pain and humiliation. This fact is in need of no further justification, just as we do not have to justify defending ourselves when under attack. We do not at such a moment have a need to explain or even reach for moral principles in order to know that what the aggressor is doing is wrong. Our trust in moral intuitions mainly derives from the fact that we aim to protect, and avoid the suffering of people with whom we – in part – identify.

This brings us to the question as to why, when intuitions based on moral principle and intuitions deriving from concrete dyads clash, we will always go with the latter. This is related to the fact that we have a need to defend and protect individuals and groups who awaken our empathy. In our moral considerations, we first and foremost take their safety and integrity into account. Here, being consistent or rational takes a step back. Under no circumstances, even at the risk of seeming irrational and incoherent to ourselves, are we willing to directly harm a perceived needy person who we care for, and who we feel is part of our own self in one way or another.

In weighing moral situations, we are somewhat like a general who mobilizes his forces in defense of his country. A choice of strategic and tactical decisions is open to him, but in the end any decision must be for the better protection of the people of his country. The same goes for us: we may be guided by numerous intuitions, but the intuition that eventually wins the day relates to the protection of those individuals or groups we perceive as C. What threatens them we will reject, and what promotes their well-being and safety we adopt.

Looking once more at the example of the trolley, it is obvious that participants fully understand that the death of one person is to be preferred over the death of five. Still, most will not be willing to personally push the victim onto the rails, regardless of the number of lives saved. Pushing this person onto the train track would constitute a gross violation of expectations. The victim here is innocent, she is unaware of the plan that will lead to her death. A radically asymmetrical dyad emerges between her and the person who will push her. It is the victim's great vulnerability and neediness together with the attacker's power over her that generate such dismay and condemnation. Participants prefer not to get their hands soiled and violate the moral position concerning dependence and vulnerability, to saving as many lives as possible. They cannot choose to personally act inhumanely towards one individual, even at the price of several other lives.

One more issue needs clarification. How is it that we are so sure of our moral intuitions, even when we know that were we born in another culture or had we received a different education, we would have been guided by altogether different moral intuitions?

In his *On Liberty* (1859), John Stuart Mill introduces an insight concerning a person lacking a sense of criticism. Such a person:

> devolves upon his own world the responsibility of being in the right against the dissentient worlds of other people; and it never troubles him that a mere accident has decided which of these numerous worlds is the object of his reliance, and that the same causes which made him a churchman in London would have made him a Buddhist or a Confucian in Peking.
>
> (p. 17)

We might expect that since we "accidentally" hold the moral intuitions of a certain culture or society or historical period, we would feel less confident about them. If I am aware that I would take the same moral position as my opponent had I been born and raised like him or her, then I should have a greater tolerance to opinions that differ from mine. If it is only by accident, historical and otherwise, that I have these moral intuitions, then why should I believe myself more in the right than those who hold other opinions?

Mill (1859) writes:

> Judgment is given to men that they may use it. Because it may be used erroneously, are men to be told that they ought not to use it at all? To prohibit what they think pernicious, is not claiming exemption from error, but fulfilling the duty incumbent on them, although fallible, of acting on their conscientious conviction. If we were never to act on our opinions, because those opinions may be wrong, we should leave all our interests uncared for, and all our duties unperformed.
>
> (p. 34)

George Sher (2001) puts it very well:

> The fact that people's moral beliefs vary systematically with their background and life experiences shows considerably more, for in becoming aware of this, I acquire a positive reason to suspect that when you and I disagree about what morality demands, my taking the position I do has less to do with the superiority of my moral insight than with the nature of the causes that have operated on me.
>
> (p. 67)

For Sher (2001), "my awareness that a different upbringing and set of experiences would have caused me to acquire a different set of moral beliefs provides evidence that the processes through which I acquired my actual moral beliefs are probably not reliable" (p. 64).

Why, then, doesn't the fact that we know that had we been raised in another culture we would have held different moral views not affect the firmness of our moral convictions? The answer is that when these moral judgments emerged, there was hardly any room for rational, critical thinking or a determined effort to reach truth (for a philosophical consideration of this question, see Sher, 2001). Critical thinking only enters the stage once the moral judgments are installed, and only in order to confirm them. Since our confidence in our moral judgments does not rely on reason or brilliant, subtle arguments, we don't have any problems with the fact that someone else might have equally powerful but very different opinions.

Our uncommonly strong confidence in our own moral judgment is deeply entrenched in our animal nature. Many types of social animals will defend members of their tribe as if they were their own offspring.

To disregard our moral intuitions or to set aside every one of our moral beliefs just because we do not have any special reason to favor them over those of others will be wrong for two reasons.

First, as Sher (2001) suggests, it would merely be discounting one set of practical judgments in favor of another whose members are no less compromised by their own life experiences and social upbringing.

Second, once we stop listening to our moral intuitions, we would stop caring for everything that matters to us: for all the individuals and groups whom we hold dear and whose rights and security we wish to protect. It is, for instance, unclear whether women would have attained equality in the West, if the US would have abolished slavery, or indeed if King John would have met the barons' demands and signed Magna Carta, had we switched off these intuitions. All these events were the result of decisions by people who trusted their moral intuitions.

This section wouldn't be complete without us addressing the critiques of emotivism, which argue that moral concepts are nothing but bogus ideas that don't really mean anything other than something which could just as well be expressed by a series of exclamation marks or rude words (Mayo, 1986).

As with every approach that swings the pendulum in only one direction – in this case in the direction of the emotions – philosophers who supported emotivism in the first half of the twentieth century were precise about some matters but missed out on a number of components essential to the understanding of moral judgments.

As Alasdair MacIntyre (1981) points out, Ayer does not explain why moral feelings are aroused in the first place, or what the difference is between moral emotions and other feelings.

In his book *After Virtue* (1981), MacIntyre writes:

> "Moral judgments express feelings or attitudes," it is said. "What kind of feelings or attitudes?" we ask. "Feelings or attitudes of approval," is the reply. "What kind of approval?" we ask, perhaps remarking that approval is of many kinds. It is an answer to this question that every version of emotivism either remains silent or, by identifying the relevant kind of approval as moral approval – that is, the type of approval expressed by a specifically moral judgment – becomes vacuously circular.
>
> (p. 13)

So, the emotivist theory has nothing to say about what distinguishes moral emotions from non-moral ones. And this strongly suggests that emotion is only a secondary rather than a primary feature of morality.

Another important argument in MacIntyre's critique of emotivism can in fact be leveled against the entire range of sentimentalist models. In MacIntyre's view, "emotive meaning . . . is devoid of meaning." In his *A Short History of Ethics* (1998), MacIntyre accuses emotivism of confusing the word "meaning" with the word "use."

MacIntyre (1981) posits that the notion of "emotive meaning" is itself not clear. What makes certain statements guides to or directives of action is not that they have any meaning over and above a factual or descriptive one. It is that their utterance on a specific occasion has import for, or relevance to, the speaker or hearer's interests, desires and needs. "The White House is on fire" does not have any more or less meaning when uttered in a news broadcast in London than it does when uttered as a warning to the President in bed, but its function as a guide is quite different. Emotivism, that is, does not attend sufficiently to the distinction between the meaning of a statement that remains constant between different uses and the variety of uses to which one and the same statement can be put (MacIntyre, 1998, p. 259).

Ayer's argument as to why moral judgments are devoid of meaning is a different one. In his view, it is because they express nothing *other than* emotions. Let us examine this claim in the light of the model offered in this book. As an example, Ayer cites the statement "stealing is wrong." He argues that such a statement merely expresses a feeling, something that could just as well be done by frowning when the word "stealing" is uttered, using a tone of disapproval when talking about the act of stealing or adding a series of exclamation marks at the end of the statement.

The word "wrong" then, is used only to express the speaker's anger and intent to reprimand.

However, the model presented here explains that the statement "stealing is wrong" has a profound dyadic meaning. As I argue in Chapter 5, one of the ways in which the mind establishes dyads is in terms of the action taken by one side of the dyad vis-à-vis the second side. The sign $\rightarrow$ expresses this action. Utterances such as "he stole," "he hit" and "he pushed" provide us with enough information to identify that there exists asymmetry between the parties. The $A \rightarrow C$ is deep-rooted within these utterances. In fact, "stealing is wrong" expresses a specific instance of a more basic rule that "one must not harm anyone." Whoever harms another person can be accused of a moral failure because he or she has violated the expectations we have of the way in which the strong acts towards the weak. Indeed, the violation of expectations frequently leads to negative sentiments, condemnation and hostility towards whoever is responsible for such a violation.

The emotivism espoused by Ayer and Stevenson places feeling, taste and inclination at center stage. In their view, all our moral judgments are directed by feelings. That, argue Ayer and Stevenson, is tantamount to saying that such actions are not directed by reason. However, as the current model argues, feelings in this context arise from a deeper layer linked specifically to the process of moral judgment: the dyadic rules. These unchanging and unchallengeable rules are acknowledged as universal. What I ought to do now, and what I hold to be right or wrong now, is constrained by certain rules that dictate what I ought always to do, or always hold to be right or wrong. The dyadic rules go beyond the particular case, in a way in which pure feelings do not.

As I have shown, the emotional component in moral judgment has deep roots in the human psyche. It is neither detached nor arbitrary, as it is described by emotivists. The emotive component is supported by an array of rules of communication, cognitions and a computational mechanism, all of which are required in every moral judgment.

The dispute over capital punishment

Let us look at the dispute over capital punishment and see how the claims of both supporters and opponents of the death penalty construe differently the computational task in the process of reaching a moral judgment. I am using this as an example to illustrate that in both camps, the parameters by which moral judgments are reached are similar and compatible with the dyadic rules. Yet despite the very simple and predictable formulation of the computational task, the information that streams into that computation is rich, complex and, as we shall see, at times unexpected.

Using the dyadic rules, we begin with an analysis of a news story published on 27 April in *The New York Times* about a murderer sentenced to death (see Blinder & Fernandez, 2017). I will illustrate the debate on the death penalty in two ways. First, a concrete case reported in the media, including various positions regarding the death penalty in the event of murder. Second, I will proceed to demonstrate how abstract principles regarding the death penalty always hark back to the dyadic rules.

The story

Following an execution in the US state of Arkansas, it is the duty of the local coroner to pronounce the death of the condemned man. Seventeen years after pronouncing the death of a murder victim and family friend, Mr. B, an Arkansas coroner, confirmed the death of the victim's murderer, Mr. W, following the latter's execution. The coroner viewed the killer's execution as a satisfying moment that had been keenly awaited by the community since Mr. B's murder.

From this opening the dyad in the story becomes:

Mr. W → (murder) Mr. B

At the same time, Mr. W is depicted in two ways: as a murderer and as someone who has been executed. The components of childlike and adultlike are extremely dramatic, creating possibilities for conflicting judgments. This opens two alternative channels of moral judgment, between which the reader will have to choose.

Disruption and reparation

The coroner's words clearly convey that he is in favor of the death penalty in this case.

According to his moral judgment, the state, as the strong side, hadn't violated the expectations he had of it by behaving towards Mr. W as it did. The principle expressed by the coroner has already been mentioned in Chapter 3, namely on infant development: disruption must be followed by repair – a principle that underlies every act of retribution. The victim has died, and it is impossible to return to everyday routines until reparation has been made. This reparation has to be proportional to the moral failure. The principle of disruption and repair is behind every form of punishment. How punitive the sentence needs to be for the observer to be pacified and accept that "repair" has occurred will depend on cultural, social and personal values.

The murderer's childlike components

Mr. W was executed at 11:05 p.m. after the US Supreme Court rejected an appeal from his lawyers, who sought to block the execution on the ground that their client was mentally disabled and ineligible for the death penalty.

Mr. W's lawyers present arguments contradicting the views expressed by the coroner about the treatment of their client. They generate an entirely different dyad:

state → (execution) Mr. W

Mr. W's high level of childlike components makes his execution seem unjustified and immoral. According to his lawyers, Mr. W is mentally unfit. If he is, we may reformulate their position. The state would be violating our expectations as to how the strong must behave towards the weak.

The victim's childlike components

In reporting the execution of Mr. W, the local media claimed that out of eight planned executions in the space of less than two weeks, none had aroused the level of community interest more than the execution of Mr. B's murderer. The victim had been an IRS employee and an assistant warden in the prison where Mr. W was awaiting his execution. Though according to the coroner emotions surrounding an execution are rarely intense in his community, he told a reporter, "When it hits your home, it's a little different."

This information strengthens the dyad Mr. W → (murder) Mr. B through two components. The first component is that the murdered person is a local resident and that the murder occurred in the area where the execution is due to take place. This could explain the local inhabitants' support for the execution of the murderer. The second component is the victim's nickname "Pee Wee." The name is associated with childhood, thus linking the victim to his child-related components, and therefore strengthening his childlike components.

The aggressor's stand after committing the murder

In 1978, Mr. W emptied a revolver after a robbery in neighboring Jefferson, killing a 19-year-old woman, Ms. H. When the convicted murderer was spared the death penalty and sentenced to life in prison, he mocked Ms. H's relatives, turning to them and saying, "You thought I was going to die, didn't you?"

In any situation in which expectations have been violated, the observer will pay attention to the aggressor's view of his victim. This is also a part of the disruption and repair process since the perpetrator can also initiate reparation by expressing genuine sorrow and regret. On the other hand, in instances, such as the above, in which the attacker maintains his or her aggressive stance towards the victim (or the victim's family), it increases the observer's sense of disruption, perhaps no less than that produced by the deed itself.

The above quotation renders the culmination of the horror the observer felt towards Mr. W. Even those who are staunchly opposed to the death penalty will be hard put to remain indifferent to such an avowedly unrepentant attitude. In my view, Mr. W's shocking comment to the victim's family may even have exceeded the horror of Mr. B's murder. While the murder may be explained by Mr. W's wish to remove every obstacle standing in the way of his flight from jail, his response to the family of the murdered woman is shocking and inhumane as a result of a severe violation of the dyadic rules.

An attempt to lessen the gravity of the judgment through the expression of remorse

A possible turning point for the dyad's construal and a mitigation of the moral/legal judgment may occur if and when Mr. W expresses remorse and accepts responsibility for his actions. Sentenced to death for Mr. B's murder, Mr. W later wrote a letter to the *Pine Bluff Commercial*, an Arkansas newspaper, and confessed to another killing that had until then not been resolved.

"I don't want to make any excuses or shift the blame," Mr. W said in the 2005 letter. "I just want to be honest and accept responsibility for my actions." Some of the other prisoners facing the death penalty, he told the paper, had chosen not to ask for clemency in the knowledge that these petitions were usually turned down. He, on the other hand, saw an opportunity in such a plea. He wanted to appear before the clemency board to show that he was a changed man. God had transformed him. Revealing this truth, he wrote, meant more to him than being spared the execution, since he would die eventually anyway. His "victory" lay in standing up for God in front of man. As to the families of his victims, Mr. W wanted them to know that he was sorry for having robbed them of their loved ones, shallow as that expression of remorse may sound.

The confession, as well as Mr. W's professed religious transformation, had no discernible effect on the Arkansas Parole Board, which ruled that his application for clemency was "without merit." His adoption of a religious stance may testify to a change he went through. The change signals Mr. W's acceptance of the observer's point of view. In the past, his murderous deeds and the scornful way he related to the family of the victim showed that the object standing in front of him was not the object perceived by the observer – a human being defined by his vulnerability and his weakness. By expressing remorse, Mr. W signals his acceptance of the dyadic rules in relation to the victims he murdered. He is also helping the police/society by revealing that he has been responsible for an additional murder in a case that hitherto remained unsolved. But all of this proved to be to no avail. Perhaps the parole board did not believe that his remorse was genuine. Alternatively, the board may simply have thought that what Mr. W thinks about his actions and his victims is of no interest in view of the enormity of his crimes.

Rethinking the dyad's components: the victim's daughter opposes the death penalty

During his flight from the police in Missouri, Mr. W killed yet another person – Mr. G. The victim's daughter urged the state governor to stop the execution. She told a local Internet site, *Springfield News*, that the family was in no way asking the governor to ignore the pain suffered by the victims of Mr. W's other acts of murder. However, in the case of the murder of her father, the family had chosen to find a way other than the execution of the murderer to alleviate their pain.

Given that Mr. W's brutal murders, together with his initially scornful attitude towards the victim, created such a profound sense of shock, any lessening of the severity of the sentence naturally required dramatic arguments from unexpected sources. Among these was the refusal to approve of the death sentence by the daughter of one of the victims. To be convincing, this attitude must take into account the suffering of the victims. Therefore, Mr. G's daughter took pains to relate to and recognize that suffering. But even this was not sufficient.

A new victim: the murderer's daughter

An additional argument made by the victim's daughter in her attempt to commute Mr. W's death sentence was to bring Ms. J, the killer's daughter, another victim of the murder, into the picture. In an item in the *Springfield News Leader*, it was reported that the daughter of the victim had discovered that the murderer had a 21-year-old daughter named Ms. J, whom Mr. W hadn't seen for 17 years, and that he had never met his 3-year-old granddaughter. The victim's daughter was said to be hoping that Ms. J could visit her father before the execution.

The victim's daughter generated a new dyad: if the state were to execute Mr. W, it would cause terrible suffering to his daughter J:

state → (execution of father) Ms. J

Presenting this new dyad might change the computation of the central dyad that is in dispute, state → (execution) Mr. W, because executing Mr. W will harm another needy person – his daughter.

As we can see, there is much ambivalence and confusion in the story, as though perspectives quickly shift in contrasting directions.

This ambivalence can also be found in the US legal system. It is so indecisive about capital punishment that it has, as a result, created a mechanism that encourages jurors to hear all about the criminal's child-like components. After jurors in a capital case have sentenced the defendant, there is a separate mini-trial, which is called the penalty phase, in which jurors decide whether to impose the death penalty. During this mini-trial, the state tries to bring compelling evidence to justify and support the imposition of the death penalty. The defendants and their lawyers must present mitigating evidence to convince the jurors that the defendants do not deserve capital punishment. The defendants and their lawyers can bring anything that might help to convince the jurors to avoid the death sentence. The Supreme Court even ruled that the state must pay for experts who could present evidence to mitigate the sentence. In 2003, Justice Sandra Day O'Connor struck down a death sentence against a convicted murderer because of his lawyers' "failure to investigate his background and present mitigating evidence of his unfortunate life history." O'Connor wrote that "among the topics counsel should consider presenting are medical history, family and social history, employment and training history, prior adult and juvenile correctional experience, and religious and cultural influences" (Toobin, 2008, p. 36).

Toobin (2008) writes:

> It is now more or less mandatory for defense attorneys to hire social workers and investigators to compile mini-biographies of their clients, known as "social histories." In general, the investigators pay particular attention to a defendant's childhood in an effort to determine whether he suffered abuse.
>
> (p. 36)

Through Mr. W's case, I have tried to convey the idea that although arguments may differ in what is justified, they do not differ in what does the justifying. This explains the constancy of justification; everyone uses the same justifiers. These justifiers are well grounded, without the need to base them on actual inference in order for the observer to justify it. Thus, if one thinks that Mr. W's life must be saved because of the suffering of his daughter, it seems that we are not puzzled by this argument. It seems to be self-evident, even though we might not be convinced by it.

A principled moral debate

When one looks at the principled debate regarding the death penalty, and not just at individual cases, it becomes clear that the arguments too are subordinate to the rules of the dyad.

Here is a general argument from a Catholic Internet site that supports capital punishment:

> We have the responsibility to punish those who deserve it, but only to the degree they deserve it. Retributivists do not justify the death penalty by the general deterrence or safety it brings us. And we reject over-punishing no less than under-punishing. How obscene that aggravated murderers who behave well inside prison watch movies and play softball. Regardless of future benefits, we justify punishment because it's deserved. Let the punishment fit the crime . . .
>
> (Dallas News, 2014)

There is an echo here of the process of disruption and repair in that the crime is so severe that reparation cannot apparently be anything less than the death penalty. An expectation that has been so blatantly violated demands, a return to the order of the dyadic rules through the imposition of a capital punishment.

In general, in principled debates, the arguments against the death penalty are strengthened by trying to make a perspective shift. This is accomplished by generating new dyad victims. These dyads create a distance between the observer's shock of the horrible act, drawing attention to other victims.

For example, Ernie Chambers, JD, said:

> Over 150 people in the last few years have been taken off death row because they were innocent. I know there are people who want to believe that no innocent person has ever been executed in this country. But when you have this many people conclusively proved by DNA evidence to be actually innocent, there is no escaping the conclusion that innocent people have been executed . . .
>
> (ProCon, 2017)

This is, I would say, one of the most common and powerful arguments put forth by opponents. Drawing attention to mistaken executions demonstrates the great injustice of this practice without having to resort to the defense of murderers. This type of argumentation is also applied in other moral discussions.

In moral claims, the search will always be focused on finding some area of human action that violates the observer's expectation as to the correct treatment of the needy in relation to the controversial issue of the death penalty. A further example relates to the discrimination against African Americans.

Martin O'Malley, JD, former Governor of Maryland writes: "Our nation's legacy of slavery and racial injustice finds continued offense in our use of the death penalty. Our death row population is more than 40% black – nearly three times the proportion of the general population" (O'Malley, 2015). Thus:

state → (discrimination) black people

The computational task that functions in line with the dyadic rules is very flexible, and can develop and change in accordance with changing circumstances. It is like an empty vessel into which self-interest, greed, fear and prejudices are poured to justify immoral acts. However, the system may also develop in a more positive direction. From this point of view, the abolition of capital punishment in most countries, and the growing opposition to it wherever it is still practiced, is a significant achievement for humanity.

If we look at the history of the death penalty throughout the ages, we can see that there has been a great leap forward in relation to this form of punishment.

According to Randa (1997), the first known legal codification of the death penalty dates back to more than 4,000 years ago (c. 2050 BCE) during the reign of Ur-Nammu over Sumer (in modern-day Iraq), and covered such crimes as murder, robbery and adultery – when committed by a woman. The far better known and far more punitive Hammurabi Code dates back to the eighteenth century BCE. This code imposed the death penalty on 25 crimes, though murder was not one of them. The first recorded imposition of the death penalty was in the eighteenth century BCE in Egypt. A member of the nobility was found guilty of practicing magic and ordered to commit suicide. Egyptian commoners in that period were executed with an axe. The Mosaic Law was codified between *c.*500 BCE and the seventh century AD. Like in the above earlier codifications, the Mosaic death penalty was applicable to a variety of crimes. Also, like its forerunners, the various techniques of execution were extremely cruel and inhumane, including stoning, beheading, drowning at sea, burying alive and dismemberment. The Athens Code, formulated in the seventh century BCE, made death by execution the punishment for *every* codified crime. No less draconian were the Roman laws of the fifth century BCE. As in ancient Egypt, the nobility was less harshly treated than were free commoners and slaves. The crimes liable to be punished by death ranged from libellous publications and cheating a client, to robbery when committed by a slave, perjury, and the premeditated killing of a freeman or a parent.

Great Britain and its expansive empire was the setting for executions for a very broad range of crimes, the gallows being the most commonly used method. By the eighteenth century, British law listed 220 crimes as punishable by death. These included stealing 40 shillings from someone's house (approximately equal to $1,500 today), cutting down a tree or counterfeiting tax stamps. During the era of general parliamentary and legal reform in Great Britain (1830s and onward), the death penalty was abolished for more than 100 crimes in the first legislative act of that period (1825). British reformists were joined by similarly minded European legislatures throughout the nineteenth and twentieth centuries. As of now, the death penalty has been abolished throughout Europe, with the exception of Belarus and Russia. In these latter countries, the death sentence has been suspended so that no executions have taken place there since 1999 (Randa, 1997).

The elasticity of our moral capacities is tremendous. The fact that the psyche can create a dyad in which a cruel murderer who is sentenced to death is seen as a victim of a cruel punishment demonstrates the plasticity and flexibility of our moral knowledge and practice. The trend towards abolition of the death penalty, particularly in the Western world, is not merely a step forward, but a quantum leap. It shows us the dyadic rules as a generous open-ended protective system for any perceived dependent, regardless of his or her wrongdoing. The computational system has become more and more sensitive over the last 100 years.

Change in our moral understanding often involves assigning new meaning to an object (human or non-human). It might start with attachment to that object, but it also brings new ways of thinking about it. It is rarely earning something completely new. The Nonhuman Rights Project, for example, was founded "to secure actual legal rights for nonhuman animals through a state-by-state, country-by-country, long-term litigation campaign." Its mission is:

> To change the common law status of at least some nonhuman animals from mere "things," which lack the capacity to possess any legal rights, to "persons," who possess such fundamental rights as bodily integrity and bodily liberty, and those other legal rights to which evolving standards of morality, scientific discovery, and human experience entitle them.
>
> (Choplin, 2018)

This new way of thinking is not an evolution from one moral way of thinking to another. It is rather an extension of our existing cognitive apparatus to include more objects to be likened to living a human form of life.[1]

As we will see in the next chapter, this is one of the most decisive factors in the process of making a right/wrong judgment.

Note

1   It goes without saying that this is merely one side of the story. In history's darkest periods, wars, genocide, the expulsion of millions of citizens from their homes, refugees living without any form of rights, ignominious poverty, all damaged the system's sensitivity to others, especially out-group members especially strangers and out-group members.

Chapter 7

The like-me criterion and turned-off dyads

Until now, we have been looking at a fairly simple model of moral judgment. It is a model applicable to everyone. The judgments so far discussed include a comparatively uncomplicated assessment of a fairly simple moral situation and some sort of objective calculation of the relative childlike and adultlike features of each of the sides involved.

However, moral judgment is complex and messy. What is considered a grave moral failure in one culture is normative in another. And in addition to the cultural factor, there is an historical dimension: a variety of acts that are injurious to humans, permissible less than 100 years ago, are absolutely off limits today (formal slavery, for example).

There is a further difficulty with one of the model's other assumptions. It supposes that once one of the sides is identified as matching a child schema, the observer tends to favor him or her and defend him or her in one way or another. We all know how fallacious this description is. Very few people or groups in distress arouse sympathy. In every major city, one can see people in the streets, sometimes children, clearly leading a life of abject poverty, their presence ignored by more fortunate passers-by. More often than not, the response to the deprived is one of disapproval and absolute indifference.

Extensive research has confirmed that most people believe in the "just world," in which the social environment is fair and people get what they deserve (Hafer & Begue, 2005; Lerner, 1980; Lerner & Miller, 1978). Because people want to believe that the world is fair, they will look for ways to explain or rationalize away injustice, often blaming the person in a situation who is actually the victim. It suggests that people may treat others badly precisely because they want to sustain their belief in justice. Melvin Lerner and Carolyn Simmons (1966) conducted a key experiment in the 1960s in which participants watched on a television monitor as a woman appeared to be receiving painful electric shocks from a researcher. In fact, the events were only simulated by actors. People who watched this described the victim's character quite negatively, and mostly so when they also believed that in suffering she was behaving for the sake of others (she agreed after the instructor told her that many students' credits are depending on her). The authors concluded from these findings that people have a powerful desire to believe that the world is a just place in which people get what they deserve. When an individual continues to suffer through no fault of his or her own, this threatens his or her belief in a just world. In response, people may try to restore justice by helping or compensating victims. When this is not possible, they may reinterpret the situation by, for example, considering the victim as a bad or otherwise unworthy person. In this manner, his or her fate seems more deserved and people's sense of justice is preserved.

Even when a genuine concern for the other is expressed, its origins are unclear. Take, for example, highly involved activist groups organized to defend animal rights, the poor, people who have lost their houses in fires or earthquakes, or refugees fleeing the war in Syria. What led these individuals to relate specifically to these needy groups and not to others who are no less dependent? What is the foundation of the emotional link between a socially involved individual and the population he or she is attempting to help? And what can be said about the moral standing of a person who is indifferent to, and therefore uninvolved in, the suffering of non-kin others?

In this chapter, I will be attempting to shed new light on, and bring order to, the ostensibly chaotic component of moral judgment. I will use the theory I have presented in the previous chapters to isolate the chaotic/subjective/emotional component from the other stable, fixed and universal components of moral judgment. I will show that the chaotic/subjective/emotional component is mainly attached to the observer's possible sense of identification with and belonging to (based mostly on likeness) the parties involved.

The subjective component of moral judgment

If we strip away the cultural, personal and subjective components of moral situations, our model would achieve near-perfect universality in terms of the moral judgments it yields. If we follow it, all we have to do is to objectively calculate the components of childlike and adultlike features for each of the sides and activate an array of expectations vis-à-vis the side matching the adult schema. Since the raft of expectations is universal, a quite similar moral judgment in any given moral situation would be reached by everyone. This means that everyone will recognize some breach of trust on the part of the adult-related party. This model assumes the existence of what Bernard Gert (2004) termed a "common morality," a concept that presupposes broad agreement among moral agents on the vast majority of moral issues. Gert posits that as long as the issues are not debated in the light of a particular religious or other belief system, everyone can agree that murder, the infliction of pain causing debilitating disabilities, and depriving someone of his or her entitlement to freedom or any other such basic right are all morally wrong. There may, of course, be acceptable justifications for any such act. However, here, too, there is universal acknowledgment that the only way any such action can be justified is if the explanation offered by one agent is accepted as a justification for all other moral agents violating common morality.

Of course, there is universal agreement among moral agents as to what constitutes morally good acts: the saving of a life, alleviating suffering and pain, or taking steps to prevent them, curing disease, increasing human freedom and happiness, and so on.

Such agreement is phrased in very general terms. It does not refer to specific cases. Not included is the detailed story of the relations between one person and another. It therefore does not bear on real situations of conflict.

This universal type of agreement yields the common response to one issue that arises in every two-sided relation, namely that one person is not allowed to harm another, be it by causing him or her pain, not honoring a promise, lying or any other form of injury (where harm is defined at a less general level of specification).

One can therefore formulate a moral principle that is the foundation of all the cases cited by Gert: the strong party must not harm the weak party, other than in circumstances that can justify such an action. This general law, when formulated in such an abstract way, would certainly gain overwhelming support across all groups and cultures.

If so, there is some agreement about the range of expectations. There is a universal consensus as to what the strong party in a dyad must not do to the weak side. Certainly, people from all cultures would agree to a set of expectations, so long as it is phrased in general terms under the heading of "causing distress to another."

Things become increasingly complicated when we scrutinize the situation more closely by obtaining an increasingly detailed account of the incident. Which of the two sides is the strong party and which is the weak one? What was it that led the strong side to harm the weak party, and what were the circumstances in which the act took place?

Let us for a moment imagine a moral situation independently of the social/relational contexts in which it occurs. For example, "a driver crosses a junction on a red light and injures a passenger" or "a thief forces an elderly person to hand over his old age pension." Suppose that we gradually incorporate components of identity, gender and ethnicity. We would then see that people's views become more diverse as more such specific components of the story are added. As people are exposed to additional details related to the moral situation, the influence of the subjective component will strengthen, and the areas of disagreement between them will become more evident. Were we to ask respondents to judge a situation in which A killed B with a pistol, we would gain almost total agreement in respect of the moral failure such an act involved. However, if we were to also add that the shooter was a white American officer and the victim was an Afro-American man, a certain variation in response would start to appear. Thus, moral situations that lead to consensus are typically sparse in terms of information and detail. But while they achieve uniformity of opinion, such moral situations are very schematic and lack the complexity and richness of information that characterize real life. We will not even be able to name the sides because names tend to divulge gender, religion and ethnicity. In actual life, moral situations are always presented in a context. No observer can be neutral or objective.

The weightiest factor in the processing of a moral judgment is the emotional engagement between the observer and each of the parties. This depends on the like-me criterion: the likeness in terms of ethnicity, religiosity, race or gender between the observer and the two parties. Every observer and each party are rooted in a certain context – cultural, ethnic, political, social and so on – or are associated with one group or another in the dispute.

The cruellest Nazi, like any person, certainly had dyadic knowledge, but it was limited to the so-called Aryan population. Being told of a thief who robbed an elderly Aryan of her old-age pension, this Nazi would, in all probability, be shocked and form the morally appropriate dyad. But Nazis did not identify Jews as childlike, that is, as part of their moral community. The psychological mechanism that forms dyads, determines their contents and decides who can be counted as a like-me individual is itself subjective, capricious, unstable and given to emotional swings, and cannot therefore be relied on. It functions only in certain instances and under certain conditions and towards certain populations. Victims who endure little suffering may generate feelings of great compassion, while victims who have had to suffer great distress and often unimaginable hardships may fail to trigger the mechanism, and to form an active, potent dyad in the observer.

The victim's objective distress, or his or her vulnerable and childlike features, are not the decisive factors in recognizing the harmed party as C. The suffering party will most often gain this recognition if he or she is a "like-me other" (one of our own).

From the beginning of life, like-me and dependency do not really manifest themselves as distinct entities. They both fall within the ambit of our experience of dyads and dependents. When green and red lights combine, they produce yellow, but our consciousness, when presented with yellow, is not aware of the two distinct colours from which it is made up. Similarly, our feelings towards dependents do not neatly split into a like-me criterion and a dependency criterion. When I see a member of my family or group in distress, I perceive the person at once as a "like-me distressed person." Like-me and dependency are the most fundamental components of our moral judgment.

This is a disposition we begin to acquire in infancy when dependency and like-me coexist in the mother's powerful feelings of care for her baby. According to Winnicott (1963), as pregnancy reaches term, and for a number of weeks following the infant's birth, the mother's complete attention is focused on caring for her child. During this period, she feels that the newborn is a part of her own being. She identifies the infant with herself and instinctively knows how the child feels. These feelings, Winnicott claims, are based on her own experiences as a newborn.

So, from the mother's point of view, dependency and like-me are inseparable in the first months of life. From the baby's perspective, all the matching phenomena that were described in Chapter 3 are part of the like-me relations between the infant and his or her mother. Winnicott (1971/2005) asked, "What does the infant see when he looks at his mother? He sees himself" (p. 151). Paraphrasing this sentence, we can say that every time we react empathically to a person's distress, we are, to a greater or lesser extent, identifying with some aspect of the victim's plight.

As we saw in Chapter 3, recent research findings show that even in the first 12 months of life, and prior to the acquisition of language, the sense of liking someone is based, in various ways, on similarity (in English, indeed, liking, like and similar are cognates). According to this research, infants demonstrate a preference for others who like the same foods, wear similar clothes or play with similar toys (Mahajan & Wynn, 2012).

Meltzoff and Brooks (2001) suggest that newborns can identify others as like-me because of their ability to mimic the actions of other humans: I can act like him or her, and he or she, likewise, can act like me. Meltzoff (2006) claims that when they see others behaving in a way similar to their own behavior – "acting like me" – babies interpret the internal state associated with such behaviors on the basis of their own self-experience. Humans, including preverbal newborns, attribute meaning to the acts of others through recognition of those others as like-me rather than through an exclusively (or initially) carefully thought-out, gradual, course of reasoning.

Like-me in the first months is based on the infant's familiarity with his or her caregivers. Even within the first 15 hours of life, a newborn can already identify his or her mother's voice and prefer it to a stranger's (DeCasper & Fifer, 1980). Similarly, a mother's smell holds more attraction than the smell of a stranger (MacFarlane, 1975), and her face is welcomed far more readily than that of an unknown person (Field et al., 1982).

Research in social psychology has found that there is a strong relationship between perceived similarity and liking in adulthood (Byrne, 1971; Newcomb, 1961; Sunnafrank, 1983). From Bauman and Skitka (2012), we learn that people feel a weaker sense of moral obligation to those who they perceive as less like themselves.

Moreover, perceived similarity plays a role in an individual's decision about others he or she wishes to be friendly with, and influences a wide range of socio-cognitive processes. People identified as similar raise positive expectations and are regarded as trustworthy, reasonable and clever. "Dissimilarity" raises suspicions because it foregrounds difference and otherness (e.g. Brewer, 1979; DeBruine, 2002; Paris et al., 1972).

But it is not just our moral judgment in which the like-me criterion is brought to bear so crucially. All our understanding of the other, our ability to anticipate his or her actions and bestow meaning to his or her behavior, are based on this criterion.

According to research carried out by Azevedo et al. (2013), the like-me criterion has a neural basis. These researchers found that the sight of an arm belonging to a person of one's own race being given a highly painful injection led to greater bilateral anterior insula activity and autonomic reactivity than if the person being injected was a member of a recognizably different ethnic and/or social group.

The attribution of childlike and adultlike features is not objective, although usually it bears some resemblance to reality. As I have mentioned again and again, it is not sufficient that one party to a dyad is identified as a victim, helpless or needy. Even if these are truly the features of that party and the observer sees them clearly, certain conditions are required in order to elicit a judgment with a matching motivational emotional component.

Let us for a moment return to the example of Mark breaking into Robert's house and stealing his pension money. For the sake of the argument, let's imagine that there is something about the elderly Robert that causes the jury to dislike him while fully recognizing that he is elderly and utterly dependent on the pension money stolen by Mark. He may be smelly, drunk or a misanthrope. Alternatively, it may have come to the jury's attention that he abused his wife sometime in the past. If so, he will be perceived as low in childlike features and high in adultlike features. This makes it likely that he poses a danger, at least to his close family, and this reduces his entitlement to protection.

None of these factors are linked in any way to the dyad involving Mark and Robert. They don't alter the existing agreement in relation to the dyadic rules. And yet they may most definitely lessen the emotional engagement with Robert's suffering in the jury's mind.

Therefore, there is a highly influential factor that has an ongoing impact on the computation of childlike and adultlike features. Our relations with the involved parties can be affected by components that are irrelevant to the brute facts of the moral situation. We saw an example of this in a study by Berry and Zebrowitz-McArthur (1986), which found that participants tended to mitigate the attribution of blame when the accused happened to have a baby face.

If so, details that are irrelevant to the moral situation and connected solely to Robert himself (Has he a baby face or bad breath? Is he or is he not an alcoholic?) won't alter the dyad's directionality. Robert will continue to be identified as a victim and Mark as someone who violated expectations. But these details *are* liable to change the motivational/emotional component of the moral judgment, and change the computational result dramatically.

However, in other cases, not only will the weak and needy not be recognized as such. There are circumstances in which cultural norms act as an encouragement to harm them. Rai and Fiske (2011) posit that there are many situations in which people believe that hurting or killing others is not merely *justifiable*, but is absolutely and fundamentally *virtuous*. And in virtually every culture, there are norms that *obligate* members of the culture to hurt or kill certain others in order to protect crucial relationships. In short, people may come to regard pain and death as good, and indeed morally necessary. Rai and Fiske provide us with a lengthy list of these cases, including killing in wartime, torture, vengeance, honor-related violence, lovers' quarrels, violent punishment for disobedience, retributive justice, circumcision and clitoral excision, initiation rites, self-flagellation, suicides motivated by shame or guilt, violence committed under orders, execution, ethnic cleansing, hate crimes, drone assassinations, human sacrifice, and violence attributed to either metaphysical or heroic powers.

Descriptions of such cases show that injury by the strong of the weak, even if it causes huge suffering, even if is intentional and results in death, is not in and of itself sufficient to form the dyad $A \rightarrow C$. The objective situation always requires subjective interpretation, and if the victim doesn't arouse the appropriate emotional response in the observer, or fails in general to arouse empathy, the moral mechanism fails to identify him or her as a victim. This is to an extent a circular argument, but we can avoid such circularity if we spell out the conditions in which the mind construes a strong/weak dyad and when it fails to respond to the real suffering of another person.

Rai and Fiske (2011) described some of these conditions. Many of them are linked to the social/relational contexts in which moral situations occur. The authors identify four fundamental and distinct moral motives: (1) *unity* – the motive that leads people to care for and support the integrity of ingroups by avoiding or eliminating threats of contamination and providing aid and protection based on need or empathic compassion; (2) *hierarchy* – the motive that moves people to respect rank in social groups where superiors are entitled to deference and respect but must also lead, guide, direct and protect subordinates; (3) *equality* – the motive for balanced, in-kind reciprocity, equal treatment, equal say and equal opportunity; and (4) *proportionality* – the motive for rewards and punishments to be proportionate. Thus, benefits received must be proportionate to contributions made and judgments are to be based on a utilitarian calculus of cost and benefit. According to Rai and Fiske, the four moral motives are universal. However, cultures, ideologies and individuals differ on *when* such a motivating force is to be actualized and *how* it is put into practice.

To a great extent, these are the conditions that determine the formation of dyads. For example, according to Rai and Fiske, in honor cultures, a woman who has sexual relations outside marriage, even against her will, defiles her family, which is shamed and shunned. Other families will not marry members of the shamed family, and often will not eat, drink or socialize with them. The only way to remove the family's shame and reintegrate the family into the community is to kill the defiled woman. From this, it is clear that in such a society, the neediness and vulnerability of a woman who shames her family cannot be taken into account. For the sake of the integrity of the society and many of its leaders, its rituals, its survival and preservation, the fears that influence it from below – the fear of fragmentation, of loss, of anarchy – are more powerful than the well-being and safety of an individual, however vulnerable, dependent and weak that individual may be. In such cases, a member of the clan or the in-group is troubled by the threat to the integrity of the group as a whole and the fear of it splitting. These emotions supersede any feeling of sympathy towards the victim. The individual is simply perceived as posing a danger to the entire tribe.

There are many other examples across cultures where victims are not perceived as such because of other social pressures – for instance, the exploitation of the labor of Asian women or children by affluent Western companies with a clean corporate self-image, and the problems faced in Europe and the US due to the influx of large numbers of refugees.

The security of the community or tribe is one of the major and most decisive considerations in moral judgments. Societies/communities that are under attack and feel threatened are far less tolerant of the other.

In his Nobel lecture in 1950, *What Desires Are Politically Important?*, Bertrand Russell told his audience:

Interwoven with many other political motives are two closely related passions to which human beings are regrettably prone: I mean fear and hate. It is normal to hate what we fear, and it happens frequently, though not always, that we fear what we hate . . . Fear is in itself degrading; it easily becomes an obsession; it produces hate of that which is feared, and it leads headlong to excesses of cruelty. Nothing has so beneficent an effect on human beings as security. If an international system could be established which would remove the fear of war, the improvement in everyday mentality of everyday people would be enormous and very rapid. Fear, at present, over-shadows the world.

(Russell, 2014)

Fear is one of the major causal factors in paralyzing the moral system and in the violation of expectations regarding the treatment of the needy.

On the battlefield, this paralysis or silencing is widespread. Having to use violence against civilians on the battlefield can lead to moral distress and internal conflict in light of the gap between citizens' expectations and the violent military reality on the ground. But there have been occasions when soldiers openly expressed the pleasure they derive from their aggressiveness and their deviation from accepted social constraints (Abu Ghraib, for example). Such soldiers see violence as unequivocally legiti-mate (Elitzur & Yishai Koren, 2007).

In Chapter 2, I described Darcia Narvaez's (2008) triune ethics the-ory. The first primary ethics, according to Narvaez, is security, or self-protectionist ethics. When a threat appears, the security ethics tends to take charge, looking for what is advantageous for the self to adapt to and survive intact. The security ethics is the default system for the organism when all else fails. When people are fearful for their own safety or their self-beliefs, they are less responsive to helping others and more focused on self-preservation (e.g. Mikulincer et al., 2005).

Turned-off dyads

Let us examine a far more complex event involving what I have termed *turned-off dyads*. Occasionally, an observer construes the dyad without difficulty, and yet it fails to arouse any emotional or motivational compo-nent in him or her. The observer remains indifferent so that the suffering of the victim doesn't trigger identification and empathy and the aggressor's clear violation of expectations fails to arouse moral condemnation or anger. Such dyads are, one might say, turned-off dyads. It seems that the observer is aware of all the relevant aspects of the moral situation, is correctly adhering to the dyadic rules as he or she knows them, and yet appears to lack the expected motivational drive. The structure remains identical to dyads that include a motivational component. Often, even when evident injury or harm is being caused, it may be overlooked with a shrug or even lead to an expression of pleasure or amusement at the sight of the other's distress. Think, for example, of a homeless man, neglected and sick, begging passers-by for money – a situation we often encounter in cities. Almost certainly, many of those who pass by feel contempt and distaste for him. The sight of his dirty and neglected appearance disturbs them, and perhaps some of them even feel they are in danger in his presence. He may remind them of things they would prefer to forget, and makes them feel that their stable and secure lifestyle is more precarious than they would wish to acknowledge. Many don't even notice him at all – as if he were invisible.

However, even people who are variously deterred by the sight of a homeless person surely notice his or her neediness and vulnerability. We have observed that the dyadic structure also exists in those instances in which the moral situation involves only a victim and no aggressor. In such cases, the mind completes the picture by inserting the missing link – a figure who is considered responsible to care for and be concerned about the victim's fate. The possible missing link may be the state's welfare system.

The case of the homeless shows that empathy for the needy and motivation to help them, especially if they are strangers, requires a special set of qualities that most people lack. If the distress of homeless people would truly trouble the public, they would do more for them in the form of protests and voting for political representatives who promise to deal with their problem. Instead, homeless people are mostly met with indifference.

Thus, objective suffering, evident neediness and unconcealed distress often manage to form dyads, but these dyads are not potent, not emotionally charged, and hence, I would argue, remain turned off. The victim needs to touch the observer's deep feelings and sense of likeness so as to awaken his or her conscience and identify with this distress. Somehow, he or she needs to be acknowledged not merely as an objective dependent, but rather as a dependent whose pain and suffering affects the well-being of the observer.

People can also be indifferent to moral situations in which there is a severe blatant moral failure. For example, one can assume that there will be passers-by who will remain indifferent to the sight of someone kicking a cat in the street. If we were to stop them and ask what they thought about the situation, they might very well effortlessly form a correct dyad and identify all the childlike features in relation to the cat and the adultlike features vis-à-vis the aggressor. A decisive majority would immediately perceive the aggressor as having violated their expectations and being morally wrong. However, the suffering of the cat, in and of itself, doesn't always elicit a forceful response. In some people, it fails to trigger any kind of emotion, compassion, or sense of identification.

We are all psychopaths: the primacy of the parameters over the content

One can explain much of the published research on psychopathy cited in Chapter 1 in this way. It would seem that the psychopath knows how to organize social data into moral situations by using the dyadic rules. He or she understands very well how to construct a dyad. Psychopaths do this effortlessly and intuitively, exactly in the same way as a person who is not a psychopath. However, people with psychopathy create turned-off dyads because the suffering of the victim does not trigger their sympathy or concern.

The truth of the matter is that we all, in some way or another, at some time or another, adopt a psychopathic viewpoint. When we come across the suffering of the homeless or of many others, we often behave as the psychopath does. We are conscious of all the components of the situation, but that alone does not affect us. We remain unmoved.

The fact that we do not always have the predictable, concurrent emotional experience clearly demonstrates that it is the cognitive part of our brain that predominates and assumes precedence over the brain's emotional/motivational region. In other words, core knowledge includes the identification of the dyad, but not necessarily the emotional impact that it carries. Moreover, contrary to what the supporters of sentimentalism say, the emotional charge is not necessary to understanding the situation as moral.

We understand that things went wrong between the two parties, we clearly see the victim's distress, we judge it correctly – but we just don't care.

An emotionally charged dyad is one of the key factors most relevant to the process of reaching a moral judgment because without it the judgment lacks a motivational component. Sentimentalists might argue that a turned-off dyad cannot in any way be considered a moral judgment. Though the moral situation translates itself into a dyadic structure, this structure, they may claim, has no significance without the motivational component accompanying it. This issue, however, is more appropriately dealt with in terms of philosophy rather than psychology. Common sense suggests that it probably is a good idea to talk about different levels of dyadic formation. The most extreme case is a motivationally charged dyad in which the observer perceives the victim as part of his or her own self (like a parent does with his or her child); then there are more moderate cases in which the observer's identification is less powerful; finally, there are dyads in which identification ranges from moderate to light to utter indifference about the fate of the victim – the latter being typical of a turned-off dyad that lacks emotional significance.

Why is the cognitive part of our brain more important and primary in moral judgment than the emotional part?

Strickland et al. (2012) bring evidence that points to a broader fact about human cognition, namely that people generally exhibit a tendency to understand events in terms of agents and patients, even when those events have no moral significance. We rely on dyads and the characteristics of the child/adult relationship simply in order to familiarize ourselves with the social world, so as to be exact about what we attribute to others. This would mean that beyond moral judgment, a person's needy/independent positioning or, in Gray et al.'s (2012b) terminology, patiency/agency informs us about that person's intentions, the extent of responsibility attributable to him or her, his or her level of activity, and his or her willingness to help or harm us.

One of the most important types of knowledge provided by information about the childlike and adultlike features of others is the extent of danger posed by them. The vulnerable and weak pose no danger, while the strong and independent can cause harm.

There is, therefore, a survival value in structuring dyads and differentiating the needy and harmless from the strong and dangerous. This has a precedence over the moral judgment.

The animal world and us

How people in different cultures treat animals is a good example of our perception of childlike features as being completely biased by cultural differences.

One example that might be useful to demonstrate the interplay between likeness, dependency and moral judgment is to explore the different ways we deal with cruelty to various non-human species. Since the seventeenth century, Western society seems to have heightened its sensitivity to some animals that have become included within our terms of moral reference. But numerous others remain excluded from this rubric, and we humans remain indifferent to their suffering and are often cruel to them.

Spiders, for example, are despised, and humans tend to thoughtlessly kill them. The French entomologist Jean-Henri Fabre once took two tarantulas, each with a brood of spiderlings on their back, and put them in the same case to test their sense of territoriality (Bilger, 2007). The stronger tarantula attacks the weaker one, and:

> closed her lethal engine and grinds the head of the prostrate foe. Then she calmly devours the deceased by small mouthfuls. Now what do the youngsters do, while their mother is being eaten? Easily consoled, heedless of the atrocious scene, they climb on the conqueror's back and quietly take their places among the lawful family. The ogress raises no objection, accepts them as her own. She makes a meal of the mother and adopts the orphans.
>
> (Bilger, 2007, p. 69)

A spider may in fact be smaller, vulnerable and helpless. But it doesn't belong to the group of "our babies," and therefore is not deemed worthy of protection or rights. Apparently, spiders are not biologically programmed, as are mammals, to extend their self to their offspring. It is impossible for humans to empathize with behavior that is not governed by some version of the dyadic rules. These rules make us human. Species that do not conform to this pattern of behavior are therefore perceived by us as either wicked (spiders) or cold (fish).

There is no doubt that fishing involves the hurting of a defenseless animal. For some people, fishing is simply a fun-filled, pleasurable sporting activity. But imagine if we were to treat cats in the same way as we do fish by attaching small pieces of meat to a hook as bait to be snatched by the cat, which, while satisfying its hunger, is ensnared by the fishing rod, doomed to be stunned to death and served up as a meal for human consumption. In most Western societies, we would probably be charged with cruelty to animals. Yet fishing is accepted by most humans as a legitimate sport. In contrast, hunting mammals is a controversial issue, legally restricted in many countries and despised by many people.

Why have we developed a heightened sensitivity to cats but not to fish? The answer is that cats are perceived as like-me objects whereas fish are not. Cats are mammals, fish are not. Cats have body features, facial expressions and patterns of behavior that fish simply don't possess. So, fish are not creatures we can easily identify with because they lack the most common human characteristics. Their expressionless faces, muteness, lack of emotions and the fact that their body structure is very unlike that of humans make it almost impossible for us to empathize with them. Maybe the most important feature lacking in fish is that, unlike birds and mammals, where offspring require some form of parental assistance, most fish species do not seem to provide parental care.

However, dyadic rules are very elastic, especially in our pluralistic era, with its widespread freedoms of emotional engagement. This includes human and non-human creatures being emotionally engaging for some people. Until very recently, this was not thought possible. With some effort, people can be attached to almost anything: insects, trees, buildings and even robots. In order to be included in the moral community, the creature has to be defined as C. All this requires on the part of moral agents is some imagination and some facts on the basis of which they may identify the similarities between the creature or object and themselves. In fact, the already mentioned elasticity of the dyadic rules means that there is no limit to the number of species and objects that can be included, thereby enabling us to view them as C – and that, of course, includes fish.

How can one convince humans that fish should be creatures of interest to them? The certain answer is that this will only be possible when one can show that fish resemble humans. Failing that, an attitude of indifference is guaranteed.

One fascinating attempt to draw our attention to our resemblance to fish is Neil Shubin's book *Your Inner Fish* (2008). In Shubin's view, there are no vast leaps forward in anatomical evolution, including, of course, in the evolutionary process from fish to human. The process is gradual, advancing by very small changes to a gene, a cell or a bone, as the organism adapts to new tasks. At the end of this lengthy journey, a new species eventually comes into being. The new species carries marks relating it to its evolutionary predecessor. Thus, a continuity that may, and often does, stretch over eons can be established. According to Shubin (2008), these inherited features are still visible in the human body, noting that "Our hands resemble fossil fins, our heads are organized like those of long-extinct jawless fish and major parts of our genomes still look and function like those of worms and bacteria" (p. xx).

Jonathan Balcombe, in his book *What a Fish Knows* (2016), undertook an even more challenging task: to draw an outline of "fish psychology" and demonstrate the extent to which that psychology resembles human psychology. "After reading this," the book's back cover announces:

> you will never be able to deny that fishes love their lives, as we love ours, and that they, too, are vividly emotional, intelligent, and conscious. Balcombe's eloquent, persuasive, highly readable tour de force has a single, enlightening message: fish deserve more respect, care, and protection.

Balcombe's work is based on scientific studies augmented by his own extensive experience of fish. We tend to view fish as emotionless creatures, their vacant eyes reflecting no feelings. They supply us with nutritious, healthy food. Balcombe upends our assumptions. He portrays fish as creatures with feelings, social networks and even the capacity to be somewhat cunning. He proposes that our indifference to fish reflects a bias that obscures the fact that the experience of fish and many lower-order animals is not so remote from ours. We commonly imagine that fish lead brief, uneventful lives with a focus on securing nourishment and repetitive spawning. The truth, says Balcombe, is much more complex. Fish, he claims, indulge in carefully prepared courtship rituals and establish lifelong friendships with other fish. They also cooperate in planning activities such as hunting, attempt to get preferential treatment from others, can be mendacious, and take punitive action against any perceived wrongdoers. Balcombe's examples illustrate consciousness and intentionality among fish, together with a sense of playfulness. Among the examples is a type of fish called a *Midas cichlid* that repeatedly swims towards a trusted human, showing signs of wanting to be stroked, and sometimes demonstrating pleasure when it is momentarily plucked out of the water.

Two like-me features that are crucial to whether or not we include animals in our moral community are parenting and reaction to pain. These are the two factors that our affective like-me system is most sensitive to. We overwhelmingly assume that fish neither care for their young nor respond to pain. However, Balcombe shows that in a quarter of all fish species, there is in fact a tendency to caring, with variations as to how it is accomplished. Sometimes it is limited to the simple act of hiding eggs but not staying to protect the newborn. However, the care of the spawning fish may extend to protecting them for months in safe structures prepared well in advance. In some cases, caring includes carrying the newborn and ensuring it is fed (Balshine & Sloman, 2011). As for pain, Balcombe points to a number of studies suggesting that the fish's response to pain isn't merely reflexive – involuntary withdrawal from the source of the pain – but seems a version of expressions such as "ouch" – in other words, a conscious cognitive response.

The conclusion to be drawn from all of this is that it is difficult to convince humans to show interest, let alone to include a living object as being part of the moral situation, without it being based on some kind or other of "likeness" to themselves.

Indeed, resemblance between a creature of any kind and humans will reinforce the interest taken in it. We are so egocentric that we find it difficult to be interested in a creature that doesn't resemble us. Look, for example, at the movement for animal rights. They do excellent work with cows, pigs, sheep, foxes, bears and other mammals. But there are almost no such groups defending the rights of fish or insects. It would seem that they are far more mobilized to defend animals that resemble us, creatures that care for their offspring. Other species fail to gain the same level of support and compassion.

But even the human response to mammals is in some ways both puzzling and erratic. Look, for example, at current animal cruelty laws in New York State. While prohibiting the infliction of pain on domestic pets, state law permits fox trapping; it outlaws the electrocution of animals whose fur is marketable, but has no objection to furry animals such as hamsters and rats being culled by electrocution. In New York, you're not allowed to decoratively tattoo your dog, but you are free to do so on the skin of your cow, branding them for practical purposes.

Cultural differences with respect to the treatment of mammals

Take the case of the culling of Marius the giraffe at Copenhagen Zoo (Parker, 2017). To control population zoos sometimes cull animals by euthanizing them. Many zoos in Europe adhere to a practice known as "breed and cull"; because of the medical risks of contraception and because animals can become infertile if they don't breed, and in order to limit depriving animals in captivity of their natural behaviors, these zoos allow them to mate and raise infants. Zoos in Europe who are members of the European Association of Zoos and Aquaria (EAZA) cull 20 or 30 animals a year. These are usually goats, antelopes and reindeer, but also lions, tigers, zebras and bears. This practice in most zoos tends to be kept under wraps (Parker, 2017).

Copenhagen Zoo, however, dissects animals such as lions and giraffes in front of a family audience as part of a weekend-long event called "Animals Inside Out." In Denmark, culled animals are viewed as opportunities to learn about the species and as food for other captive animals.

Ian Parker (2017) described in *The New Yorker* how in 2014, the death of a giraffe known as Marius became a social media sensation, causing panic in the international zoo business. It also revealed Denmark's indifference to public opinion.

When the story of Marius the giraffe's impending slaughter was published, the zoo was inundated by thousands of emails expressing protest, including death threats against the zoo management. The zoo nevertheless stuck to its policy. Surprisingly, the zoo's position was supported not only by a majority of the country's leaders, but also by the nation's biggest animal welfare organization. Unlike US zoos, which control the birth rates of animals in captivity by contraception, the Danes believe that animals in captivity should be allowed to behave as they do in their natural habitat, including mating and raising their progeny. In the words of Bengst Holst, Copenhagen Zoo's scientific director, "When you're dead you're dead. Animals don't have any expectations of what happens after death, or that they could have had a longer life" (Parker, 2017, p. 45). In Holst's view, the only boundary that one can draw is between:

> human beings and the rest. Some people say "The apes, they are so close to us, they should be in our group," but the apes are also very close to the rest of the African primates, so if we take them on, too, then you go down the ladder. And once we have agreed on killing

animals for consumption, hundreds of thousands of years ago, we have agreed that we can, for a reason, kill an animal, take a healthy life. If there's a reason for it, we can do it with an ape or an elephant or a horse or a dog.

(Parker, 2017, p. 45)

At least so far as Holst is concerned, killing these animals does not elicit any emotional responses. In expressing this view, Holst challenges what seems to him as some humans' irrational moral feelings for animals. Yet such feelings are widespread and generally accepted, and in all probability account for the fiercely oppositional public response to Marius' culling.

Holst is undoubtedly fully aware of zoo animals' vulnerability and dependency, as well as their perception in the public eye. By drawing a line between humans and animals, he is, in effect, telling us something about his own and his colleagues' emotional/motivational system. They refuse to view the animals as being "our babies" (the child position in the dyad) who warrant protection and mercy.

Personifying animals is exactly what the popular film industry does in the animation of such characters as Donald Duck, Mickey Mouse, the three little pigs, Bambi, Wall-E or Nemo. For the most part, these figures are *cute*, an attribute derived precisely from the way in which their gestures and various other characteristics bear a close and suggestive resemblance to humans. The key factor on which like-me hinges in mammals, and to a great extent also in birds, is that these animals are born helpless and need a parent who will raise them and be concerned for them. Their offspring are vulnerable and arouse feelings similar to those aroused by human newborns. The vulnerability of the offspring and their cuteness is what make them like us in our own eyes. On the other hand, as the following true story illustrates, there are those for whom the lives of animals are no less significant than those of humans.

Having slipped through a Cincinnati zoo's perimeter fence, a 3-year-old boy fell into a moat. There, he found himself at the mercy of a 200 kg male mountain gorilla by the name of Harambe. The horrific spectacle was watched by a crowd of alarmed, screaming onlookers. But in fact, the gorilla appeared to be standing over the boy, as if protecting him from the steadily louder anguish coming from the crowd. Harambe then took hold of the boy's ankle and dragged him across the water, then carried him up a ladder, out of the moat and onto dry land. The zoo authorities, assuming that Harambe posed a real threat to the boy's life, ordered that he be killed. The child was briefly hospitalized and found to have sustained no serious injuries. The shooting aroused strong feelings in the local community. Some questioned whether the boy had really been at risk; others called for either the zoo or the parents to be criminally prosecuted for killing the gorilla. On social media, the boy's mother was harassed by people who saw her as responsible for the animal's death. In October 2016, a Facebook group calling itself "Honoring Harambe" was formed and displayed pictures taken by a member of the group, whose post read "am still heartbroken over this" and the mantra "May we always remember Harambe's sacrifice." No criminal charges were ever brought against either the zoo or the parents.

It is important to note that the significant support for the view that killing the gorilla was morally wrong was intimately related to the fact that the child had not been injured. Had he been harmed, would the moral computation have tipped the scales in favor of killing the gorilla? And in those circumstances, would any form of protest have arisen? Even though the example is somewhat extraordinary, its structure is entirely what we would expect in moral dilemmas of this type when they appear in everyday life. Again, we are faced with the gap between richness of content and the simplicity of the parameters of the dyadic rules, their uniformity and the fact that they repeat themselves time and time again.

Most moral dilemmas do not involve a conflict between feelings and logic. The crux of almost every moral dilemma is captured by the question "Who resembles us?" or "Who is part of our extended self"? In this case, a 3-year-old boy or a gorilla?

The elasticity of dyadic rules is so impressive that, with the aid of technological manipulations, even robots can be "cute," and that is all that is needed to be recognized as C.

HitchBOT was a Canadian "hitchhiking robot" created by David Harris Smith of McMaster University and Frauke Zeller of Ryerson University. It gained international attention for successfully hitchhiking across Canada and in Europe, but in 2015 an attempt to hitchhike across the US ended shortly after it began when the robot was destroyed by vandals in Philadelphia, Pennsylvania.

The robot had a cylindrical body composed of a plastic bucket, with two flexible "arms" and two flexible "legs" attached to the torso. The top section of the cylindrical body was transparent, containing a screen that displayed eyes and a mouth, making the robot approximately humanoid in external appearance, but gender-neutral.

The robot was able to carry on basic conversation and talk about facts, and was designed to be a robotic travelling companion. It had a GPS device and a 3G connection, which allowed researchers to track its location. It was equipped with a camera, which periodically took photographs to document its journeys. It was powered either by solar power or by cigarette lighter sockets in cars.

The robot was not able to walk – it completed its hitchhiking journeys by "asking" to be carried by those who picked it up. It was created as a social experiment. The robot's "hitchhiking" was reported by the press in many countries. When in 2015 the hitchhike across the US was truncated, there was an outpouring of sympathy and support from thousands of people. They tweeted how sad they were that hitchBOT "is dead because humans are awful" and "I'm so sorry some awful person in my city did that to you. Please know not everyone in Philly is this terrible."

A researcher named Kate Darling (2016) and her team observed how people treated Pleo robots – advanced machines, shaped like cute baby dinosaurs, that react to external stimuli. First, they asked participants to name the robots and play with them. Once they were done, she asked them to torture and kill the machines. Most people hesitated.

Research carried out on cuteness of infants by Kringelbach et al. (2016) can help us understand how humans come to have feelings of empathy towards "cute" robots.

This account shows that cuteness is a basic mechanism that helps to trigger protective feelings. In addition to visual cues, such emotions are also promoted by the sound of infant laughter and even our sense of smell (Riem et al., 2012). Evidence assembled by these researcher shows the criteria used to define an infant's face as "cute" include such features as a head that appears to be out of proportion in relation to body size, large round eyes, rounded cheeks and a small chin. The feelings of empathy elicited by "cuteness" among adults gradually paves the way for more complex forms of relations, beginning with "instinctive parenting" and, as time goes by, engagement between adult and child in relations of attachment and various cognitive functions. It would appear that as infants mature, the extent and power of perceived "cuteness" diminishes.

In light of this uncovered evidence, Kringelbach et al. (2016) suggest that the concept of cuteness be viewed as forming a biologically important and beneficial stimulus that could assist caregivers and possibly advance the supervision of various complex emotions. In speedily triggering caregiving in ways that mere intuition cannot, a child's cuteness actually helps him or her to survive.

Turned-off dyads and moral principles

Earlier in this chapter, we saw that the ability to form turned-off dyads was a critical flaw in humans. It leads to a state of moral indifference. The mind correctly identifies the moral failure, notices the suffering of the weak side, but remains indifferent and passive as if the event was none of its business. However, this downside of our mental apparatus can also turn into one of humanity's great accomplishments. Turned-on, active dyads are based on empathy and the like-me criterion. But as we have seen, empathy is an inadequate moral guide in almost all realms of life, whether it's public policy, private charity or interpersonal relationships. Paul Bloom, in *Against Empathy* (2016), argues that empathy, being biased, pushes us in the direction of parochialism and racism. The existence of turned-off dyads shows that we can reach a proper moral judgment without solely relying on empathy.

If, in constituting a dyad, we can somehow detach our feelings, and by that avoid the dominance of the like-me criterion and our personal interests, we might be able to phrase a general moral principle. In fact, it would not be so much a case of detachment, but rather an extension of the like-me criterion to members we are not usually affiliated to. The extension will not be due to their cuteness, but rather to our conviction in the rightness of the moral principle.

We can constitute rules that settle relations between two sides (for example, between the authorities and a citizen) that are based on the principles of equality and justice rather than being decided by the legislator's preferences and personal inclinations, or just because we perceive the victim as tender, vulnerable and cute. This mental capacity can be used to achieve positive objectives such as educating people and societies as a whole to behave in line with a set of principles. In moral situations, the principle of equality and justice will prevail over personal interests, personal needs, group affiliation or party membership.

In examining turned-off dyads, we were looking at moral judgment bottom-up: a specific dyad creating a moral situation leading to a moral judgment by the observer. When we turn this around and view things top-down, we see that a set of principles from "above" may guide us in making a moral judgment by minimizing – to the extent possible – the influence of our personal interests, our ethnic or national affiliation, and other subjective needs and perspectives.

Such principles come into play when we are required to form a moral judgment that bypasses the motivational/emotional component, basing the judgment solely on a rational decision. From this perspective, a dyad subordinate to moral principles, being directed by neither emotion nor motivation related to the specific situation, can also be considered "turned off." Here, only the motivation to uphold the moral principle informs the judgment. In other words, the dyad that is emotionally and motivationally charged must be in sync with a "cold" rational perception of the moral failure. In the event of a contradiction between the two judgments, we must give preference to the "cold" turned-off dyad. It is, in fact, the foundation of the idea of impartiality, the most important of the principles underpinning moral law. This law can only be applied if we can avoid being prejudiced by our feelings for or against the sides.

Ultimately, the hope for a just society must be to rise above the particular case and find one principle that will direct the moral judgment. These moral principles based on turned-off dyads are one answer to the exclusion of entire populations from the moral community.

We have to include every human being within our protected moral community not because we love them or don't love them, or because they do or do not belong to our group. We must include them for the simple reason that this is what the moral law/principle determines we should do. Which means that I have to recognize every human being as C not because he or she is like me, but because his or her suffering is, in principle, acknowledged – if not always emotionally.

Identifying and observing this one overarching principle is in fact what Kant attempted to do. Kant differentiated between what he termed "duty" and "inclinations." According to Kant, a person's action can only be said to have moral value if it is supported by a sense of duty. Actions based on duty have to be consistent with actions controlled by reason. By contrast, Kant argues, if an action is based on an individual's "inclination" it is hard to know whether duty also played a role, and therefore difficult to assign such an action moral value. However, in a situation in which inclination and duty are incompatible, the power of the sense of duty is decisive. As Kant (1785/2002) writes, "the sublimity and intrinsic dignity of the command in duty are so much the more evident, the less the subjective impulses favor it and the more they oppose it" (II.42).

The duty to act morally actually means to act in line with the requirements of reason. According to Kant, an action cannot be rational unless it falls under a universal principle that commits one to act in the same way in all similar circumstances. According to Norman (1998), Kant wishes to capture a much stronger sense of the universality of the principle than is achieved with the principle of consistency. He wants our moral choices to be impersonal. A moral choice and its justification cannot be specific to individuals. Moral justifications are, by their very nature, justifications for anyone and everyone.

Thus, Kant believes that the motivational/emotional component ("inclinations," in his terms) cannot be a good basis when facing a moral dilemma. Instead, Kant urges us to rise above this component and search for the moral law based on pure reason. Kant has in mind our ability to reach moral judgments without involving our feelings, or at least without allowing them to determine the judgment. He especially values moral judgments that show a preference for duty at the expense of our natural tendency to act in accordance with our feelings.

Kant's views on moral duty were far-reaching. Not only does the moral choice have to be detached and independent of our feelings and needs; it must also be devoid of any objective other than aiming to obey the moral imperative (Norman, 1998). Kant's famous categorical imperatives are direct commands to act not in pursuit of some objective, but rather to do what the moral law orders one to do. Implied in this is the notion that in obeying the moral law, one is merely obeying reason and exercising one's own free will. Kant believes humans to be divided beings, split between reason and inclination. When acting in line with reason, our moral conduct is an expression of our free will. But in Kant's view, humans may, in pursuance of inclinations, behave irrationally, and therefore possibly immorally. In such circumstances, the individual must, according to Kant, obey reason and subject the lower self to the higher self (Norman, 1998).

Another model is presented by the American philosopher John Rawls (1971), and what he termed as a "contractarian" view of justice. Rawls' aim is to offer a more abstract concept of the social contact than suggested by Locke, Rousseau and Kant. He coins the term "the original position" – a hypothetical situation that is designed to be a fair and impartial point of view to be accepted in our reasoning about fundamental principles of justice. In this original position, people – or "contracting parties" – have no sense of altruism or motivation to help others. They have no interest in one another's lives.

Moreover, in the original position, people have no knowledge of their social status, what class they may belong to, what assets they possess to navigate their way through life, nor do they possess a concept of the good. Thus, argues Rawls, principles of justice are decided upon from "behind a veil of ignorance." Massive inequality between rich and poor would not be accepted by Rawls' hypothetical individual because as far as they knew, they could well end up at the bottom of the pile (Norman, 1998).

Reaching a moral judgment through moral principles *does not change the basic parameters of the computation process*. It merely changes the weight of each parameter. Whether or not people listen to the voice of their conscience or give preference to their own interest or group, they perform the same moral operations to reach a moral judgment. Kant's significant contribution to the debate and, to an extent, Rawls' too, was not a new model serving as a basis for moral judgment. Rather, their call was to constrain our moral computation of a dyadic situation. This constraint is intended to limit the influence of the subjective like-me criterion, as well as the personal connections between the observer and each of the sides.

For example, in Israel, an ultra-orthodox Jewish community was not prepared to enroll children who do not belong to their particular ethnic group in the community's schools, which are official state-sponsored schools. Members of the community who support the discrimination are unable to form the dyad:

A (community) → C (non-community's children)

refusal to admit to school

At most, community members have some awareness that excluded children would suffer a form of harm. They could form a turned-off dyad in their minds, by which the exclusion of the discriminated children will not trigger any emotion or real concern. A host of excuses and justifications will lead them to "turning off" the dyad.

Kant would probably think that the failure to include all children, irrespective of their religious affiliation, amounts to a moral failure. Were we to justify such an action, we would have to provide a viable argument in favor of refusing to admit children into an educational institution due to their ethnicity. Since it is very difficult to defend such a rule, the discrimination is likely to constitute a moral failure.

In the case of the school that discriminated against children on the basis of their ethnicity, the Israeli Supreme Court intervened and ordered the school to admit these children. The state threatened to deny the school its budget allocations and even impose fines if it were to continue to refuse to enroll pupils "from a certain ethnic background."

One of Kant's formulations concerning the categorical imperative is "Act only on that maxim whereby you can at the same time will that it should become a universal law" (Kant, 1785/1959, p. 421). We cannot apply Kant's moral imperative without recognizing the discriminated children as human beings (C) who have rights to be educated in a state school like any other child.

Here, emphasis shifts to the harm done to the discriminated child; thus, discrimination results in a distinctive dyad in which the school management (the strong side) has violated expectations of how they should conduct themselves vis-à-vis the discriminated children (the weak side). The dyad becomes active by extension of the like-me criterion through the law and the moral principle.

Removing the personal element from moral judgment and turning it into a universally accepted rule will not, however, always work in favor of the weak side. Imagine a situation in which a devoted father doesn't have the money to feed his children. He has to borrow money from the bank in the knowledge that he will not be able to repay the loan. If we base our judgment on the universal principle, we will have to reach the conclusion that, in effect, morally speaking, the father's action was wrong.

If we think the father has a rational justification for his action, then we must accept that everyone else would be equally justified in taking such a loan whenever their family needed food. Unless that is accepted, there is no rational basis for justifying the father's conduct. But why? We could, on the face of it, in our moral calculation, understand the father's motivation. After all, he only acted in the interest of his hungry children. How can it be that moral calculation judges in favor of the bank against the concerned father and his needy children?

Kant himself acknowledges that the universal principle needs to be put into practice, and that during implementation one must take into account facts about the world in which the principle is being applied. In the case of not fulfilling promises, Kant's view is that if people break promises every time they run into difficulty, no one will take the concept of a promise seriously. In an economy that relies on differential promises reflecting the different abilities of rich and poor to return loans, the poor will be the first to lose out!

I'm not suggesting that the best interests of the poor are the central important reason in arguing why loans must be returned and promises kept. I'm simply saying that the reasoning behind every moral question that involves universality will, at some point or another in the chain of argumentation, also concern itself with the weak and needy, and the fact that a universal principle cannot circumvent asymmetric dyads.

Many thinkers have pointed out that Kant's moral philosophy, which was intended to direct our moral judgments, cannot be put into effect. Prinz (2007) writes, "A purely rational rule cannot have a motivational effect on us. It would leave us cold. And if we are emotionally indifferent to morality we might fail to act morally" (p. 134).

At the same time, Kant clarifies something very important in relation to moral judgment. If we are conscious of Kant's requirement in our assessment of moral situations – even if Prinz is right and we cannot give full effect to that requirement – we may tilt the computation of a moral situation in a more universal and rational direction. In other words, a direction that is (relatively) detached from the specific characteristics of the dyad in question. We can work within Kant's moral psychology, bringing to bear his view of the tensions between reason and inclination. This can be modified to suggest that rather than striving for reason to exclude inclinations, we argue that reason should moderate the influence of our inclinations.

It is doubtful if turned-off dyads based entirely on abstract principles are feasible. In any event, they occupy a minor place in people's common moral judgment. At the same time, their corollary, the law, is far more common and influential. A society without an agreed law, one with various ethical approaches, could not function as a society. It would become a Hobbesian state of "war of all against all." In part, the law must include an agreement that all citizens will be given certain rights. In other words, the law must protect citizens against the arbitrariness of rulers and other citizens.

Of course, moral principles are not the same as laws. Laws are limited in time and space, whereas moral principles are ubiquitous and not bound by time. Laws are codified, whereas moral principles are not. However, they do have much in common. Both legal and moral principles apply to large populations, never just an individual or a specific group.

In democracies, all citizens have rights. The state and the judicial authorities are committed to protecting these rights. This means that the system of dyadic expectations is applied to everyone. The government, so to speak, participates in forming dyads, imposing them on citizens. Thus, the state obliges those who plan to construct a public building (e.g. a restaurant or cinema) to make it accessible to disabled citizens, even though this comes at considerable financial cost. This bears no connection whatsoever to the property owners' personal attitude to disabled citizens. By means of legislation, the state creates a new dyad between property owners (the strong party) and the disabled population (who need support). Of course, not all laws are right and just. Sometimes in order to overcome a financial or military crisis, states tend to legislate laws that in hindsight seems to be unjust (such as the Patriot Act, legislated by the Bush administration, which actually gave the government unlimited power that enabled security forces to spy on virtually every American and abuse people's rights to privacy). But overall, this is an exception, especially when compared to dictatorships.

One of the most important virtues of democracies is their consistent and strict moderation of the capriciousness of any individual's computational mechanism. It is not up to you personally to choose who you identify as C and who you regard as A in line with your preferences. The laws of the state make that decision. Whether or not an act is deemed to have violated a set of principles is not decided by the whims of an individual or in line with his or her ethnic or religious affiliation. The judgment is based on what the law dictates.

Rulers cannot simply give preference to those who are close to them and abuse those in whom they have no interest or are opposed to their rule. The law, not the individual mind, determines who should and should not be considered and who is not C. Because a plurality of citizens accepts the principles of democracy, there is significant public sensitivity to any infringement of these principles. Which is to say that the public is highly sensitive to any tendency on the part of those in government to give preference to the capricious and subjective component of their singular mindset at the expense of the fixed and uniformly accepted component.

As a consequence, democracies, in spite of all their income inequality, injustices and other social problems, rarely declare war on, or murder, their own populations. The transfer of power from one elected group to another similarly chosen party is virtually always a peaceful transition. Moreover, the evidence clearly shows that democracies are more consistent in their respect for human rights than are other forms of government.

Chapter 8

The prototype of evil

- Danny, a boy with impaired eyesight, is a pupil in a regular class. Roy takes advantage of the teacher not being in the room and puts a chair in Danny's way to deliberately trip him up. Danny falls over the chair and is injured. Roy's response is to burst out into loud laughter.
- Harry is irritable. He's had a bad day. When he sees a homeless person in the street, he kicks him hard.
- Peter and Rose's divorce was ugly. To undermine Rose's maternal duties, Peter secretly gives their 4-year-old daughter Sarah stimulants, as a result of which the child has outbursts of anger and violent behavior. Peter is happy for this opportunity. In front of a judge, he blames the mother's dysfunctionality for their daughter's behavior.

It is plausible to assume that most people will think that these situations involve acts of evil rather than just commonly recognized moral failures. While the injury inflicted on these victims cannot in any way be compared to the actions of serial killers or, say, the crimes committed by the Nazis, we use the same adjective, evil, to describe them. Why are these extremely different transgressions captured by a shared definition?

The term "evil" is often used to encourage an intolerant and extreme stance towards an enemy or someone who violently opposes you. Over a period of thousands of years, the concept of evil was closely linked to a religious view of life. In Judaism and Christianity, evil is viewed as human conduct in defiance of God's Commandments. An act of evil violates that holy code.

However, despite the evident religious connotations attached to the concept of evil, widespread usage of the term has survived. People in Western societies employ the term in a variety of contexts. The Holocaust has become the ultimate paradigm of evil (Gampel, 2016, p. 1). However, the term is also used to describe war crimes, horrific acts of murder, cruel violence, sexual abuse and attempts to cause suffering simply to gain pleasure from a victim's acute distress. One must assume that the concept has survived because people find it useful. Perhaps it describes a category of moral failures of a certain kind better than any other concept does.

And yet, even though the term is quite common, psychologists have refrained from using empirical methods to deal with the subject of evil. In the professional discourse, evil has been consistently viewed at best as an elusive topic, and at worst a dangerous one, and thus should not be, nor need it be, turned into a scientifically researched field of enquiry (Govrin, 2016).

This chapter deals with the following question: What is it that glues together disparate acts of evil? In other words, can we point to certain characteristics that are common to all instances of perceived evil? And if so, can we say, as I shall argue that we can, that this commonality constitutes a prototype of evil? It is important to point out that the fact that one person terms a certain moral failure as "evil" and another disagrees doesn't constitute a problem from a perceptual point of view. The two people concerned can agree on what the common features of all instances of evil are, even if they disagree about the existence or otherwise of these characteristics in a given moral situation. Therefore, cultural differences in relation to moral values do not necessarily cancel out the agreement that exists between people in relation to the perception of evil.

There are four parts to this chapter. In the first part, I show that it makes a great deal of sense to perceive evil as a coherent concept incorporating a number of salient features that, combined, create a prototype of evil, a dyad with unique characteristics. In the second part, I show that four co-occurring features of a dyad generate the most salient features of the prototype of evil: extreme asymmetry between victim and perpetrator; a specific perceived attitude of the perpetrator towards the victim's vulnerability (Govrin, 2016); the observer's inability to recognize or identify with the perpetrator's motivation; and insuperable differences between the observer and perpetrator's judgment following the incident. In the third part, I describe the perception of evil as a cognitive bias, an inherent gap between the attribution of the observer and the actual experience of the perpetrator. The philosophical and cultural significance of this gap is discussed in the final part of the chapter.

This chapter's aim is to inspire a greater interest among psychologists in the concept of evil, to view it as an important subject for scientific research and to stimulate an understanding of this phenomenon from a variety of perspectives.

Evil as prototype

Elsewhere, I explained why philosophers had, and continue to have, a tough time defining evil (Govrin, 2016). Definitions of evil are plagued by three problems. First, they are circular and employ formulations that describe evil's emotional impact (often in the shape of adjectives such as "shocking" and "outrageous") but not its essence; for example, according to Eve Garrard (2002), "evil acts are not just very bad or wrongful acts, but rather ones possessing some especially horrific quality" (p. 321).

Second, many of the philosophical definitions of evil are quantitative, in the sense that they distinguish evil merely in terms of excessive wrong-doing. As Calder (2013) argues, "If evil is just very wrong we can do without the term 'evil.' We can say everything we need to say using terms such as 'very wrong' or 'very very wrong'" (p. 178).

Third, other definitions are partial and do not capture the gestalt of the concept. Luke Russell (2007) maintains that no philosopher has been able to creditably depict an act of evil that is qualitatively distinguishable from commonly encountered acts of wrongdoing.

Why is it so hard to define "evil"?

The difficulty with formulating a definition of evil is that most definitions rely on classical philosophical structures. The definitions I have cited try to isolate and apply an appropriate law or rule. They attempt to locate a set of necessary and sufficient conditions that would effectively define evil.

Schein and Gray (2014) call this kind of model an "if/then" paradigm. Such theoretical accounts view the mind as if it were a highly skillful machine able to effortlessly calculate acts of evil by subjecting a given situation to a series of simple tests, with an example being classified as evil only if it passes all the tests in turn. Let us suppose that in order for an act to be classified as evil, it must be massively damaging, intentional and absent of any expression of remorse by the perpetrator. In the event that, say, the perpetrator fails to express regret, then according to the if/then criteria, the act will be deemed "evil." As Schein and Gray (2014) argue, such models were advanced decades ago by Alan Turing, since then contemporary research has shown that in reality, mental processes are far more complex (Dreyfus, 1981, 2007).

The if/then model represents a classical structure by which an appropriate law or rule is isolated. The trouble is that most human concepts do not possess a classical structure. Mark Johnson (1993) calls such a doctrine "moral law folk theory" (p. 4). This doctrine, he claims, permeates our cultural heritage, and hence underpins both lay and philosophical conceptions of moral life. Yet it is a doctrine that, he argues, is radically mistaken and morally incorrect. According to Johnson (1993), it would be ethically reckless for us to believe and behave as if we had within us a universal, ethereal faculty for reasoning that is capable of generating universally accepted laws and procedures (p. 5).

Instead of static definitions, recent research suggests that moral concepts proceed "like a swirling vortex, pulling together cognitive elements toward an underlying prototype" (Schein & Gray, 2014, p. 236). Recent views of the operation of the mind support this more disorderly and more dynamic view of how judgments are formed.

In work carried out by Spivey and Dale (2004), perception and cognition have been shown to involve continuous processes of competition, rather than successive computations. Examples showing this to be so are drawn from extensive research in visual cognition.

A better account to define moral judgment is through a class of computational approaches known as connectionism. One of the more fruitful models of this approach is the theory offered by Paul Churchland (1989, p. 104), which draws on neuroscientific findings. According to this view, we do not simply test for the presence or absence of a neat list of defining features and judge the concept applicable or inapplicable accordingly.

Churchland (1996) posits through his moral network theory that our moral knowledge is developed in a process similar to that by which we develop specific physical skills, by training the response of neuronal networks to sensory input. Such training enables us to understand and adapt to the social world in which we live. Churchland maintains that as we acquire moral knowledge, we learn to distinguish between morally "important" and morally "unimportant" categories of action, and between what is morally "bad" and morally "good." Moreover, Churchland (1989) unifies similar cases under one roof, thus creating a core "hotspot" representing an archetypal example of that particular category.

Unlike Churchland, Clark (1996) argues that a prototypical model cannot be understood as an actual specific case. Instead, Clark suggests that the critical factor involved is the statistical median of a group of exemplars. Such a measure is computed by viewing each specific exemplar as consisting of several features that regularly appear together, leading to the formation of a kind of artificial model that links the characteristics that are statistically the most significant. Thus, the archetypal pet may possess both dog and pet features, and the archetypical crime may include personal injury and loss of property. In Clark's view, specific models and "rich sophisticated know-how" remain key factors, but their role is to provide information on the basis of which these simulated models are formed. New cases then fall under the umbrella of a specific category (such as "pet" or "crime"), depending on how closely its features conform to those of the simulated model. Clark (1996) writes:

> Features common to several training examples will figure in more episodes of weight adjustment than the less common features. As a result, the system will become especially adept at encoding and responding to such features. Features that commonly occur together in the exemplars become strongly mutually associated. The system extracts the so-called central tendency of the body of exemplars, that is, a complex of common co-occurring features.
>
> (p. 113)

Such a concept of prototype corresponds with a model of information storage in the brain called state-space representation, which draws on neuroscience (Churchland, 1989; Clark, 1996).

Churchland (1989) posits that the brain's representation of color, for example, is perceived as involving a three-dimensional (3D) state space in which the dimensions reveal: (a) long-wave reflectance; (b) medium-wave reflectance; and (c) short-wave reflectance. According to Churchland, each such dimension may correspond to the action of three distinct types of retinal cone. Within such a 3D space, white and black reside in diametrically opposed locations, while red and orange are quite close together. Our perceptions regarding the perceived similarity/difference relations between colors may thus be understood as mirroring distance in this color-state space.

According to Churchland, new instances are categorized as basically falling under a concept or category according to the perceived distance of the instance from a prototypical example.

Churchland's theory has been criticized by Larson (2017) on the grounds that it fails to identify which features of moral prototypes are crucial for categorization. Larson point out that Churchland is wrong to assume that comparable actions such as lying, cheating and betraying are a reliable way of categorizing "morally bad" behavior since those very same actions may be viewed in certain circumstances as "morally good" – for example, lying to a hostage taker to save the lives of the hostages. Such a lie is clearly in a different category than lies that are morally wrong. Larson posits that mere words such as "lying" or "cheating" do not capture the essential elements of moral failure.

Instead of thinking that perceivers of evil apply a rule-based, context-free moral vision, we must find what kind of fast, highly focused, context-related information perceivers are considering when judging whether a moral failure is evil or just an act of severe wrongdoing. Although the categories of moral failure and evil overlap, evil tends to have greater weight and emotional response.

The tendency of philosophers to look for defining features should be replaced, then, by an inclination towards human moral psychology. We cannot understand evil without knowing a great deal about how the mind operates when facing moral situations, what crucial factors the mind weighs, and how and what kind of interplay exists between motivations, emotions and cognitions when making right/wrong judgments.

Here, I wish to base the perception of evil on a prototype model. As Schein and Gray (2014) have suggested, prototypical models forecast human cognition more accurately than do paradigms based on the "if/then models" (p. 236) in every field of research in which the predictive capacity of these two models has been compared. I suggest that evil is no exception.

Burris and Rempel (2008) were the first to explore evil as a prototype. But they based their model on conscious responses. They initially asked approximately 200 students to list whatever came to mind when they thought of evil. Students' responses were coded into possible meaningful categories. Evil is perceived as applicable to events involving intentional harm, is associated with negative emotional reaction, and with religious (Satan, Adam and Eve) and secular (money, black) symbols. They posit that the term "evil" can be applied to acts viewed as coinciding with a prototypical model of harm, intent and perceived lack of justification. People apply the label evil whenever enough of these central features of the evil prototype are salient in a given situation.

In my view, the traits singled out by this research are necessary but insufficient. First, Gromet et al. (2016) found that an observer who takes pleasure in the suffering of others will be judged evil even if he or she was not responsible for the victim's suffering, which is to say that even in the absence of "intentional harm," the behavior of those involved is categorized as "evil." If so, classifying an act as "evil" must in some way be linked to the position thought to be held by the perpetrator towards the victim's suffering. Second, the characterization "perceived lack of justification" is insufficient. Severe negligence resulting in death or injury can also be judged as lacking justification but is not considered evil. Also, the perpetrator will have many justifications, considered by him or her to be valid, for having harmed the victim. Why, in so many cases, does the observer refuse to accept the perpetrator's explanations? Perceived lack of justification is too narrow a characterization to describe the huge cognitive discrepancy and emotional crisis between the observer and the perpetrator. Third, these characterizations do not consider the power relations between the two sides and the specific traits of each one of them.

Let us assume several cases:

A 7-year-old child shot another child for no apparent reason.

An individual suffering from a psychiatric disorder shoots someone for no apparent reason.

A case in which the murderer and the victim are both convicted criminals.

Each of these cases is characterized by intentionality, harm and lack of justification. However, we cannot rule out the possibility that the observer will not classify these behaviors in the same way since in each case the relations between the two parties differ.

The proposition advanced here is that in every moral judgment reached, the observer must assess relations between two sides. The parameters relating to evil and every moral judgment cannot in and of themselves supply us with an all-inclusive list of the traits relevant to acts of evil and the perpetrator's motives unless they are combined with a theory explaining how the observer goes about learning to assess the relationship between two people.

The central argument I develop is that the perception of evil must be understood through acquaintance with the nature of moral judgment. Elsewhere (Govrin, 2016), I argued that evil is not only defined by the intention of the aggressor and his or her wickedness, or the magnitude of the harm caused. Each of these in isolation cannot serve our purpose. Rather, we need to find the perceptual properties that guide us in recognizing and discriminating evil from ordinary wrongdoing. These perceptual properties are governed by the dyadic rules. Like the perception of color and sounds, this is not something we are necessarily aware of, and here, too, we might find, as in other cognitive faculties, the priority of the pre-verbal over the verbal.

The perception of evil is based on the same parameters as every moral judgment. This provides us with a computed outcome of a moral judgment in relation to an event in which the four salient features discussed below were found to be present at one and the same time.

Four salient features of evil

I. Asymmetry

Think of all the following dyads:

rapist → victim

Nazi → Jew

child molester → 4-year-old child

There is one feature that is common to these crimes: an extreme perceived asymmetry between victim and perpetrator, the first salient feature required for the perception of evil. Whenever the observer identifies evil, the victim or dependent is perceived as weak, helpless, defenseless and needy, and at times innocent. The perpetrator, on the other hand, is perceived as strong and all-powerful. This type of extreme asymmetry may manifest itself through binaries such as armed/unarmed, adult/child, vulnerable/powerful, weak/strong and so on.

To constitute the dyad, the computing system takes both sides' features into account and checks their power relations. Any adult-associated characteristic, when somehow linked to the victim, is likely to moderate the asymmetry, and vice versa: child-associated features attributed to the perpetrator will have the same unsettling effect. Think, for instance, about the subtle differences in each of the similar statements below:

The man pulled out his gun and shot the child in his head.

The man pulled out his gun and shot the mayor in his head.

The man pulled out his gun and shot the armed policeman in his head.

The 5-year-old child pulled out his gun and shot the policeman in his head.

The 5-year-old child pulled out his gun and shot the baby in his head.

Changes in the power relations that mark a situation are likely to affect moral judgment. The more obvious the difference in power, the more easily and faster is the judgment. These expectations are molded on the parent/child dyad, where one side is strong and has unlimited power, while the other is extremely vulnerable, weak and helpless. Where either side is attenuated by being ascribed one or more clashing features, expectations will change and moral judgment becomes harder to compute.

But even here, there might be gestalt shifts. When victims are "associated" with an evil actor, moral judgment will work against them and in favor of the perpetrator, despite the asymmetry of power.

For example, suppose that we have the following information: thousands of innocent citizens were killed because of massive aircraft raids. Entire regions of the ancient beautiful city became hills of debris. At first, the asymmetry of power between the two parties (citizens of nation A, army of nation B) is obvious. Then we are told that it was the Allied forces that sent the planes to bomb the German city of Dresden during World War II. The asymmetry of power is still present: the immensely powerful joint air forces of the Allies against innocent, helpless German citizens. However, the foreground becomes background, and so the fact that they were citizens of Nazi Germany and the reality of that country's severe war crimes have a strongly moderating effect on people's moral judgment, and make them consider the power conjunction quite differently. The information that the victims were Germans and that the bombing took place during World War II are not simply added on or incorporated into the original judgment. Rather, new meaning is given to the original judgment. What happened was a "component shift" (DesAutels, 1996, p. 135): a mental shift in how we perceive the dyad. This changed the computations of the different components, and as a result the entire moral judgment.

Many other factors can moderate the asymmetry of force. For example, if the observer associates considerable personal distress with the aggressor – a distress that played a role in his or her reprehensible action – then this will weigh in in his or her favor. This then may well add vulnerable and needy features to the perpetrator and change the moral judgment, as, for example, in the case of a husband killing his wife's lover. All this is also relevant to the next condition, namely the question of the accessibility of the perpetrator's state of mind to the observer.

2. The perpetrator's perceived attitude to the victim's vulnerability

Another salient feature necessary for an observer to attribute evil relates to his or her perception of the perpetrator's attitude to the victim's dependency and vulnerability.

From the perspective of the observer, the perpetrator recognized the signs of extreme dependency displayed by the victim – helplessness, weakness – and nevertheless (and sometimes *because* of them) he or she knowingly and intentionally harmed him or her.

The observer's impression is that the perpetrator clearly recognized (as did he or she him or herself) a weak and helpless human being (or group). From the observer's perspective, the aggressor acted in full awareness of the victim's vulnerability.

But while in the observer this vulnerability and weakness arouse empathy and a desire to come to the victim's defense, the aggressor's perceived feelings are the very opposite. In some cases, the victim's vulnerability fails to arouse his or her concern; in others, it even causes the aggressor to attack and injure the victim. Thus, the observer judges the perpetrator as hostile and aggressive towards the weak and needy. The aggressor's apparent awareness of the victim's neediness and vulnerability together with the suffering inflicted on the victim are what disturbs the observer and leads to the collapse of basic dyadic expectations, namely that harming the dependent and weak is morally unacceptable and constitutes an act of evil.

This is a qualitative, not a quantitative, basis for attributing evil. It is the key condition distinguishing acts of evil from other grave moral failures. Thus, evil is not fundamentally in the act itself, nor in the gravity of the damage done, but is rather to be found in the perceived relation of the aggressor to the victim's vulnerability and weakness, and towards those who are needy and dependent in general. As Lazar (2017) writes on evil, "When we speak of catastrophe or collapse, we refer to an event that destabilizes thought and judgment, which does not allow presence and orientation" (p. 202).

Bollas (1995) posits that "the evil person horrifies his victim and those who study him precisely because he lacks a logical emotional link to and is removed from his victim, even if transformed to fury" (p. 189). Bollas's account mainly refers to serial killers, in which:

> The evil one searches for someone who is in need and presents himself as good . . . when the victim takes up the offer of assistance, he becomes dependent on the provider; we may regard this form of dependence as malignant since the murderer feeds in order to destroy.
>
> (p. 211)

In fact, as already mentioned, the two conditions to which I have so far referred – extreme asymmetry between perpetrator and victim, and the perpetrator's perceived attitude vis-à-vis vulnerability and neediness – are linked, the one influencing the other.

Between the two, it seems that the latter is more informative and more salient.

As mentioned previously, Gromet et al. (2016) showed that people who derived pleasure from inflicting suffering on others, or were apathetic to that suffering, tend to be regarded by participants as immoral and evil, whether their enjoyment was explicit or implied. That same judgment was also applied to people who merely observed a scene of suffering if they were perceived to have derived pleasure from the event.

At the same time, as Gromet et al.'s research shows, there are circumstances in which the observer may derive a benefit from the suffering of the victim (for instance, where the observer is promoted at the expense of the victim) but would not be judged as evil.

To illustrate how participants judge differing types of pleasure and their moral consequences, Gromet et al. (2016) describe a number of moral situations involving colleagues at work. In one situation, a worker is seriously injured in an accident, as a result of which he cannot for the time being return to work. The injured worker and a colleague are in competition for promotion. The accident removes the injured man from the competition and the promotion goes to his colleague – we could term this an "indirect pleasure." In a second hypothetical situation, the two workers are not in competition and the uninjured worker doesn't gain anything from the other's misfortune other than "pleasure" – this could be said to yield "direct pleasure." In a third situation, the unharmed colleague has a mixture of emotions: pleasure at being promoted as well as sympathy for the victim and the injuries he sustained.

Only when direct pleasure was gained did the majority of people questioned (75%) judge the colleague's response as evil. Participants had a clear preference to avoid physical or social contact with the actor who derived direct pleasure from his or her victim's distress. They expressed more comfortable feelings about being in the vicinity of the actor who gained "indirect" pleasure from such suffering and felt most comfortable about being associated with the person who reported mixed emotions.

In his book *Evil: Inside Human Violence and Cruelty* (1997), Roy F. Baumeister maintains that the most difficult and troubling issue in the debate about evil is whether people derive pleasure from inflicting harm on others, and, if they do, how significant the pleasure derived from such act is in explaining the concept of evil. The tortuous arguments involved in this debate have led Baumeister to the view that sadistic pleasure is genuinely felt and takes time to acquire. However, overall, it accounts for only a minor fraction of acts that are categorized as "evil." Accounts by perpetrators convinced Baumeister that even if these accounts cannot be regarded as an admission that pleasure was derived from harming others, references to pleasure by the aggressors were too numerous to ignore. Evidence cited by Baumeister from Hans Toch's research on violent offenders showed that 6% of Toch's sample were classifiable as bullies (Toch, 1992). While most aggressors put an end to their violence when the victim shows signs of weakness and suffering, the bully uses that moment of helplessness on the part of the victim to intensify the violence, as if for him or her the pleasure from his action is just beginning.

Baumeister describes another example, the Ku Klux Klan. In its early days, it was simply a social club with no particular political or racial agenda. At first, they spent time playing practical jokes on one another. In the course of time, this was extended to the general public, and finally included blacks as a target for their mischievous acts. The violence that gained the Klan such notoriety didn't begin until later.

In all of these cases, the incongruity between the observer's and the aggressor's attitude towards the victim is extreme. The same thing that causes the observer to be distressed and horrified is a source of pleasure and satisfaction to the aggressor; subsequently, the observer is taken aback by realizing the incongruity between him or herself and the perpetrator. Here, the suffering of the victim is not the decisive issue in the perception of evil, even though it is a weighty factor in the formation of the gestalt as a whole. The decisive factor is the stance the aggressor adopts regarding the victim – a blatant undisguised violation of expectations, and the satisfaction he or she gains from this violation.

The perceived stance of an individual towards the components of dependency and vulnerability in a victim appears to be the weightiest consideration in assessing acts of evil and in moral judgments in general.

All the observer's effort in any moral judgment is aimed at understanding the aggressor's attitude to the victim's dependency/neediness component.

3. The perpetrator's mind is inaccessible to the observer

The third salient feature required to match a prototype of evil involves the observer's complete lack of understanding of the aggressor's motives.

The perpetrator's motives appear senseless to the observer. To the observer, it seems that the perpetrator was either acting in an intentionally sadistic way, with a desire to harm, or displaying moral indifference. For the observer, the perpetrator's act just doesn't make sense – he or she can't figure how the perpetrator doesn't see and perceive what he or she, the observer, sees and perceives. It is in precisely this sense that the perpetrator's mind feels sealed to the observer.

As Lazar (2017) writes:

> When we name an action evil [as opposed to crime], we actually mean that we do not know how to contain it within the existing order. Evil is an action which seriously threatens our trust in the world, a trust which we require in order to orientate ourselves within this world. Evil is characterized as that "thing" which massively attacks and collapses fundamental values cherished by man and society. Evil shakes the foundation, unravelling the important moral-emotional-relational tapestry of life, confusing any effort to build a cohesive explanatory scheme.
>
> (pp. xix–xx)

Even if the observer finds reasonable psychological motives to explain the aggressor's behavior, the sense of bafflement remains. Often in such cases, the motives remain somehow external, in the sense that they do not resolve the mystery surrounding the transgressor's actions. The observer understands but at the same time does not understand, is aware of the motives but remains guarded and unconvinced. For example, in *The Roots of Evil* (1989), Ervin Staub emphasized the predisposing societal conditions for genocide. Arguably, harsh living conditions as well as cultural factors may trigger certain psychological processes and provide motives that cause one group of people to assault another group, thus launching a series of attacks that culminate in genocide (Staub, 1989, p. x). In situations of economic hardship and rapid social change, people become more motivated to defend themselves physically and psychologically. They are more likely to engage in destructive acts if they: share a sense of both superiority and insecurity; have a history of devaluing others and aggressive behavior; are more oriented to obey authority; and their culture is monolithic rather than pluralistic. Eager to regain a sense of comprehension of the world and their legitimate place in it, they are more susceptible to genocidal ideologies, particularly when promulgated by authoritarian governments that have the power to propagate a uniform definition of reality.

Staub sheds new light on the murderer's motives, and very accurately describes the psychological dynamics underlying genocide.

However, explanation and understanding do not share the same meaning, and there is much debate within philosophy and psychology regarding their differences. Two principal theories of categorization emerge from this research: the *theory-theory of mind* and the *simulation theory of mind* (Zahavi, 2010). The theory-theory of mind posits that our perception of others primarily involves unemotional rational methods, progressing by deduction from one conviction to the other. According to Zahavi, the simulation theory of mind does not accept the idea that our comprehension of the behavior of others is largely hypothetical, and argues that our own minds serve as a model when attempting to understand the minds of others. We approach others as if we share their beliefs and desires, thus assuming a resemblance between us. (Kögler & Stueber 2000; Zahavi, 2010). Some researchers believe the two models are not mutually exclusive. In any case, explanations such as Staub's seem to match the principles of the theory-theory, but not those included in the simulation theory. We understand the moral failure without reference to our own selves and feelings. We are unable to perceive an analogy between how we think and act and this particular terrible deed (Gallagher, 2005; Gallagher & Zahavi, 2008; Zahavi, 2005).

Alvin Goldman (2006) has argued that an essential condition for mind reading "is that the state ascribed to the target is ascribed as a result of the attributor's instantiating, undergoing, or experiencing, that very state" (Goldman & Sripada, 2005, p. 208). According to Goldman, "an attributor arrives at a mental attribution by simulating, replicating or attempting to do so" (Goldman & Sripada, 2005, p. 194).

This exactly is the process that is obstructed in perceptions of evil. The observer may feel frustrated and shocked because of the extreme lack of correspondence between the two minds.

When perceiving evil people's huge frustration is obvious. He or she normally has no problems in successfully setting the circuits of simulation and projection into motion. Where people encounter the type of moral failure they identify as evil, this reliable everyday mechanism becomes useless. They simply fail to understand another person through themselves.

As Dilthey (2010) also emphasized, when attempting to comprehend the behavior of the other, that person's psychological state is not our principal interest. Rather, we are seeking to decipher the meaning of his or her conduct and the extent of its legitimacy, given that we live in a world we share and of which we have a common understanding. Understanding as well as self-understanding depends on a public scope of symbols, expectations and practices. It is in this profound sense that we fail to understand the true mind of the aggressor who commits what we consider an act of evil.

4. The aggressor's refusal to accept responsibility for his or her deeds

Where the perpetrator's attitude after the act lacks remorse and regret and when he or she refuses to accept responsibility for his or her deeds, it might lead to the formation of two incompatible positions within the observer and the perpetrator. After the act, the perpetrators will be afforded an opportunity to alter the dyadic computation: they can express sincere regret about what they have done, accept responsibility and alter their stance towards the victim.

Perpetrators in some cases understand that they have seriously failed to meet the expectations of how a strong person conducts him or herself towards a weaker one. By consequence, they understand that they have wholly and offensively ignored the fact that they were in the role of the strong one and the victim was weak, that there is an extreme imbalance of power between the two of them. They learn to see the victim's pain for the first time, the suffering they have inflicted and the indifference or cruelty with which they treated the victim. In doing so, they come much closer to the observer's position. They might be appalled by their own actions, just like the observer.

Sometimes this can have the effect of reassuring the observer. Remember that from the observer's point of view, the most problematic aspect of the situation is the fact that the perpetrator's action manifestly violated the rules of the dyad, the most blatant violation being the aggressor's refusal to recognize dependency/vulnerability as worthy of protection. That not only turns the aggressor into a dangerous and inhumane person, but also undermines the observer's worldview. The perpetrator's actions have shattered what the observer considers to be obvious, certain and axiomatic to the understanding of human nature. If the aggressor expresses sincere regret and is prepared to pay a price for his or her misdeed, compatibility between observer and aggressor could be reinstated. While the transgression is still perceived as very serious and remains unforgivable, some aspect of the fundamental moral matrix within which the observer conducts his or her affairs is restored. The observer feels more at ease as the dyadic rules have triumphantly re-emerged within the perpetrator's mind. The expression of regret may also affect another one of the four criteria for attributions of evil: it may reduce the perception of extreme asymmetry between the sides because, having expressed regret, the aggressor is now perceived as more humane and vulnerable. It is as if the aggressor has once more become part of the human community: the object he or she perceives is like that seen by the observer.

On the other hand, the perception of evil is reinforced if the aggressor refuses to alter his stance. It might be said that the aggressor's attitude to – or computation of – the relevant dyadic situation diverges crucially from that of the observer. For example, perpetrators might see themselves as a victim or emphasize factors that were out of their control.

Diana Scully's (1990) interviews with convicted rapists yielded two categories. *Deniers* justified their actions because the victim was willing or got what they deserved. Rapists' claims that their victim seduced them or had a reputation of promiscuous behavior are examples. Deniers did not think they really had committed rape and were said to be "unaware of their victim's feelings." In contrast, *admitters* acknowledged they committed rape but excused their actions by denying responsibility and blamed alcohol or some personal problem they had for their behavior; some even claimed that rape itself had become an addiction.

Observers are likely to remain indifferent to such explanations. The explanations do not make it any easier for the observer to recognize or identify with the aggressor's position. At times, they may have the opposite effect and reinforce the attribution of evil.

It is hard to imagine any explanation that could cause the observer to feel more affinity with someone who raped and murdered his victim. Explanations, as mentioned, will only tend to underline how different the experience of the aggressor is from that of the observer. The aggressor, too, acts within the rules of the dyad. He has his own moral judgment as to what happened. For example, if he was under the influence of alcohol, the implication is that he was less responsible for his actions, which is to say that his adultlike components were weakened. One can say that both deniers and admitters are responsible for significant moral failures. Deniers are responsible for not acknowledging the dyad as a whole; they do not seem to grasp the asymmetry of power between them and the victim, the vulnerability of the victim, the suffering, and the serious and inexcusable harm. Admitters are responsible for their refusal to recognize that what they did cannot be justified and is morally inexcusable. The perception of evil comes as a response to the second moral failure no less seriously than it does to the first.

And so, the observer finds him or herself emotionally shaken once more by the way the aggressor perceives his own moral failure.

In *Unspeakable Acts* (1996), Douglas Pryor tries making the minds of the men who sexually abused children more accessible to readers. He does so by preparing the reader for a reading experience that is hard to digest emotionally:

> Some men cried when they described what they had done; others became extremely angry with themselves; still others shook their heads in disbelief at what they were saying. What I discovered was the human side of the men; I found that their life had often been filled with what to them was pain and turmoil, and that many, though not all, I believe, were genuinely sorry for the acts they had committed.
>
> (p. 10)

These interviews give us a glimpse into the mind of the pedophile criminal. From Pryor's book, we learn that most of the men interviewed had
been sexually abused as children. But in my view, what makes their position more understandable to readers is rather the aggressor's expressed
stance, with hindsight, vis-à-vis the crime he or she committed. That
stance is fully compatible with the position adopted by the observer. The
pedophiles who participated in this research express horror at their own
actions, admit their moral failure. Some of them seem to be in shock
because of what they did, and this matches the observer's response. If
there is an attitude that can alter the observer's moral computation in these
cases – which is not at all certain – it can only be by the aggressor perceiving the dyad in much the same way as the observer perceives it with the
same degree of horror and the same level of incredulity in the face of his
or her blatant violation of expectations.

This is also illustrated in the case of war crimes.

In the following review of testimonies or defenses of Nazi criminals,
significant differences in all the above-mentioned aspects are manifest.
This may lead to variation in the attributions of evil.

Dr. Leon Goldensohn was a US army psychiatrist who reviewed the
mental health of two dozen high-ranking Nazis indicted for genocide and
tried in Nuremberg (Gellately, 2004).

Herman Goering, commander of the Nazi air force, explained to
Goldensohn that Germans regard loyalty and obedience to orders as their
highest and most sacred duty. In his view, the court did not understand this
and was mistaken. Goering wanted the court to take into account everything he had said, including his admission that exterminating women and
children was not an appropriate thing to do, even when one had taken an
oath of loyalty. He himself found it difficult to believe that women and
children had in fact been exterminated. Others, such as Goebbels and
Himmler, had convinced Hitler to carry out such extreme actions
(Gellately, 2004, pp. 60–61).

Hans Frank, the governor general of Poland, claimed that in Germany
itself, nothing was heard about the persecution of the Jews. Other countries had a free press, unlike in Nazi Germany (Gellately, 2004, p. 166).

The Nazi foreign minister, Joachim Von Ribbentrop, also distanced
himself from the extermination of Jews. He argued that in the long run,
from an historical perspective, the extermination of Jews would always
be a stain on the history of Germany. Von Ribbentrop testified that the

important historical issue was not the extermination of the Jews, but rather the fact that the German people had been oppressed and deprived of hope (Gellately, 2004, p. 221).

Otto Ohlendorf was the commanding officer of Einsatzgruppe D on the Eastern Front. He told interrogators that the Jews were shot in military style, one bullet per Jew. He claimed that he had personally taken care that no unrestrained behavior would be committed (Gellately, 2004, p. 281).

Oswald Ludwig Pohl headed the SS head office for economic and administrative affairs, and was the chief administrator of all the concentration camps. In his defense, he told his interrogators that he had known many mixed couples. Many of them had been his friends. Before their marriage, his wife had worked for the famous Berlin Bank Jakob Goldschmidt, which was Jewish-owned. He further wanted his interrogators to know that some of his wife's current friends were Jewish, obviously regarding this as sufficient, positive proof of his feelings about Jews (Gellately, 2004, p. 386).

Reading the interviews with the Nazi leadership is no easy task: moral judgment and assessment of the dyad continues after the incident between the aggressor and the victim has ended. The aggressor naturally depends on the observer and tries to convince him or her to alter the computation of the dyad in his favor. But the observer is also dependent on the aggressor: he wants to return to the social order he is familiar with, to go back to the stable moral assumption according to which the weak and needy possess a high level of moral power. The interviews with the Nazis are so difficult to take in because from the perspective of the observer, the moral failure continues, and the order that he or she would like to see restored remains undermined. Not one of them recognizes the horror of the acts committed or his personal responsibility for what has happened. For them, the extermination of the Jews is a minor matter relative to their preoccupation with clearing their names. From this point of view, severe punishment can also repair the disrupted dyadic rules. In the case of crimes against humanity, it would seem that capital punishment expresses the desire of the general public for some form of reparation.

Now compare these testimonies to Albert Speer's, who, having begun his career as an architect, was appointed in 1942 as Reich Minister of Armaments and War Production. Though his lawyer thought otherwise, Speer decided that it was in his best interest to admit that as a member of the Nazi regime, he was in part responsible for the crimes committed. He also thought it best to distance himself from Hitler, while conceding that there had been a time when, like almost everyone else, he had been captivated by the Führer. Speer focused on his having been part of a system: as he had not been the leader, he rarely mentioned his own personal guilt.

In an early phase of the Nuremberg trials, Speer told the court that towards the end of the war, he had attempted to assassinate Hitler, but that the plot had failed. This was another bid to demonstrate to the prosecutors that he was somehow different from the other defendants.

Speer's approach paid off. He was dealt with more leniently than the others, and sentenced to 20 years in prison rather than being hung for his crimes. It remains a question whether Speer's approach was merely a tactic to win the sympathy of the court, or whether he was genuine in his admission that the regime of which he had been an important part was responsible for genocide. In his book *Inside the Third Reich*, Speer (1970) wrote, "I had closed my eyes . . . Because I failed at that time, I still feel, to this day, responsible for Auschwitz in a wholly personal sense" (p. 480).

Speer seems to have been successful in convincing the judges that he accepted the stance of the observer. He took issue with Goering's line of defence and challenged it by his recognition that the entire Nazi leadership was responsible, and he expressed profound sorrow and regret. At the same time, he was successful in convincing the judges that he had had no direct involvement in, or indeed knowledge of, the extermination of the Jews. To what extent that claim was true remains controversial, as does the question as to whether Speer really tried to assassinate Hitler.

Bear in mind that as is the case with every moral judgment, there is no question of expecting an objective assessment of the four perceptual traits of evil. Different judges will weigh the importance of the various traits differently.

There are also personality factors that influence the judgment of an act of evil. Webster and Saucier (2013; see also Campbell & Vollhardt, 2013; Webster & Saucier, 2015, 2017) developed an individual difference scale of belief in pure evil (BPE), assessing the degree to which individuals attribute sadistic tendency to other people. Individuals who more strongly believe in pure evil (who score higher on the BPE scale) exhibit a more antisocial/aggressive orientation towards others. Such individuals believe that the world is a viler, more dangerous place and report more aggressive (versus peaceful) attitudes, from matters of foreign policy to the criminal justice system. Two studies have shown that people who in general have a stronger belief in pure evil recommend harsher punishments for a variety of crimes (murder, assault, theft), support the death penalty more strongly and are more vehemently opposed to criminal rehabilitation (Webster & Saucier, 2013).

Evil as cognitive bias

Are the observers' attributions of evil appropriate? Are observers right to assume that the person the perpetrator sees before them is the same as the person they see – a vulnerable and weak victim? Is it true that where the observer identifies evil, the aggressor violates the dyadic rules and lacks the natural, human instinct in the face of suffering and distress? My main argument is that the observer is wrong in making these attributions (Govrin, 2016). The perception and attribution of evil are forms of cognitive bias, and they are not independent of human creation and invention.

Baumeister (1997), for the most part, examines the way in which perpetrators understand actions of theirs which have been judged to be "evil." As is not uncommon in other severe cases of criminality, those responsible for such actions frequently believe that their conduct was wholly or almost wholly justified in response to what they perceived as an act of aggression by their "victim." In Baumeister's view, difficult as it may be for some observers to swallow, such opinions often contain an element of truth. Most people's view of evil is straightforward: a cruel, violent aggressor attacking a helpless victim. But not all perceived acts of evil conform to this description. Violence between two sides is often the result of ever-worsening relations between two sides, for which both parties to the conflict bear a share of the responsibility. Thus, the side perceived by observers as the aggressor may, at least in part, be justified in claiming "provocation." Basing himself on a host of recorded cases, Baumeister argues that in reaching their judgment in such instances of perceived evil, the observer tends to underestimate the influence of the aggressor's situational circumstances and exaggerate the extent to which the perpetrator's perceived temperament was responsible for his or her actions.

Even aggressors who derive sadistic pleasure from the suffering of their victim perceive the victim in a totally different way than does the observer. Most abusers, for example, have themselves experienced severe abuse in their childhood, and it seems that the helplessness of the victim and his or her weakness contribute to the illusion that they are now on the side of the strong and that of the abuser, and not on the side of the victim (Bollas, 1995). In other words, they attribute an entirely different connotation to the victim than does the observer.

Our perception of evil is not rational. It is an error. It is not based on logic; as Roth (2017) explained, it "is not open for debate" (p. 182). However, like many other biases, this is not a design flaw of our mind, but a design feature (Haselton et al., 2016).

It supports the assumption that the perception of evil is domain-specific and was favored by natural selection over an accurate and objective perception of the perpetrator. In terms of our own survival, we are fortunate to err. If people would perceive evildoers in an "objective" way, taking the perpetrator's perspective into account, they would probably be in danger. More than anything, the perception of evil involves fear: it signals an existential threat. Humans have an inborn tendency to experience fear in the face of certain stimuli such as, for instance, snakes, spiders, water and closed spaces. These fears are not consciously controlled. They occur even when the same objects are not dangerous (e.g. a non-poisonous snake) and even when we have had no earlier experience with them.

Nesse (2001) argued for what he calls a "smoke detector" principle in bodily systems. He cites a number of examples related to medical conditions, such as allergy and cough, where a defensive system is often battle-ready, even though there is no real danger. These protecting systems appear to be over-responsive.

That said, the perception of evil is also not without its dangers. Behind the most horrific violence people have inflicted on each other, there is a claim by perpetrators that their enemy deserved that fate because of their evilness. In the years before the Holocaust, the Nazi campaign of incitement painted Jews as evil, dangerous and an enemy of the nation, thus justifying their conduct. And so, the perception of evil, which is so crucial in maintaining the stability and security of human society, is also responsible for humanity's worst crimes.

The banality of evil: an attempt to alter the computation of evil?

At times, acts of evil are the result of unquestioning obedience to authority and a banal, unreflected set of motives. The notion of "the banality of evil" was introduced by Hannah Arendt in her book on the trial of Nazi

SS-Obersturmbannführer Adolf Eichmann, *Eichmann in Jerusalem* (1963). The book was based on Arendt's articles for the *New Yorker* magazine covering the Eichmann trial in Jerusalem in 1961, when she first saw Eichmann in court. Like many others, she had expected a sadistic and satanic mass murderer who hated Jews and derived pleasure from his contribution to the extermination of the Jewish people. To her surprise, Eichmann manifested himself as an entirely different personage, ordinary to the point of "gray," and ostensibly normal. The moral chasm between Eichmann's mediocre personality and the horrifying deeds that he initiated and took part in led Arendt to describe him in terms of "the banality of evil."

The most notable aspect of the term is the incongruity between the words "banality" and "evil," which, when combined, seemingly create an oxymoron. In using the word "evil," Arendt – who narrowly escaped the fate of her fellow Jews when she fled from the Third Reich – did not doubt the brutality and inhumanity of the Holocaust and the suffering of the dehumanized victims. But in her analysis of Eichmann, Arendt was referring generally to the attempt by totalitarian regimes (Nazism and Stalinism) to obliterate man's independent thinking and the spontaneity that, in Arendt's view, make us human. Arendt believed that the aim of evil regimes was to turn humans into automatons. Through the hell of the extermination camps, the Nazis sought to turn their victims into some kind of zombies, people drifting between life and death – *Muselmänner*, as they were described by their captors. The Nazi objective was to turn certain human beings – Jews, homosexuals, the mentally disabled and others – into creatures that react automatically and are exclusively preoccupied with the most basic of needs: survival. The totalitarian regime directed the same mechanism at its own people. Soldiers, too, and camp guards had to become obedient, brutal robots. In Arendt's view, Eichmann, however high placed in the state hierarchy, was no exception to this.

In the event, as Arendt saw it, Eichmann was motivated by nothing more than banal personal interests: a wish to be promoted, to be part of something big, an aspiration to find his place in the world and a desire to become powerful. All of these are entirely common and unsurprising motives that may lead a person to good, evil or morally neutral deeds. In Eichmann's case, they led him to become one of the leaders and main executors of a plan to exterminate an entire race. Gradually, he climbed the ladder of promotion in the SS.

Another aspect of Arendt's notion of the banality of evil was what she called "thoughtlessness." By this, she meant the inability to see things from the point of view of another person. Eichmann's thoughtlessness took the form of engendering – mainly from within Eichmann himself – constant, repetitive mantras. Arendt's impression was that Eichmann was unable to give an honest, personal answer to the questions he was asked. As the trial proceeded, he simply "spouted" formulaic responses to all questions. Arendt thought that the banality of Eichmann's answers was linked to his inability to see reality from the perspective of others. Eichmann, Arendt believed, lacked the cognitive ability to think about a situation in any way other than that which he had become accustomed to, and lacked the emotional capacity to identify with an alternative view and empathize with it. His responses, therefore, were mere clichés, utterly predictable and banal.

Arendt's observations aroused harsh responses and fierce criticism. One reason for this was surely the above-mentioned oxymoronic effect of the juxtaposition between "banality" and "evil" in such a traumatic context.

As Richard Wolin (2014), professor of history and political science, wrote in the *Jewish Reviews of Books*:

> If Eichmann was "banal," then the Holocaust itself was banal. There is no avoiding the fact that these two claims are inextricably intertwined. But can it plausibly be said that the mass graves at Babi Yar, the manacles of Theresienstadt, the ovens of Dachau, and the torture implements at Buchenwald were, in the main, a product of "thoughtlessness"? Arendt's defenders would have us believe, counter-intuitively, that it was the *mentalité* of dutiful "functionaries," rather than impassioned anti-Semites, that produced the horrors of Bergen-Belsen, Treblinka, and Auschwitz. But the vast preponderance of available historical evidence tells a very different story.

This links up with a fierce debate concerning the motives of the Nazis and the German people who collaborated in the extermination of the Jews, between Christopher Browning (1992) and Daniel Goldhagen (1997). Shortly after the end of the Eichmann trial, Stanley Milgram, a psychologist at Yale University, began a series of experiments that were greatly influenced by that event. Milgram (1963) wanted to find out how much pain an ordinary person would be willing to inflict on a fellow human simply because he or she was ordered to do so. The study found that more often than not, as long as the authority giving the orders was viewed as legitimate (teachers, scientists, the boss at work, close family members), the order would be obeyed, even if doing so violated the individual's most cherished moral beliefs.

These findings were strongly reinforced in Christopher Browning's (1992) book *Ordinary Men: Reserve Police Battalion 11 and the Final Solution in Poland*. As Browning was to discover, German Police Battalion 101 was made up of less than 500 middle-aged men considered too old and inexperienced to take part in the major frontline battles, and were therefore consigned to the German *Ordnungspolizei* (Order Police) in their hometown of Hamburg. Most of them had never fired a shot or been fired upon. In June 1942, their lives were to change dramatically. The final decision on exterminating European Jewry had been taken in January of that year. But 75–80% of the intended victims were still alive, the vast majority of them in Poland, mostly in scattered small towns and cities. Rounding up such populations required significant forces. With the bulk of Germany's armies beleaguered on the Eastern Front, the regime turned to the 20 or so battalions of *Ordnungspolizei* to deal with these Jewish populations. In June of 1942, Battalion 101 left Hamburg for Poland for what they were told would be an unspecified "special action." Three weeks later, in the early hours of July 13, they found themselves on the way to the Polish village of Józefów. Once there, they discovered that their mission was to annihilate the village's entire Jewish population of 1,500. The battalion commander, himself astonished by the orders received, told the men that they could refuse to carry them out. Only 15 out of the 500 took up that option. Some of those who'd backed out in Józefów chose, on later similarly horrific occasions, to participate in actions that became increasingly routine. Browning reached the conclusion that the men of Battalion 101 participated in numerous massacres not because they were bloodthirsty animals or because of an ingrained hatred of Jews. Their motive was, above all, obedience to authority and group ethos, together with peer pressure.

The fiercest critic of Browning's thesis was Daniel Goldhagen in his book *Hitler's Willing Executioners* (1997). Goldhagen agreed with Browning that most of those involved in the extermination of the Jewish people were ordinary men who came from all sections of German society. However, Browning and Goldhagen fundamentally disagreed as to what drove these ordinary men to engage in mass murder. In Goldhagen's view, deeply rooted anti-Semitism in German society well before Hitler came to power, rather than obedience to authority, was the explanation for the mass murder of European Jewry. Goldhagen termed this German form of anti-Semitism "eliminationism," a variant that called for the elimination of Jewish influence or of Jews themselves from German society. When the Nazis took power, they found themselves masters of a society already imbued with notions about Jews that could be mobilized for the most extreme form of "elimination" imaginable.

On April 8, 1996, the US Holocaust Research Institute hosted an evening of dialogue to examine the issues raised by Daniel Goldhagen's book (Goldhagen et al., 1996). Aside from Goldhagen himself, the participants were all prominent Holocaust scholars, including Christopher Browning. In the course of the symposium, Goldhagen asked whether any of his listeners really believed that those responsible for the massacre in Srebrenica in former Yugoslavia participated against their will. The same applied to the slaughter of Tutsis by Hutus in Rwanda, the Turkish massacre of Armenians during World War I and the decimation of the Cambodian people under the Khmer Rouge. The Holocaust, Goldhagen argued, was the only genocide in history about which it is claimed the killers did not believe their actions desirable or just. And yet all the evidence suggested that the German forces acted no differently than those involved in other acts of genocide, the evidence often coming from testimonies provided by the killers themselves. Goldhagen argued that the Holocaust was different from other genocide and mass killings in some significant ways, but that did not alter the fact that in their willingness to kill, they were no different from other mass murderers. There was no evidence to suggest that the Germans were forced to kill their victims. On the contrary, Goldhagen maintained, there was evidence that in a number of cases, officers told their men they didn't have to carry out the order to kill. Himmler himself, he argued, allowed those who felt they couldn't carry out the orders to be excused. For Goldhagen, what needed to be explained was that ordinary Germans, even when they knew they didn't have to, nonetheless participated in the murders. That, in Goldhagen's view, put paid to the idea that the killing was due to coercion. There was evidence that the men involved showed initiative, acted with zeal and were actively cruel to their victims. Goldhagen dismisses the idea the German forces acted like automatons: they were men who made choices about whether or not to kill and how the victims were to be treated. Soldiers routinely took photographs of their barbaric activities – often against the orders of the superior officers – and proudly showed these to their comrades in arms. Thus, in Goldhagen's view, the Holocaust cannot be explained by such notions as coercion, obedience to authority, personal profit or the search for promotion.

For Goldhagen, the perpetrators' anti-Semitism alone explains their willingness to carry out orders, their zeal, and the initiative they took in brutalizing and killing their Jewish victims. Had the same men been ordered to slaughter Danish people or the citizens of Munich, they would have refused to do so. Therefore, Goldhagen argues that the perpetrators' conception of the victim was a crucial factor in their willingness to obey orders and to do so in the way they did. Any explanation that fails to place the anti-Semitic component of Nazi ideology at center stage cannot, in Goldhagen's opinion, possibly succeed to cast light on the perpetrators' motivation.

In response to this, Christopher Browning argued that while he agreed that the ethnic identity of the victims should not be ignored, there were other factors that Goldhagen had chosen to overlook.

One such factor consistently ignored by Goldhagen was the context of dictatorship itself. In Browning's view, Goldhagen analyzed German behavior as if there was no dictatorship and that all forms of expression were spontaneous and free. Browning argued that the dictatorship's use of a variety of mechanisms – such as manipulative rituals, pageantry and propaganda in an effort to create a uniform image of Jews – should not merely be regarded as evidence of a pervasive anti-Semitism throughout German society, as Goldhagen had implied. The repression practiced by the Nazi dictatorship, argued Browning, was real. As an example, he mentioned the dissident anti-Nazi group "the White Rose," who distributed leaflets condemning the regime, and were arrested, tortured and beheaded. While conceding that some members of the killing units were given the option of not participating in the murders, he argues that anyone who encouraged others not to shoot was court-martialed for defeatism and subversion of the public morale.

Goldhagen's book became the subject of fierce debate. His critics didn't mince their words. Norman Finkelstein (1998), for example, called Goldhagen's thesis "crazy."

In the view of such notable historians as Eberhard Jäckel – respected for his study of Hitler's role in German history – and the American historian Raul Hilberg – widely regarded as the world's preeminent authority on the Holocaust – Goldhagen's book was of no value. Some accused him of a lack of objectivity due to being Jewish and the child of Holocaust survivors.

But Goldhagen's work was also enthusiastically received and applauded.

In 1997, Goldhagen was awarded the Democracy Prize by the German *Journal for German and International Politics,* which asserted that "because of the penetrating quality and the moral power of his presentation, Daniel Goldhagen has greatly stirred the consciousness of the German public" (Ruber, 1997). Goldhagen received the award from the German sociologist Jürgen Habermas and the German literary scholar Jan Philipp Reemtsma. Elie Wiesel praised the work as something every German schoolchild should read.

Why did Goldhagen's book arouse such fierce controversy? Why does knowing the real motive of the killers make such a difference? To a large extent, motivation explains the perpetrator's attitude towards the victim. One of the criteria I established for an act to be considered as evil was the specific way in which the aggressors are perceived to engage or disengage themselves with the victim's dependency. The observer believes that the perpetrators are fully aware of the victim's vulnerability and weakness. And yet instead of responding as expected by preventing pain, they deliberately attack him. This leads the observer to conclude that the aggressors are evil, not because the neediness and dependency of the other failed to inhibit them, but because these very features actually led to an outburst of aggression and a desire to deliberately inflict injury. This is what turns common moral failure into an act of evil.

Browning (1992) attempts to show that three of the perceptual traits included in the prototype of evil are missing in the behavior of "ordinary" Germans during the Nazi era. First, there is no extreme asymmetry between victim and perpetrator, given that the German people were themselves victims of the Nazis and their regime of terror and fear. Second, since "ordinary" Germans only participated in the horrific deeds because they were obeying authority and the group's ethos, one shouldn't consider them to have been either indifferent or sadistic in their attitude towards their Jewish victims. Third, since their participation in the horror was not prompted by hatred of Jews, but rather by obedience to the Nazi orders, their minds became far more accessible to the observer. After all, Milgram (1963), in his famous experiment, found that ordinary American people would administer an electric shock to a learner that gave a wrong answer. Two-thirds of his participants continued to the highest level of 450 volts. The obvious conclusion invited by this line of argument is that the actions of "ordinary" Germans while the Nazis were in power should not be regarded as evil.

Of course, Browning never tried to defend ordinary Germans who participated in the genocide. After all, Germans who participated in the genocide showed no empathy whatsoever to the Jews' suffering and no regret, one of the most defining features of perceived evil. However, Browning's account does shake the polarity between the innocent victim and the murderous perpetrator because it shows that the role of ordinary Germans in the genocide was an accident, and that almost anybody could have taken their place (see also Arendt's answer to Eichmann's defense, Arendt, 1963, p. 278). It also gives access to the perpetrators' minds.

The moral dyad Goldhagen refers to in relation to the Germans and the Holocaust differs from the dyads formed by Arendt and Browning. The latter two argue that the Germans and some Nazis followed orders, were technocrats, feared authority, and that genocide was almost inevitable under Hitler's totalitarian regime.

Their analysis implied that normal people – and most people are, by definition, normal – would act similarly in similar circumstances.

Goldhagen's description of the Nazi collaborators led to a very different computation, from that of Arendt and Brown.

As said, his thesis is that the central causal agent of the Holocaust was the German people's enduring pathological hatred of the Jews.

Beyond the facts, as is the case in all moral disputes, there is, here, a debate over the form of the dyad. I have to say that, at least in my own mind, it matters little whether the Germans actively participated in the murder of the Jewish people because they obeyed authority, feared the regime, or because killing Jews was a source of gratification to them. As I compute the dyad, and I believe many others, the result stays the same either way. The massive scale of the murder and the horrific acts of brutality that accompanied the killings bend my own computation in favor of a judgment of evil, regardless of the oppressors' and perpetrators' motives. However, there is a question exactly at this point whether we can ever morally/politically allow ourselves to disregard motives and historical/political context.

Of course, these two motives, it would seem, appeared together in various combinations. Let us look briefly at four possible situations. A German who shot Jews to death derived some pleasure from the act and, at the same time, was driven from compliance to authority and to the group's ethos. A second German doing the same thing derived enormous pleasure and was only slightly compliant. A third German was just motivated by plain compliance to authority and to the group's ethos, while a fourth felt nothing but pleasure without the slightest compliance. In my own personal computation, I believe such issues as fear and pleasure are irrelevant. If they were at all relevant, we would all have to lessen our condemnation of SS leader Heinrich Himmler's actions in light of his avowal, in hindsight, that the final solution had become "the most painful question of my life," that he "hated this bloody business" that had disturbed him to the "depth of his soul," but everyone must do his duty, "however hard it might be." Finkelstein quotes biographer Richard Breitman, who claimed this is proof that:

> Himmler . . . was not a simple, bloodthirsty, sadistic monster . . . If a sadist is one who delights in personally inflicting pain or death on others, or in witnessing others inflict them, then Himmler was not a sadist. Himmler was the ultimate bureaucrat.
>
> (Finkelstein, 1998, p. 62)

Do such views really alter the conceptualization of Himmler as evil? Is the observer supposed to change his or her moral computation of Himmler in the light of such ideas? Would it really make any difference if Himmler was sadistically gratified by the death of Jews? In my own moral computation, given the scale of the atrocities and the number of victims, the moral computation remains unaltered, irrespective of whether or not Himmler was a sadist. Still, thinkers might put their emphasis on other questions: How does this type of evil come into being? How is it perpetrated? Where can we identify it (and perhaps prevent the worst excesses)? What different forms does it take?

Arendt, it would seem, felt the same about Eichmann's evil acts. While agreeing with the court's judgment that Eichmann should be executed, Arendt disagreed with the reasoning behind this verdict, and was uncomfortable with the theatrical nature of some of the court's proceedings. Her critique was of the nationalist/political motive behind the staging of the trial (in Jerusalem, as a showcase to boost a form of Zionism that she felt very uncomfortable with). She thought that the trial should have focused on the acts Eichmann committed, acts that included devising a policy of genocide. As for Eichmann himself, Arendt was critical of his unfaltering obedience and his failure to distance himself from the laws that the regime required him to follow. At a certain point in the trial, Eichmann told the court that his concept of obedience derived from his reading of Kant.

Central to Arendt's critique of Eichmann was his failure to think for himself. That, in her view, was his crime. By not thinking, not judging, not making use of "practical reason," he had been anything but Kantian in his behavior. Whether or not his intentions were criminal, or what his inner thoughts may or may not have been, or what other social factors may have led Eichmann to do what he did, cannot alter the final judgment. As Arendt (1963) summed it up, "there still remains the fact that you have carried out, and therefore actively supported, a policy of mass murder" (p. 279).

The prototypical model of evil can be applied to many instances. Evil may indeed be in the eyes of the beholder, but this chapter suggests that judgments of evil are not arbitrary, nor do they arise from a neat list of defining features. Rather, evil is a special perceived dyad, a case of proto-type-based reasoning, and is judged quickly, effortlessly and without deliberation. The model can assist us to break down the concept of evil into its various component parts and then re-examine the extent to which the deed matches the model. Our spontaneous judgment of evil might prove to be false, but only if we are consciously aware of how our automatic perceptual system reached such a judgment can we reconsider our verdict.

Epilogue

Moral judgments have an odd quality. We find it easy to reach them but much more difficult to explain them. Our ability to reach rapid, almost instantaneous decisions, judging between good and bad, is far greater than our capacity to think about those decisions and find consistent rational principles on which our actions are based. We are not in control of most of our moral judgments. Indeed, they control us.

Moral judgments simply happen. We don't initiate or choose them. Moral judgments seem uninterested in our opinions; they run their course detouring our conscious selves. In their mode of resolution, they differ from other judgments we make, in which we assimilate reservations such as economic, educational or environmental. Moral judgments defy control and possess us. By the time we think about the moral judgment we have reached, we are already under its sway. Reflection comes too late. We reach the moment of conscious thought *shortly after* having made the decision, and by then it is very difficult to change. The first immediate moments when the moral situation is presented to us are fateful.

When we see a homeless person being kicked, a driver crossing a red light and running over a child, or a youth drowning a cat, we come up with an intuitive, automatic judgment. Only once we have made the judgment can we explain: one mustn't kick an innocent person, we must obey traffic rules, or one isn't allowed to abuse animals. But none of these arguments crossed our minds before we already knew for certain that all these actions were morally forbidden. We made the instantaneous moral judgment with reference to an essentially different database.

There are a number of interesting philosophical approaches that have made sense of this – for example, moral intuitionism as it is presented in Robert Audi's *The Good in the Right* (2004). Audi (2004) defines a moral intuition as a non-inferential, firm, comprehended and pre-theoretical moral belief (pp. 33–36). To call a moral belief non-inferential is to make a descriptive psychological claim about its cause, namely that "it is not – at the time it is intuitively held – believed on the basis of a premise" (p. 33).

The central claim of moral intuitionism is that some moral intuitions do not need any actual inferential basis in order to be either justified or known. Moral intuitionists usually also claim that certain propositions are self-evident. A proposition is self-evident if somebody who adequately understands it is justified in believing it and knows it if the belief is based on that understanding. This philosophical approach articulates something very important, namely that there is an entire psychic area that is nonverbal and beyond the reach of symbolization and language. Here, arguments do not have an important position and explanations are superfluous. There is knowledge without justification, without a foundation that validates it. Even the most elaborate and abstract moral principles will remain unacceptable in the absence of earlier knowledge that is self-evident and based on experience and immediate perception (i.e. moral intuitions). The interesting question is: What is the nature of these intuitions?

It would seem that of all human motivations, there is only one that requires no justification – the need to protect one's life and the life of one's offspring. The need to protect the life of one's own child is so basic, so primary, so obvious, so universal and shared by all living creatures, that we find it self-evident.

According to Patricia Churchland (2011), self-caring and well-being are based in neural circuitry. An animal will neither survive for any length of time nor reproduce when it is unmotivated to preserve itself. This neuronal organization evolved, in the case of mammals, into concern for the well-being of helpless offspring. In some species, this evolved further to include kin, mates or friends – and eventually even strangers. Morality is the outcome of this widening movement in the social behaviors associated with caring for others.

Our moral intuitions are fast, intense, powerful, deliberate and carried out with self-conviction, because we act under the assumption that we are in a battlefield and must defend something. This explains the emotional charge of moral arguments: the observer feels someone, who has in some sense become part of him or herself, is in danger.

Perhaps this explains why moral intuitions are more decisive than rational explanations, why emotion and motivation are more important than language and explanations.

The evolutionary logic of the original dyad has covered unimaginable distances. Thus, someone living in Boston can volunteer to rescue victims of an earthquake in the Philippines whom he or she has never met.

Culture, no doubt, grew out of our biological inheritance, but it does not follow that our genes benefit from our current values – "our reasons aren't the reasons of fish just because fish are our ancestors" (Dennett, 1995, p. 472).

What do we stand to gain when we support – or oppose – legislation on abortion or capital punishment? Why should we care about the victims of an earthquake on the other side of the globe? The archaic origins of such attachments – protection of offspring and kin – have long since stopped to matter. The self is no longer under physical threat, and it is doubtful whether our concern for, say, convicts on death row will affect our personal security. These attachments, it would seem, now have their inherent motivational power, regardless of their origins in the drive for the preservation of self, kin or tribe. But the underlying mechanism remains the same.

As humanity evolved, all sorts of early behavioral patterns, including the dyadic rules, assumed new significance and new roles not fully in line with their original evolution-shaped intention.

If, however, our intuitions are uncontrollable and inevitable, then what's the point of understanding them? If they are so crucially grounded in the need to protect and defend our closest kin, then how can we hope to affect and alter them? Can the attachment approach to moral judgment, a theory that describes our intuitions and throws light on its mysteries, help us alter our moral judgments, or at least the way we perceive our moral opponents?

The answer is complicated and would require another book.

But one possible contribution of the present theory concerns the way in which we conduct a dialogue with those who have different opinions than our own. We may use this theory to develop a different way of listening. Perhaps at times, this new listening will alter moral judgments them-selves; at other times, it can alter our convictions or attitudes towards them. My suggestion is very general and does not pretend to fit all situations. We are not obliged to listen indiscriminately to any and all moral positions with the same degree of patience and openness. Some are dangerous: they are not based on a love of humanity, and they must be rejected outright. Developing another way of listening also does not imply that one must be ready to accept moral positions to which one objects, that somehow threaten one's existence or squarely oppose one's own values.

What a different type of listening may involve is that in certain cases, we might be able to adjust our moral computation by taking into account, rather than the psychology of the victim, that of the observer, our other-minded interlocutor. For that to happen, we must have some minimal ability to realize the circumstances about observers, and to trust their goodwill, sincerity and reliability. We can only do this if we try to get out of ourselves and if we are curious to learn something new. Harsh criticism should be replaced by curiosity, respect and openness. Rather than relating to our opponent as someone who espouses positions that differ crucially from ours, we approach him or her as a human being with fears, profound attachments, strong loyalties, and a need to defend an individual or a group with which we don't identify. In short, we relate to all the psychological motives that have led this person to this present position.

We must change our perception of the speaker: The speaker is not merely someone who threatens our values, but has his or her own feelings and fears, and they are reflected in a moral position. One way or another, and beyond our differences, we share a psychological reality. In this way, our opinion about this person may change, not because we lose faith in our own values, but because we are facing another person whose moral choices are informed by a very similar psychology. We are both human beings. We are both programmed by the same evolution to extend ourselves to other individuals, or groups who we believe to be somehow endangered and who we deeply care about.

References

Ahn, W. (1998). Why are different features central for natural kinds and artifacts? The role of causal status in determining feature centrality. *Cognition, 69*, 135–178.

Ahn, W. K., Taylor, E. G., Kato, D., Marsh, J. K. & Bloom, P. (2013). Causal essentialism in kinds. *The Quarterly Journal of Experimental Psychology, 66*(6), 1113–1130.

Aknin, L. B., Hamlin, J. K. & Dunn, E. W. (2012). Giving leads to happiness in young children. *PLOS One, 7*(6), e39211. https://doi.org/10.1371/journal.pone.0039211

Allmark, P. (1995). Can there be an ethics of care? *Journal of Medical Ethics, 21*(1), 19–24.

Arendt, H. (1963). *Eichmann in Jerusalem: A report on the banality of evil.* New York: Viking Press.

Arrington, R. L. (1989). *Rationalism, realism and relativism: Perspectives in contemporary epistemology.* Ithaca, NY: Cornell University Press.

Asch, S. E. (1956). Studies of independence and conformity: A minority of one against a unanimous majority. *Psychological Monographs, 70*(9), 1–70.

Audi, R. (2004). *The good in the right: A theory of intuition and intrinsic value.* Princeton, NJ: Princeton University Press.

Ayer, A. J. (1936/1946). *Language, truth, and logic.* London: Gollancz.

Azevedo, R. T., Macaluso, E., Avenanti, A., Santangelo, V., Cazzata, V. & Aglioti, S. M. (2013). Their pain is not our pain: Brain and autonomic correlates of empathic resonance with the pain of same and different race individuals. *Human Brain Mapping, 34*(2), 3168–3181.

Baillargeon, R. & DeVos, J. (1991). Object permanence in young infants: Further evidence. *Child Development, 62*(6), 1227–1246.

Baillargeon, R., Scott, R. M., He, Z., Sloane, S., Setoh, P. Jin, K. & Bian, L. (2015). Psychological and sociomoral reasoning in infancy. In M. Mikulincer & P. R. Shaver (Eds.), *APA handbook of personality and social psychology: Vol. 1. Attitudes and social cognition* (pp. 50–79). Washington, DC: American Psychological Association.

Bakeman, R. & Brown, J. V. (1977). Behavioral dialogues: An approach to the assessment of mother-infant interaction. *Child Development, 48*(1), 195–203. 10.2307/1128898

Balcombe, J. (2016). *What a fish knows: The inner lives of our underwater cousins.* New York: Scientific American.

Balshine, S. & Sloman, K. A. (2011). Parental care in fishes. In A. P. Farrell (Ed.), *Encyclopedia of fish physiology: From genome to environment, volume 1* (pp. 670–677). San Diego, CA: Academic Press.

Banerjee, K., Huebner, B. & Hauser, M. (2010). Intuitive moral judgments are robust across variation in gender, education, politics and religion: A large-scale web-based study. *Journal of Cognition and Culture, 10*(3), 253–281.

Barrett, L. F. & Bar, M. (2009). See it with feeling: Affective predictions during object perception. *Philosophical Transactions of the Royal Society of London, 12*(364), 1325–1334.

Bauman, C. W. & Skitka, L. J. (2012). Corporate social responsibility as a source of employee satisfaction. *Research in Organizational Behavior, 32*, 63–86.

Baumeister, R. F. (1997). *Evil: Inside human violence and cruelty.* New York: Henry Holt & Company.

Beauchamp, T. L. & Childress, J. F. (2001). *Principles of biomedical ethics.* New York: Oxford University Press.

Beebe, B. (1985). Interpersonal timing: The application of an adult dialogue model to mother-infant vocal and kinesic interactions. In T. Field. & N. A. Fox (Eds.), *Social perception in infants.* New York: Ablex Publishing Corporations.

Beebe, B. & Lachmann, F. (1988a). The contribution of mother-infant mutual influence to the origins of self- and object representations. *Psychoanalytic Psychology, 5*, 305–337.

Beebe, B. & Lachmann, F. (Eds.) (1988b). *Mother-infant mutual influence and precursors of psychic structure.* Hillsdale, NJ: The Analytic Press.

Beebe, B. & Lachmann, F. (2002). *Infant research and adult treatment: Co-constructing interactions.* Hillsdale, NJ: The Analytic Press.

Beebe, B. & Stern, D. (1977). Engagement – disengagement and early object experiences. In N. Freedman & S. Grand (Ed.), *Communicative structures and psychic structures* (pp. 35–55). New York: Plenum.

Beebe, B., Jaffe, J., Feldstein, S., Mays, K. & Alson, D. (1985). Interpersonal timing: The application of an adult dialogue model to mother-infant vocal and kinesic interactions. In T. Field (Ed.), *Infant social perception.* New York: Ablex.

Beebe, B., Jaffe, J. & Lachmann, F. (1992). A dyadic systems view of communication. In N. Skolnick & S. Warshaw (Eds.), *Relational perspectives in psychoanalysis* (pp. 61–81). Hillsdale, NJ: The Analytic Press.

Berger, P. & Luckmann, T. (1967). *The social construction of reality: A treatise in the sociology of knowledge.* Garden City, NY: Doubleday.

Berry, D. S. & Zebrowitz-McArthur, L. (1985). Some components and consequences of a babyface. *Journal of Personality and Social Psychology, 48*(2), 312–323. 10.1037/0022-3514.48.2.312

Berry, D. S. & Zebrowitz-McArthur, L. (1986). Perceiving character in faces: The impact of age related carniofacial changes on social perception. *Psychological Bulletin, 100,* 3–18.

Berry, D. S. & Zebrowitz-McArthur, L. (1988). What's in a face? Facial maturity and the attribution of legal responsibility. *Personality and Social Psychology Bulletin, 14*(1), 23–33. 10.1177/0146167288141003

Bilger, B. (2007). Spider woman: Hunting venomous species in the basements of Los Angeles. *The New Yorker*, March 5. Retrieved July 24, 2018, from: www.newyorker.com/magazine/2007/03/05/spider-woman.

Blair, R. J. R. (1995). A cognitive developmental approach to morality: Investigating the psychopath. *Cognition, 57,* 1–29.

Blair, R. J. R. (1997). Moral reasoning and the child with psychopathic tendencies. *Personality and Individual Differences, 22*(5), 731–739.

Blair, R. J. R., Sellars, C., Strickland, I., Clark, F., Williams, A. O. & Smith, M. (1995). Emotion attributions in the psychopath. *Personality and Individual Differences, 19*(4), 431–437.

Bless, H. & Forgas, J. P. (Eds.) (2000). *The message within: Subjective experiences and social cognition.* Philadelphia, PA: Psychology Press.

Blinder, A. & Fernandez, M. (2017). An Arkansas community looks for an execution to end its ache. *The New York Times*, April 27. Retrieved July 24, 2018, from: www.nytimes.com/2017/04/27/us/in-area-near-arkansas-prison-an-execution-is-the-one-were-waiting-on.html.

Bloom, P. (2016). *Against empathy: The case for rational compassion.* New York: HarperCollins.

Bollas, C. (1995). *Cracking up: The work of unconscious experience.* New York: Hill & Wang.

Borg, J. S., Hynes, C., Van Horn, J., Grafton, S. & Sinnott-Armstrong, W. (2006). Consequences, action, and intention as factors in moral judgments: An fMRI investigation. *Journal of Cognitive Neuroscience, 18*(5), 803–817.

Bowlby, J. (1944). Forty-four juvenile thieves: Their characters and home-life (II). *The International Journal of Psychoanalysis, 25,* 107–128.

Bowlby, J. (1958). The nature of the child's tie to his mother. *International Journal of Psycho-Analysis, 39,* 1–23.

Bowlby, J. (1969). *Attachment and loss.* New York: Basic Books.

Bowlby, J. (1973). *Attachment and loss.* New York: Basic Books.

Bowlby, J. (1980). *Loss: Sadness and depression*. London: Hogarth Press.

Bowlby, J. (1988). *A secure base: Parent-child attachment and healthy human development*. London: Routledge.

Brewer, M. B. (1979). In-group bias in the minimal intergroup situation: A cognitive-motivational analysis. *Psychological Bulletin, 86*(2), 307–324.

Brown, G. W. & Harris, T. O. (Eds.) (1978). *Social origins of depression: A study of psychiatric disorder in women*. London: Tavistock.

Browning, C. R. (1992). *Ordinary men: Reserve Police Battalion 101 and the final solution in Poland*. New York: HarperCollins.

Bruner, J. (1977). Early social interaction and language acquisition. In H. R. Schaffer (Ed.), *Studies in mother-infant interaction* (pp. 271–289). New York: Norton.

Bruner, J. (1983). *Child's talk: Learning to use language*. New York: Norton.

Burris, C. T. & Rempel, J. K. (2008). Me, myself, and us: Salient self-threats and relational connections. *Journal of Personality and Social Psychology, 95*(4), 944–961.

Buttelmann, D., Carpenter, M. & Tomasello, M. (2009). Eighteen-month-old infants show false belief understanding in an active helping paradigm. *Cognition, 112*, 337–342.

Byrne, D. (1971). *The attraction paradigm*. New York: Academic Press.

Cacioppo, J. T., Petty, R. E., Kao, C. F. & Rodriguez, R. (1986). Central and peripheral routes to persuasion: An individual difference perspective, *Journal of Personality and Social Psychology, 51*, 1032–1043.

Calder, T. (2013). Is evil just very wrong? *Philosophical Studies, 163*(1), 177–196.

Came, D. (2012). Moral and aesthetic judgments reconsidered. *Journal of Value Inquiry, 49*, 159–171.

Campbell, M. & Vollhardt, J. R. (2013). Fighting the good fight. *Personality and Social Psychology Bulletin, 40*(1), 16–33.

Carpendale, J. I. M. (2000). Kohlberg and Piaget on stages and moral reasoning. *Developmental Review, 20*, 181–205.

Choplin, L. (2018). *NhRP Statement on NY Court of Appeals decision in chimpanzee rights cases*. Retrieved from: www.nonhumanrights.org/blog/nhrp-statement-fahey-opinion/.

Chugani, H. T., Behen, M. E., Muzik, O., Juhász, C., Nagy, F. & Chugani, D. C. (2001). Local brain functional activity following early deprivation: A study of postinstitutionalized Romanian orphans. *Neuroimage, 14*(6), 1290–1301.

Chugh, D., Kern, M. C., Zhu, Z. & Lee, S. (2014). Withstanding moral disengagement: Attachment security as an ethical intervention. *Journal of Experimental Social Psychology, 51*, 88–93. http://dx.doi.org/10.1016/j.jesp.2013.11.005

Churchland, P. (1989). *A neurocomputational perspective: The nature of mind and the structure of science.* Cambridge, MA: MIT Press.

Churchland, P. (1996). Neural representation in the social world. In L. May, M. Friedman & A. Clarck (Eds.), *Mind and morals: Essays on cognitive science and ethics* (pp. 91–108). Cambridge, MA: MIT Press.

Churchland, P. (2011). *Brain trust: What neuroscience tells us about morality.* Princeton, NJ: Princeton University Press.

Ciaramelli, E., Muccioli, M., Ladavas, E. & Di Pellegrino, G. (2007). Selective deficit in personal moral judgment following damage to ventromedial pre-frontal cortex. *Social Cognitive and Affective Neuroscience, 2,* 84–92.

Cima, M., Tonnaer, F. & Hauser, M. D. (2010). Psychopaths know right from wrong but don't care. *Social Cognitive and Affective Neuroscience, 5*(1), 59–67.

Clark, H. H. (1996). *Using language.* Cambridge: Cambridge University Press.

Clark, N. (2016). Ken Loach is not exaggerating – as a carer to a disabled child, I know this really is the truth about benefits. *The Independent*, October 19. Retrieved July 24, 2018, from: www.independent.co.uk/voices/ken-loach-i-daniel-blake-welfare-benefits-system-carer-disabled-child-know-this-is-really-the-truth-a7369961.html.

Cohn, J. & Tronick, E. (1989). Specificity of infant's response to mother's affective behavior. *Journal of the American Academy of Child and Adolescent Psychiatry, 28,* 242–248.

Colby, A. & Kohlberg, L. (Eds.) (1987). *The measurement of moral judgment.* New York: Cambridge University Press.

Craik, K. (1943/2010). *The nature of explanation.* New York: Cambridge University Press.

Crick, N. R. (1996). The role of overt aggression, relational aggression, and proso-cial behavior in the prediction of children's future social adjustment. *Child Development, 67*(5), 2317–2327. 10.2307/1131625

Crick, N. R. & Grotpeter, J. K. (1995). How girls fight: Relational aggression in children. *Clinician's Research Digest, 13*(9), 710–722.

Crick, N. R., Casas, J. F. & Mosher, M. (1997). Relational and overt aggression in preschool. *Developmental Psychology, 33*(4), 579–588. 10.1037/0012-1649.33.4.579

Cushman, F., Young, L. & Hauser, M. (2006). The role of conscious reasoning and intuition in moral judgment: Testing three principles of harm. *Psychological Science, 17*(12), 1082–1089. 10.1111/j.1467-9280.2006.01834.x

Dallas News (2014) *Q&A: Death penalty proponent Robert Blecker.* Retrieved July 24, 2018, from: www.dallasnews.com/opinion/commentary/2014/04/11/qa-death-penalty-proponent-robert-blecker.

Damasio, A. (1994). *Descartes' error.* Boston, MA: Norton.

Darling, K. (2016). Extending legal protection to social robots: The effects of anthropomorphism, empathy, and violent behavior towards robotic objects (pp/ 213–232). In R. Calo, M. Froomkin & I. Kerr (Eds.), *Robot law*. Cheltenham: Edward Elgar.

Dar-Nimrod, I. & Heine, S. J. (2011). Genetic essentialism: On the deceptive determinism of DNA. *Psychological Bulletin, 137*(5), 800–818.

Davidson, R. J., Jackson, D. C. & Kalin, N. H. (2000). Emotion, plasticity, context, and regulation: Perspectives from affective neuroscience. *Psychological Bulletin, 126*(6), 890–909.

DeBruine, L. M. (2002). Facial resemblance enhances trust. *Proceedings of the Royal Society of London, 269*(1498), 1307–1312.

DeCasper, A. J. & Carstens, A. A. (1980). Contingencies of stimulation: Effects on learning and emotions in neonates. *Infant Behavior Development, 4*, 19–36.

DeCasper, A. J. & Fifer, W. P. (1980). On human bonding: Newborns prefer their mothers' voices. *Science, 208*(4448), 1174–1176.

Dennett, D. (1987). *The intentional stance*. Cambridge, MA: MIT Press.

Dennett, D. (1995). *Darwin's dangerous idea: Evolution and meanings of life*. New York: Simon & Schuster.

Department for Work and Pensions (2008). *No one written off: Reforming welfare to reward responsibility*. London: Department for Work and Pensions.

DesAutels, P. (1996). Gestalt shifts in moral perception. In L. May, M. Friedman & A. Clarck (Eds.), *Mind and morals: Essays on cognitive science and ethics* (pp. 129–144). Cambridge, MA: MIT Press.

Dijker, A. J. M. (2014). A theory of vulnerability-based morality. *Emotion Review, 6*(2), 175–183.

Dilthey, W. (2010). *Wilhelm Dilthey: Selected works. Volume II: Understanding the human world*, R. A. Makkreel and F. Rodi, Eds. Princeton, NJ: Princeton University Press.

Dreyfus, H. L. (1981). From micro-worlds to knowledge representation: AI at an impasse. In J. Haugeland (Ed.), *Mind design II* (pp. 161–204). Cambridge, MA: MIT Press.

Dreyfus, H. L. (2007). Why Heideggerian AI failed and how fixing it would require making it more Heideggerian. *Artificial Intelligence, 171*(18), 1137–1160.

Dubois, E., Buhle, M. J., Kaplan, T., Lerner, G. & Smith-Rosenberg, C. (1980). Politics and culture in women's history: A symposium. *Feminist Studies, 6*(1), 28–36.

Dunfield, K. A. & Kuhlmeier, V. A. (2010). Intention-mediated selective helping in infancy. *Psychological Science, 21*(4), 523–527. http://dx.doi.org/10.1177/0956797610364119

Dunfield, K. A., Kuhlmeier, V. A., O'Connell, L. J. & Kelley, E. A. (2011). Examining the diversity of prosocial behavior: Helping, sharing, and comforting in infancy. *Infancy*, *16*, 227–247.

Dwyer, S., Huebner, B. & Hauser, M. (2010). The linguistic analogy: Motivations, results, and speculations. *Topics in Cognitive Science*, *2*(3), 486–510.

Edwards, K. & Von Hippel, W. (1995). Hearts and minds: The priority of affective versus cognitive factors in person perception. *Personality and Social Psychology Bulletin*, *21*(10), 996–1011.

Eisenberg, N., Spinrad, T. L. & Sadovsky, A. (2006). Empathy-related responding in children. In M. Killen & J. G. Smetana (Eds.), *Handbook of moral development* (pp. 517–549). Mahwah, NJ: Erlbaum.

Elitzur, Y. & Yishai Koren, N. (2007). How can that be? IDF soldiers' atrocities during the Intifada. *Alpayim*, *31*, 25–54 (Hebrew).

Fawcett, C. & Liszkowski, U. (2012). Infants anticipate others' social preferences. *Infant and Child Development*, *21*, 239–249.

Feldman Barrett, L., Mesquita, B., Ochsner, K. N. & Gross, J. J. (2007). The experience of emotion. *Annual Review of Psychology*, *58*, 373–403.

Field, T. (1981). Infant gaze aversion and heart rate during face-to-face interactions. *Infant Behavior and Development*, *4*, 307–315.

Field, T., Woodson, M., Greenberg, R. & Cohen, D. (1982). Discrimination and imitation of facial expressions by neonates. *Science*, *218*, 179–181.

Finkelstein, N. G. (1998). Daniel Jonah Goldhagen's "crazy" thesis: A critique of Hitler's willing executioners. In N. G. Finkelstein & R. B. Birn (Eds.), *A nation on trial: The Goldhagen thesis and other views*. New York: Metropolitan Books.

Follan, M. & Minnis, M. (2010). Forty-four juvenile thieves revisited: From Bowlby to reactive attachment disorder. *Child Health Care and Development*, *36*(5), 639–645.

Frijda, N. H. (1986). *The emotions*. Cambridge: Cambridge University Press.

Gallagher, S. (2005). *How the body shapes the mind*. Oxford: Oxford University Press.

Gallagher, S. & Zahavi, D. (2008). *The phenomenological mind*. New York: Routledge.

Gallistel, C. R. & King, A. P. (2009). *Memory and the computational brain*. Malden, MA: Wiley-Blackwell.

Gampel, Y. (2016). Evil. In R. Lazar (Ed.), *Talking about evil: Psychoanalytic, social and cultural perspectives* (pp. 1–16). London: Routledge.

Garrard, E. (2002). Evil as an explanatory concept. *The Monist*, *85*(2), 320–335.

Gellately, R. (Ed.) (2004). *The Nuremberg interviews: An American psychiatrist's conversations with the defendants and witnesses conducted by Leon Goldensohn*. New York: Alfred A. Knopf.

Gelman, S. A. & Bloom, P. (2000). Young children are sensitive to how an object was created when deciding what to name it. *Cognition, 76*, 91–103.

Gelman, S. A. & Wellman, H. M. (1991). Insides and essences: Early understanding of the non-obvious. *Cognition, 38*, 213–244.

Gert, B. (2004). *Common morality: Deciding what to do*. Oxford: Oxford University Press.

Gianino, A. & Tronick, E. Z. (1988). The mutual regulation model: The infant's self and interactive regulation coping and defense. In T. Field, P. McCabe & N. Schneiderman (Eds.), *Stress and coping* (pp. 47–68). Hillsdale, NJ: Erlbaum.

Gibbs, J. C. (1995). The cognitive developmental perspective. In W. M. Kurtines & J. L. Gewirtz (Eds.), *Moral development: An introduction* (pp. 27–48). Boston, MA: Allyn & Bacon.

Gilligan, C. (1977). In a different voice: Women's conceptions of self and of morality. *Harvard Educational Review, 47*(4), 481–517.

Gilligan, C. (1982). *In a different voice: Women's conception of self and morality*. Cambridge, MA: Harvard University Press.

Gilligan, C. (1986). On in a different voice: An interdisciplinary forum – reply. *Signs, 11*(2), 324–333. 10.1086/494226

Gilligan, C. & Wiggins, G. (1987). The origins of morality in early childhood relationships. In J. Kagan & S. Lamb (Eds.), *The emergence of morality in young children* (pp. 277–305) Chicago, IL: University of Chicago Press.

Goldberg, H., Preminger, S. & Malach, R. (2014). The emotion–action link? Naturalistic emotional stimuli preferentially activate the human dorsal visual stream. *Neuroimage, 84*, 254–264.

Goldfarb, W. (1945). Psychological privation in infancy and subsequent adjustment. *American Journal of Orthopsychiatry, 15*(2), 247–255.

Goldhagen, D. J. (1997). *Hitler's willing executioners: Ordinary Germans and the holocaust*. New York: Vintage Books.

Goldhagen, D. J., Browning, C, Wieseltier, L. & Berenbaum, M. (1996). *The "willing executioners"/"ordinary men" debate: Selections from the symposium, April 8, 1996*. Washington, DC: United States Holocaust Research Institute. Retrieved July 24, 2018, from: https://collections.ushmm.org/search/catalog/bib22755.

Goldman, A. I. (2006). *Simulating minds: The philosophy, psychology, and neuroscience of mindreading*. Oxford: Oxford University Press.

Goldman, A. I. & Sripada, C. S. (2005). Simulationist models of face-based emotion recognition. *Cognition, 94*(3), 193–213.

Goodman, N. (1972). *Problems and projects*. Indianapolis, IN: Bobbs-Merrill.

Govrin, A. (2014a). The ABC of moral development: An attachment approach to moral judgment. *Frontiers in Psychology, 5*(6), 1–14.

Govrin, A. (2014b). From ethics of care to psychology of care: Reconnecting ethics of care to contemporary moral psychology. *Frontiers in Psychology*, 5, 1135.

Govrin, A. (2016). The psychology of evil. In R. C. Naso & J. Mills (Eds.), *Ethics of evil: Psychoanalytic investigations* (pp. 95–134). London: Karnac.

Govrin, A. (2018). The attachment approach to moral judgment. In K. Gray & J. Graham (Eds.), *Atlas of moral psychology* (pp. 440–450). New York: Guilford Press.

Gray, H. M., Gray, K. & Wegner, D. M. (2007). Dimensions of mind perception. *Science*, *315*(5812), 619. 10.1126/science.1134475

Gray, K. & Wegner, D. M. (2009). Moral typecasting: Divergent perceptions of moral agents and moral patients. *Journal of Personality and Social Psychology*, *96*(3), 505–520. 10.1037/a0013748

Gray, K., Knickman, T. A. & Wegner, D. M. (2011). More dead than dead: Perceptions of persons in the persistent vegetative state. *Cognition*, *121*(2), 275–280.

Gray, K., Waytz, A. & Young, L. (2012a). The moral dyad: A fundamental template unifying moral judgment. *Psychological Inquiry*, *23*(2), 206–215. 10.1080/1047840X.2012.686247

Gray, K., Young, L. & Waytz, A. (2012b). Mind perception is the essence of morality. *Psychological Inquiry*, *23*(2), 101–124.

Greene, J. D. (2005). Emotion and cognition in moral judgment: Evidence from neuroimaging. In J. P. Changeux, A. R. Damasio, W. Singer & Y. Christen (Eds.), *Neurobiology of human values* (pp. 57–66). Berlin: Springer-Verlag.

Greene, J. D. (2007). Why are VMPFC patients more utilitarian? A dual-process theory of moral judgment explains. *Trends in Cognitive Sciences*, *11*(8), 322–323. 10.1016/j.tics.2007.06.004

Greene, J. D. & Haidt, J. (2002). How (and where) does moral judgment work? *Trends in Cognitive Sciences*, *6*(12), 517–523. 10.1016/S1364-6613(02)02011-9

Greene, J. D., Sommerville, R. B., Nystrom, L. E., Darley, J. M. & Cohen, J. D. (2001). An FMRI investigation of emotional engagement in moral judgment. *Science*, *293*, 2105–2108.

Greene, J. D., Nystrom, L. E., Engell, A. D., Darley, J. M. & Cohen, J. D. (2004). The neural bases of cognitive conflict and control in moral judgment. *Neuron*, *14*(44), 389–400.

Greene, J. D., Morelli, S. A., Lowenberg, K., Nystrom, L. E. & Cohen, J. D. (2008). Cognitive load selectively interferes with utilitarian moral judgment. *Cognition*, *107*, 1144–1154.

Gromet, D. M., Goodwin, G. P. & Goodman, R. A. (2016). Pleasure from another's pain: The influence of a target's hedonic states on attributions of immorality and evil. *Personality and Social Psychology Bulletin*, *42*(8), 1077–1091.

Grossberg, S. & Levine, D. S. (1987). Neural dynamics of attentionally modulated pavlovian conditioning: Blocking, interstimulus interval, and secondary reinforcement. *Applied Optics, 26*(23), 5015–5030.

Gunnar, M. R., Morison, S. J., Chisholm, K. & Schuder, M. (2001). Salivary cortisol levels in children adopted from Romanian orphanages. *Development and Psychopathology, 13*, 611–628.

Hafer, C. L. & Begue, L. (2005). Experimental research on just-world theory: Problems, developments, and future challenges. *Psychological Bulletin, 131*, 128–167.

Hahn, U. & Ramscar, M. (Eds.) (2001). *Similarity and categorization.* New York: Oxford University Press.

Haidt, J. (2000). The positive emotion of elevation. *Prevention & Treatment, 3*(1). 10.1037/1522-3736.3.1.33c

Haidt, J. (2001). The emotional dog and its rational tail: A social intuitionist approach to moral judgment. *Psychological Review, 108*, 814–834.

Haidt, J., Bjorklund, F. & Murphy, S. (2000). Moral dumbfounding: When intuition finds no reason. *Lund Psychological Report*, 1(2).

Hamlin, J. K. (2013). Moral judgment and action in preverbal infants and toddlers: Evidence for an innate moral core. *Current Directions in Psychological Science, 22*(3), 186–193. 10.1177/0963721412470687

Hamlin, J. K. & Wynn, K. (2011). Young infants prefer prosocial to antisocial others. *Cognitive Development, 26*, 30–39.

Hamlin, J. K., Wynn, K. & Bloom, P. (2007). Social evaluation in preverbal infants. *Nature, 450*(7169), 557–559. 10.1038/nature06288

Hamlin, J. K., Wynn, K. & Bloom, P. (2010). Three-month-olds show a negativity bias in their social evaluations. *Developmental Science, 13*(6), 923–929. 10.1111/j.1467-7687.2010.00951.x

Hamlin, J. K., Wynn, K., Bloom, P. & Mahajan, N. (2011). How infants and toddlers react to antisocial others. *PNAS Proceedings of the National Academy of Sciences of the United States of America, 108*(50), 19931–19936. 10.1073/pnas.1110306108

Hamlin, J. K., Mahajan, N., Liberman, Z. & Wynn, K. (2013). Not like me = bad: Infants prefer those who harm dissimilar others. *Psychological Science, 24*(4), 589–594. 10.1177/0956797612457785

Hampshire, S. (1954). Logic and appreciation. In W. R. Elton (Ed.), *Aesthetics and language* (pp. 161–169). Oxford: Blackwell.

Hampton, J. A. (2001). The role of similarity in natural categorization. In U. Hann & M. Ramscar (Eds.), *Similarity and categorization* (pp. 13–28). Oxford: Oxford University Press.

Hare, R. (1991). *The hare psychopathy check-list revised.* Toronto: Multi-Health Systems.

Harman, G. (1975). Moral relativism defended. *Philosophical Review*, *84*, 3–22.

Harman, G., Mason, K. & Sinnot-Armstrong, W. (2010). Moral reasoning. In J. M. Doris (Ed.), *The moral psychology handbook* (pp. 206–245). Oxford: Oxford University Press.

Haselton, M. G., Nettle, D. & Murray, D. R. (2016). The evolution of cognitive bias. In D. M. Buss (Ed.), *The handbook of evolutionary psychology, volume 2: Integrations* (pp. 968–987). Hoboken, NJ: John Wiley.

Haslam, N., Rothschild, L. & Ernst, D. (2000). Essentialist beliefs about social categories. *British Journal of Social Psychology*, *39*(1), 113–127.

Hauser, M. (2006). *Moral minds: How nature designed our universal sense of right and wrong.* London: HarperCollins.

Hauser, M., Cushman, F., Young, L., Kang-Xing, J. & Mikhail, J. (2007). A dissociation between moral judgments and justifications. *Mind & Language*, *22*(1), 1–21.

He, Z. (2012). Socio-moral expectations in infants and toddlers. *Dissertation Abstracts International*. Section B: The Sciences and Engineering, 73(5-B), 3300.

Held, V. (2006). *The ethics of care: Personal, political and global.* New York: Oxford University Press.

Henry, J. P. & Wang, S. (1998). Effects of early stress on adult affiliative behavior. *Psychoneuroendocrinology*, *23*(8), 863–875.

Hepach, R., Vaish, A. & Tomasello, M. (2012). Young children are intrinsically motivated to see others helped. *Psychological Science*, *23*(9), 967–972.

Hinde, R. A. & McGinnis, L. (1977). Some factors influencing the effects of temporary mother-infant separation: Some experiments with rhesus monkeys. *Psychologichal Medicine*, *7*(2), 197–212.

Hoffman, M. L. (2000). *Empathy and moral development: Implications for caring and justice.* New York: Cambridge University Press.

Hohle, B., Bijeljac-Babic, R., Herold, B., Weissenborn, J. & Nazzi, T. (2009). Language specific prosodic preferences during the first half year of life: Evidence from German and French infants. *Infant Behavior and Development*, *32*(3), 262–274.

Hoksbergen, R. A. C., ter Laak, J., Van Dijkum, C., Rijk, S., Rijk, K. & Stoutjesdijk, F. (2003). Posttraumatic stress disorder in adopted children from Romania. *American Journal of Orthopsychiatry*, *73*(3), 255–265.

Hoksbergen, R., ter Laak, J., Rijk, K, van Dijkum, C. & Stoutjesdijk, F. (2005). Post-institutional autistic syndrome in Romanian adoptees. *Journal of Autism and Developmental Disorders*, *35*, 615–623.

Holmes, J. (1993). *John Bowlby and attachment theory.* Abingdon: Routledge.

Hrdy, S. B. (2009). *Mothers and others: The evolutionary origins of mutual understanding.* Cambridge, MA: Harvard University Press.

Huebner, B., Dwyer, S. & Hauser, M. (2009). The role of emotion in moral psychology. *Trends in Cognitive Science, 13*(1), 1–6.

Hume, D. (1739/2000). *A treatise of human nature*. Oxford: Oxford University Press.

Hume, D. (1751/1998). *An enquiry concerning the principles of morals: A critical edition*, T. L. Beauchamp, Ed. Oxford: Clarendon Press.

Ireland, T. O., Smith, C. A. & Thornberry, T. P. (2002). Developmental issues in the impact of child maltreatment on later delinquency and drug use. *Criminology, 40*, 359–399.

Jackendoff, R. (1987). The status of thematic relations in linguistic theory. *Linguistic Inquiry, 18*(3), 369–411.

Jackendoff, R. (2002). *Foundations of language: Brain, meaning, grammar, evolution*. Oxford: Oxford University Press.

Jackendoff, R. (2007). Linguistics in cognitive science: The state of the art. *The Linguistic Review, 24*, 347–401.

Jackendoff, R. (2011). What is the human language faculty? Two views. *Language, 87*, 586–624.

Jackendoff, R. (2015). In defense of theory. *Cognitive Science: A Multidisciplinary Journal*, 1–28.

Johnson, M. (1993). *Moral imagination: Implications of cognitive science for ethics*. Chicago, IL: University of Chicago Press.

Jost, J. T., Glaser, J., Kruglanski, A. W. & Sulloway, F. J. (2003). Political conservatism as motivated social cognition. *Psychological Bulletin, 129*(3), 339–375.

Kagan, S. (2001). Thinking about cases. In E. F. Paul, F. D. Miller & J. Paul (Eds.), *Moral knowledge* (pp. 44–61). Cambridge: Cambridge University Press.

Kalish, C. W. (2002). Essentialist to some degree: Beliefs about the structure of natural kind categories. *Memory & Cognition, 30*(3), 340–352.

Kant, I. (1785/1959). *Foundations of the metaphysics of morals* (Lewis White Beck Trans.). Library of Liberal Arts.

Kant, I. (1785/2002). *Groundwork for the metaphysics of morals*. Oxford: Oxford University Press.

Keil, F. C. (1989). *Concepts, kinds, and cognitive development*. Cambridge, MA: MIT Press.

Kerber, L. K. (1986). On in a different voice: An interdisciplinary forum – some cautionary words for historians. *Signs, 11*(2), 304–310. 10.1086/494222

Kiehl, K. A. (2006). A cognitive neuroscience perspective on psychopathy: Evidence for paralimbic system dysfunction. *Psychiatry Research, 142*, 107–128.

Kihlstrom, J. F. (1987). The cognitive unconscious. *Science, 237*, 1445–1452.

Kinzler, K. D., Dupoux, E. & Spelke, E. S. (2007). The native language of social cognition. *Proceedings of the National Academy of Sciences, 104*(30), 12577–12580.

Klein, M. (1932) *The psychoanalysis of children*, Hogarth. Reprinted as *The writings of Melanie Klein, Vol. 2*. London: Hogarth Press, 1975.

Knobe, J. (2003). Intentional action in folk psychology: An experimental investigation. *Philosophical Psychology*, *16*(2), 309–324. 10.1080/09515080307771

Knudsen, B. & Liszkowski U. (2012). Eighteen- and 24-month-old infants correct others in anticipation of action mistakes. *Developmental Science*, *15*, 113–122.

Koenigs, M., Kruepke, M., Zeier, J. & Newman, J. P. (2012). Utilitarian moral judgment in psychopathy. *Social Cognitive and Affective Neuroscience*, *7*, 708–714.

Koenigs, M., Young, L., Adolphs, R., Tranel, D., Cushman, F., Hauser, M. & Damasio, A. (2007). Damage to the prefrontal cortex increases utilitarian moral judgements. *Nature*, *446*(7138), 908–911.

Kögler, H. H. & K. R. Stueber (Eds.) (2000). *Empathy and agency: The problem of understanding in the human sciences*. Boulder, CO: Westview Press.

Kohlberg, L. (1968). The child as a moral philosopher. *Psychology Today*, *2*(4), 24–30.

Kohlberg, L. (1969). Stage and sequence: The cognitive developmental approach to socialization. In D. A. Goslin (Ed.), *Handbook of socialization theory and research* (pp. 347–480). Chicago, IL: Rand McNally.

Kohlberg, L. (1971). From "is" to "ought": How to commit the naturalistic fallacy and get away with it in the study of moral development. In T. Mischel (Ed.), *Cognitive development and epistemology* (pp. 151–284). New York: Academic Press.

Kohlberg, L. (1981). *Essays on moral development*. San Francisco, CA: Harper & Row.

Kohlberg, L. & Kramer, R. (1969). Continuities and discontinuities in childhood and adult moral development. *Human Development*, *12*(2), 93–120.

Komatsu, L. K. (1992). Recent views of conceptual structure. *Psychological Bulletin*, *112*(3), 500–526. 10.1037/0033-2909.112.3.500

Krebs, D. L. & Denton, K. (2005). Toward a more pragmatic approach to morality: A critical evaluation of Kohlberg's model. *Psychological Review*, *112*(3), 629–648.

Kreppner, J. M., O'Connor, T. G., Rutter, M. & English and Romanian Adoptees Study Team. (2001). Can inattention/overactivity be an institutional deprivation syndrome? *Journal of Abnormal Child Psychology*, *29*, 513–528.

Kringelbach, M. L., Stark, E. A., Alexander, C., Bornstein, M. H. & Stein, A. (2016). On cuteness: Unlocking the parental brain and beyond. *Trends in Cognitive Science*, *20*(7), 545–558.

Kuhlmeier, V., Wynn, K. & Bloom, P. (2003). Attribution of dispositional states by 12-month-olds. *Psychological Science*, *14*(5), 402–408.

Kurtines, W. M. & Gewirtz, J. L. (Eds.) (1984). *Morality, moral behavior, and moral development*. New York: Wiley.

Kyong-Sun, J. & Baillargeon, R. (2017). Infants possess an abstract expectation of ingroup support. *PNAS Proceedings of the National Academy of Sciences of the United States of America, 114*(31), 8199–8204.

Lagerspetz, K. M., Björkqvist, K. & Peltonen, T. (1988). Is indirect aggression typical of females? Gender differences in aggressiveness in 11- to 12-year-old children. *Aggressive Behavior, 14*(6), 403–414. 10.1002/1098-2337(1988)14:6<403:: AID-AB2480140602>3.0.CO;2-D

Lakoff, G. & Johnson, M. (1999). *Philosophy in the flesh: The embodied mind and its challenge to Western thought.* New York: Basic Books.

Lang, F. R., Featherman, D. L. & Nesselroade, J. R. (1997). Social self-efficacy and short-term variability in social relationships: The MacArthur successful aging studies. *Psychology and Aging, 12*(4), 657–666. 10.1037/0882-7974.12.4.657

Lang, P. J., Bradley, M. M. & Cuthbert, B. N. (1990). Emotion, attention, and the startle reflex. *Psychological Review, 97*(3), 377–395. 10.1037/0033-295X.97.3.377

Lansford, J. E., Miller-Johnson, S., Berlin, L. J., Dodge, K. A., Bates, J. E. & Ireland, T. O. (2007). Early physical abuse and later violent delinquency: A prospective longitudinal study. *Child Maltreatment, 12*(3), 233–245.

Larson, C. A. (2017). A cognitive prototype model of moral judgment and disagreement. *Ethics & Behavior, 27*(1), 1–25. 10.1080/10508422.2015.1116076

Laudan, L. (1977). *Progress and its problems: Towards a theory of scientific growth.* Berkeley, CA: University of California Press.

Lazar, R. (2017). Talking about evil in retrospect: Trying to conceive the inconceivable. In R. Lazar (Ed.), *Talking about evil: Psychoanalytic, social and cultural perspectives* (pp. 200–217). London: Routledge.

Lerdahl, F. & Jackendoff, R. (1983). An overview of hierarchical structure in music. *Music Perception, 1*(2), 229–252.

Lerner, M. J. (1980). *The belief in a just world: A fundamental delusion.* New York: Plenum.

Lerner, M. J. & Miller, D. T. (1978). Just-world research and the attribution process: Looking back and ahead. *Psychological Bulletin, 85,* 1030–1051.

Lerner, M. J. & Simmons, C. H. (1966). Observer's reaction to the "innocent victim": Compassion or rejection? *Journal of Personality and Social Psychology, 4*(2), 203–210.

Leventhal, H. & Scherer, K. (1987). The relationship of emotion to cognition: A functional approach to a semantic controversy. *Cognition and Emotion, 1*(1), 3–28.

Liberman, Z., Woodward, A. L. & Kinzler, K. D. (2017). Preverbal infants infer third-party social relationships based on language. *Cognitive Science, 41,* 622–634.

Liesener, J. J. & Mills, J. (1999). An experimental study of disability spread: Talking to an adult in a wheelchair like a child. *Journal of Applied Social Psychology*, *29*(10), 2083–2092. 10.1111/j.1559-1816.1999.tb02296.x

Lindquist, K. A., Wager, T. D., Kober, H., Bliss-Moreau, E. & Barrett, L. F. (2012). The brain basis of emotion: A meta-analytic review. *The Behavioral and Brain Sciences*, *35*(3), 121–143.

Liszkowski, U., Carpenter, M., Striano, T. & Tomasello, M. (2006). Twelve- and 18-month-olds point to provide in-formation for others. *Journal of Cognition and Development*, *7*, 173–187.

Liszkowski, U., Albrecht, K., Carpenter, M. & Tomasello, M. (2008). Infants' visual and auditory communication when a partner is or is not visually attending. *Infant Behavior and Development*, *31*, 157–167.

Lowen, L. (2017). *20 key arguments from both sides of the abortion debate*. Retrieved July 24, 2018, from: www.thoughtco.com/arguments-for-and-against-abortion-3534153.

MacFarlane, A. (1975). Olfaction in the development of social preferences in the human neonate. *Ciba Foundation Symposium*, *33*, 103–117.

MacIntyre, A. (1981). *After virtue*. Notre Dame, IN: University of Notre Dame Press.

MacIntyre, A. (1998). *A short history of ethics*. London: Routledge.

MacLean, K. (2003). The impact of institutionalization on child development. *Development and Psychopathology*, *15*, 853–884.

Mahajan, N. & Wynn, K. (2012). Origins of "us" versus "them": Prelinguistic infants prefer similar others. *Cognition*, *124*(2), 227–233.

Malle, B. F. & Knobe, J. (1997). The folk concept of intentionality. *Journal of Experimental Social Psychology*, *33*, 101–121.

Mallon, R. & Nichols, S. (2010). Moral rules. In J. Doris (Ed.), *Moral psychology handbook* (pp. 297–320). Oxford: Oxford University Press.

Martin, G. B. & Clark, R. D. (1982). Distress crying in neonates: Species and peer specificity. *Developmental Psychology*, *18*(1), 3–9.

Mayo, B. (1986). *The philosophy of right and wrong*. London: Routledge & Kegan Paul.

Medin, D. L. & Ortony, A. (1989). Psychological essentialism. In S. Vosniadou & A. Ortony (Eds.), *Similarity and analogical reasoning* (pp. 179–195) New York: Cambridge University Press.

Meltzoff, A. N. (1995). Understanding the intentions of others: Re-enactment of intended acts by 18-month-old children. *Developmental Psychology*, *31*, 838–850.

Meltzoff, A. N. (2006). The "like me" framework for recognizing and becoming an intentional agent. *Acta Psychologica*, *124*(1), 26–43.

Meltzoff, A. N. & Brooks, R. (2001). "Like me" as a building block for understanding other minds: Bodily acts, attention and intention. In B. F. Malle, L. J. Moses. & D. A. Baldwin (Eds.), *Intentions and intentionality: Foundations of social cognition* (pp. 171–191). Cambridge, MA: MIT Press.

Mendez, M. F., Anderson, E. & Shapira, J. S. (2005). An investigation of moral judgement in frontotemporal dementia. *Cognitive and Behavioral Neurology, 18*(4), 193–197.

Mikhail, J. (2000). Rawls' linguistic analogy: A study of the "generative grammar" model of moral theory described by John Rawls in "A theory of justice." Ph.D dissertation, Cornell University.

Mikhail, J. (2007). Universal moral grammar: Theory, evidence and the future. *Trends in Cognitive Sciences, 11*(4), 143–152. 10.1016/j.tics.2006.12.007

Mikhail, J. (2012). Moral grammar and human rights: Some reflections on cognitive science and enlightenment rationalism. In R. Goodman, D. Jinks & A. K. Woods (Eds.), *Understanding social action, promoting human rights* (pp. 160–202). Oxford: Oxford University Press.

Mikulincer, M. & Florian, V. (2000). Exploring individual differences in reactions to mortality salience: Does attachment style regulate terror management mechanisms? *Journal of Personality and Social Psychology, 79*(2), 260–273.

Mikulincer, M., Shaver, P. R., Gillath, O. & Nitzberg, R. A. (2005). Attachment, caregiving, and altruism: Boosting attachment security increases compassion and helping. *Journal of Personality and Social Psychology, 89*, 817–839.

Milgram, S. (1963). Behavioral study of obedience. *Journal of Abnormal and Social Psychology, 67*, 371–378.

Mill, J. S. (1859). *On liberty.* Boston, MA: MobileReference.

Mitchell, S. A. (2000). *Relationality: From attachment to intersubjectivity.* Mahwah, NJ: Analytic Press.

Moll, J., de Oliveira-Souza, R., Eslinger, P. J., Bramati, I. E., Mourao-Miranda, J., Andreiulo, P. A., et al. (2002). The neural correlates of moral sensitivity: A functional magnetic resonance imaging investigation of basic and moral emotions. *Journal of Neuroscience, 22*, 2730–2736.

Moll, J., Zahn, R., de Olivera-Souza, R., Krueger, F. & Grafman, J. (2005). The neural basis of human moral cognition. *Neuroscience, 6*, 799–809.

Murphy, S., Haidt, J. & Björklund, F. (2000). *Moral dumbfounding: When intuition finds no reason.* Unpublished manuscript, Department of Philosophy, University of Virginia.

Narvaez, D. (2008). Triune ethics theory: The neurobiological roots of our multiple moralities. *New Ideas in Psychology, 26*, 95–119.

Nelson, E., Leibenluft, E., McClure, E. & Pine, D. (2005). The social re-orientation of adolescence: A neuroscience perspective on the process and its relation to psychopathology. *Psychological Medicine, 35*, 163–174.

Nesse, R. M. (2001). The smoke detector principle: Natural selection and the regulation of defensive responses. *Annals of the New York Academy of Sciences, 935*(1), 75–85.

Newcomb, T. M. (1943). *Personality and social change: Attitude formation in a student community.* Fort Worth, TX: Dryden Press.

Newcomb, T. M. (1961). *The acquaintance process.* New York: Holt, Rinehart & Winston.

Nichols, S. (2002). Norms with feeling: Towards a psychological account of moral judgment. *Cognition, 84*(2), 221–236. 10.1016/S0010-0277(02)00048-3

Nichols, S. (2004). *Sentimental rules: On the natural foundations of moral judgment.* New York: Oxford University Press.

Norman, R. (1998). *The moral philosophers,* Oxford: Oxford University Press.

Nucci, L. P. (1982). Conceptual development in the moral and conventional domains: Implications for values education. *Review of Educational Research, 52*(1), 93–122.

Nucci, L. P. (2001). *Education in the moral domain.* Cambridge: Cambridge University Press.

Ochsner, K. N. & Gross, J. J. (2005). The cognitive control of emotions. *Trends in Cognitive Sciences, 9*(5), 242–249.

O'Connor, T. G., Bredenkamp, D., Rutter, M. & ERA Study Team. (1999). Attachment disturbances and disorders in children exposed to early severe deprivation. *Infant Mental Health Journal, 20,* 10–29.

O'Connor, T. G., Rutter, M. & Beckett, C., Keaveney, L. & Kreppner, J. L. (2000). The effects of global severe privation on cognitive competence: Extension and longitudinal follow-up. *Child Development, 72,* 376–390.

O'Connor, T. G., Marvin, R. S., Rutter, M., Olrick, J. T., Britner, P. A. & English and Romanian Adoptees Study Team. (2003). Child-parent attachment following early institutional deprivation. *Development and Psychopathology, 15*(1), 19–38.

O'Malley, M. (2015). *Why the death penalty needs to go.* Retrieved July 24, 2018, from: https://edition.cnn.com/2015/11/06/opinions/omalley-capital-punishment/index.html.

Ornellas, L. (n.d.). *Death penalty arguments: Deterrent or revenge (pros and cons).* Retrieved July 24, 2018, from: www.prodeathpenalty.com/ornellaspaper.htm.

Ou, S. & Reynolds, A. J. (2010). Childhood predictors of young adult male crime. *Child and Youth Services Review, 32*(8), 1097–1107. http://dx.doi.org/10.1016/j.childyouth.2010.02.009

Over, H. & Carpenter, M. (2009). Eighteen-month-old infants show increased helping following priming with affiliation. *Psychological Science, 20,* 1189–1193.

Pallini, S. & Barcaccia, B. (2014). A meeting of the minds: John Bowlby encounters Jean Piaget. *Review of General Psychology, 18*(4), 287–292.

Panksepp, J. (1998). *Affective neuroscience: The foundations of human and animal emotions.* Oxford: Oxford University Press.

Paris, W. D., Budapest, G. C., Konstanz, H. D. D., Bristol, C. G., Oregon, K. L. & Stirling, A. O. (1972). An experimental investigation into the formation of intergroup representations. *European Journal of Social Psychology, 2*(2), 202–204.

Parker, I. (2017). The culling. *The New Yorker*, January 16, pp. 43–53.

Pessoa, L. (2008). On the relationship between emotion and cognition. *Nature, 9*, 148–158.

Pessoa, L. (2013). *The cognitive-emotional brain: From interactions to integration.* Cambridge, MA: MIT Press.

Pessoa, L. (2015). The cognitive-emotional amalgam. *Behavioral and Brain Sciences, 38*, e91.

Piaget, J. (1932/1965). *The moral judgment of the child.* New York: Free Press.

Piaget, J. (1954). *The construction of reality in the child.* New York: Basic Books.

Pinker, S. & Jackendoff, R. (2005). The faculty of language: What's special about it? *Cognition, 95*(2), 201–236.

Pizarro, D. A., Uhlmann, E. & Bloom, P. (2003). Causal deviance and the attribution of moral responsibility. *Journal of Experimental Social Psychology, 39*, 653–660.

Plato (2004). *Republic, Book I, 344c.* Indianapolis, IN: Hackett.

Pothos, E. M. & Chater, N. (2001). Categorization by simplicity: A minimum description length approach to unsupervised clustering. In U. Hahn & R. Ramscar (Eds.), *Similarity and categorization* (pp. 51–72) New York: Oxford University Press.

Powell, L. J. & Spelke, E. S. (2013). Preverbal infants expect members of social groups to act alike. *PNAS Proceedings of the National Academy of Sciences of the United States of America, 110*(41), E3965–E3972.

Premack, D. & Premack, A. J. (1997). Infants attribute value to the goal directed actions of self-propelled objects. *Journal of Cognitive Neuroscience, 9*(6), 848–856.

Pribram, K. H. & McGuinness, D. (1975). Arousal, activation, and effort in the control of attention. *Psychological Review, 82*(2), 116–149. 10.1037/h0076780

Prinz, J. J. (2007). *The emotional construction of morals.* Oxford: Oxford University Press.

ProCon (2013). Should the death penalty be abolished or paused (moratorium) because of the alleged possibility of an innocent person being executed? Retrieved July 24, 2018, from: https://deathpenalty.procon.org/view.answers.php?questionID=001006.

Pryor, D. W. (1996). *Unspeakable acts: Why men sexually abuse children.* New York: NYU Press.

Rai, T. S. & Fiske, A. P. (2011). Moral psychology is relationship regulation: Moral motives for unity, hierarchy, equality, and proportionality. *Psychological Review, 118*(1), 57–75.

Raine, A. & Yang, Y. (2006). Neural foundations to moral reasoning and antisocial behavior. *Social Cognitive and Affective Neuroscience, 1*(3), 203–213.

Randa, L. E. (1997). *Society's final solution: A history and discussion of the death penalty.* Ann Arbor, MI: University of Michigan Press.

Rawls, J. (1971). *A theory of justice.* Cambridge, MA: Harvard University Press.

Reeves, C. (2005). Singing the same tune? Bowlby and Winnicott on deprivation and delinquency. In J. Issroff (Ed.), *Donald Winnicott and John Bowlby: Personal and professional perspectives* (pp. 71–100). London: Karnac. .

Rehder, B. & Hoffman, A. B. (2005). Thirty-something categorization results explained: Selective attention, eyetracking, and models of category learning. *Journal of Experimental Psychology: Learning, Memory, and Cognition, 31*(5), 811–829. 10.1037/0278-7393.31.5.811

Reid, T. (1788). *Essays on the active powers of men.* London: Cheapside.

Rest, J. (1984). The major components of morality. In W. M. Kurtines & J. L. Gewirtz (Eds.), *Morality, moral behavior, and moral development* (pp. 24–40). New York: Wiley.

Richeson, J. A. & Shelton, J. N. (2003). When prejudice does not pay: Effects of interracial contact on executive function. *Psychological Science, 14,* 287–290.

Richters, M. M. & Volkmar, F. R. (1994). Reactive attachment disorder of infancy or early childhood. *Journal of the American Academy of Child and Adolescent Psychiatry, 33,* 328–332.

Riem, M. M., van IJzendoorn, M. H., Tops, M., Boksem, M. A., Rombouts, S. A. & Bakermans-Kranenburg, M. J. (2012). No laughing matter: Intranasal oxytocin administration changes functional brain connectivity during exposure to infant laughter. *Neuropsychopharmacology, 37*(5), 1257–1266.

Robey, K. L., Beckley, L. & Kirschner, M. (2006). Implicit infantilizing attitudes about disability. *Journal of Developmental and Physical Disabilities, 18*(4), 441–453. 10.1007/s10882-006-9027-3

Robinson, J. S., Joel, S. & Plaks, J. E. (2015). Empathy for the group versus indifference toward the victim: Effects of anxious avoidant attachment on moral judgment. *Journal of Experimental Social Psychology, 56,* 139–152. http://dx.doi.org/10.1016/j.jesp. 2014.09.017

Roth, M. (2017). The restorative power of reading literature. In R. Lazar (Ed.), *Talking about evil: Psychoanalytic, social and cultural perspectives* (pp. 181–199). London: Routledge.

Ruber, D. B. (1997). Goldhagen wins German prize for Holocaust book. *Harvard Gazette*.

Rumelhart, D. E. (1980). Schemata: The building blocks of cognition. In J. S. Rand, C. B. Bertram & W. F. Brewer (Eds.), *Theoretical issues in reading comprehension* (pp. 33–58). Hillsdale, NJ: Lawrence Erlbaum.

Rumelhart, D. E. & Ortony, A. (1977). The representation of knowledge in memory. In R. C. Anderson, R. J. Spiro & W. E. Montague (Eds.), *Schooling and the acquisition of knowledge* (pp. 99–135). Hillsdale, NJ: Lawrence Erlbaum.

Russell, B. (2014). *Nobel lecture: What desires are politically important?* Retrieved July 24, 2018, from: www.nobelprize.org/nobel_prizes/literature/laureates/1950/russell-lecture.html.

Russell, L. (2007). Is evil action qualitatively distinct from ordinary wrongdoing? *Australasian Journal of Philosophy*, *85*(4), 659–677.

Rutter, M. (1971). Parent-child separation: Psychological effects on the children. *Journal of Child Psychology and Psychiatry*, *12*(4), 233–260.

Rutter, M. (1972/1981). *Maternal deprivation reassessed* (2nd ed.). Harmondsworth: Penguin.

Rutter, M. (1995). Clinical implications of attachment concepts: Retrospect and prospect. *Journal of Child Psychology and Psychiatry*, *36*(4), 549–571.

Rutter, M. (1998). Developmental catch-up, and deficit, following adoption after severe global early privation. *Journal of Child Psychiatry*, *39*(4), 465–476.

Rutter, M. L., Kreppner, J. M. & O'Connor, T. G. (2001). Specificity and heterogeneity in children's responses to profound institutional privation. *British Journal of Psychiatry*, *179*(2), 97–103.

Sagi, A. & Hoffman, M. L. (1976). Empathic distress in the newborn. *Developmental Psychology*, *12*(2), 175–176.

Sales, D. (2016). Prove you're disabled: Government's demand of worst injured 7/7 survivor. *The Sun*, February 14. Retrieved from: www.thesun.co.uk/archives/news/146483/prove-youre-disabled-governments-demand-of-worst-injured-77-survivor/.

Sander, L. (1977). The regulation of exchange in the infant-caretaker system and some aspects of the context-content relationship. In M. Lewis & L. Rosenblum (Eds.), *Interaction, conversation, and the development of language* (pp. 133–156). New York: Wiley.

Sander, L. (1983). Polarity paradox, and the organizing process in development. In J. D. Call, E. Galenson & R. Tyson (Eds.), *Frontiers of infant psychiatry* (pp. 315–327). New York: Basic Books.

Santayana, G. (1955). *The sense of beauty: Being the outline of aesthetic theory.* Mineola, NY: Dover Publications.

Schein, C. & Gray, K. (2014). The prototype model of blame: Freeing moral cognition from linearity and little boxes. *Psychological Inquiry*, *25*, 236–240.

Schein, C. & Gray, K. (2017). The theory of dyadic morality: reinventing moral judgment by redefining harm. *Personality and Social Psychology Review*, *22*(1), 32–70.

Scully, D. (1990). *Understanding sexual violence: A study of convicted rapists*. Oxford: Psychology Press.

Shackman, A. J., Salomons, T. V., Slagter, H. A., Fox, A. S., Winter, J. J. & Davidson, R. J. (2011). The integration of negative affect, pain, and cognitive control in the cingulate cortex. *Nature Reviews Neuroscience*, *2*, 154–167.

Sher, G. (2001). But I could be wrong. *Social Philosophy and Policy*, *18*(2), 64–78.

Sherif, M. (1935). A study of some social factors in perception. *Archives of Psychology*, *27*(187), 23–46.

Shubin, N. (2008). *Your inner fish: A journey into the 3.5-billion-year history of the human body*. New York: Random House.

Shweder, R. & Haidt, J. (1993). The future of moral psychology: Truth, intuition, and the pluralist way. *Psychological Science*, *4*, 360–365.

Shweder, R. & Haidt, J. (1994). The future of moral psychology: Truth, intuition, and the pluralist way. In B. Puka (Ed.), *Reaching out: Caring, altruism, and prosocial behavior* (pp. 336–341). New York: Garland Publishing.

Shweder, R., Much, N., Mahapatra, M. & Park, L. (1997). The "big three" of morality (autonomy, community, divinity) and the "big three" explanations of suffering. In A. Brandt & P. Rozin (Eds.), *Morality and health* (pp. 119–169). London: Routledge.

Slote, M. (2006). Moral sentimentalism and moral psychology. In D. Copp (Ed.), *The Oxford handbook of ethical theory* (pp. 219–239). New York: Oxford University Press.

Smetana, J. G. (1981). Preschool children's conceptions of moral and social rules. *Child Development*, *52*(4), 1333–1336. 10.2307/1129527

Smetana, J. G. (1985). Preschool children's conceptions of transgressions: Effects of varying moral and conventional domain-related attributes. *Developmental Psychology*, *21*(1), 18–29.

Smith, C. & Thornberry, T. P. (1995). The relationship between childhood maltreatment and adolescent involvement in delinquency. *Criminology*, *33*, 451–477.

Sodian, B., Licata, M., Kristen-Antonow, S., Paulus, M., Killen, M. & Woodward, A. (2016). Understanding of goals, beliefs, and desires predicts morally relevant theory of mind: A longitudinal investigation. *Child Development*, *87*(4), 1221–1232.

Speer, A. (1970). *Inside the Third Reich*. New York: Avon Books.

Spelke, E. S., Breinlinger, K., Macomber, J. & Jacobson, K. (1992). Origins of knowledge. *Psychological Review, 99*(4), 605–632. 10.1037/0033-295X.99.4.605

Spitz, R. (1945). Hospitalism: An inquiry into the genesis of psychiatric conditions in early childhood. *Psychoanalytic Study of the Child, 1*, 53–74.

Spitz, R. A. (1965). *The first year of life: A psychoanalytic study of normal and deviant development of object relations.* New York: International Universities Press.

Spivey, M. & Dale, R. (2004). On the continuity of mind: Toward a dynamical account of cognition. In B. Ross (Ed.), *The psychology of learning and motivation* (pp. 87–142). San Diego, CA: Elsevier.

Staub, E. (1989). *The roots of evil: The origins of genocide and other group violence.* Cambridge: Cambridge University Press.

Stern, D. N. (1977). *The fisrt relationship: Mother and infant.* Cambridge: Cambridge University Press.

Stern, D. N. (1985). *The interpersonal world of the infant.* New York: Basic Books.

Stern, D. N. (1995). *The motherhood constellation: A unified view of parent–infant psychotherapy.* New York: Basic Books.

Sternberg, R. J. (1999). The theory of successful intelligence. *Review of General Psychology, 3*, 292–316.

Stevenson, C. L. (1994). *Ethics and language.* New Haven, CT: Yale University Press.

Stolorow, R. (1997). Dynamic, dyadic, intersubjective systems: An evolving paradigm for psychoanalysis. *Psychoanalytic Psychology, 14*, 337–346.

Strevens, M. (2000). The essentialist aspect of naive theories. *Cognition, 74*, 149–175.

Strickland, B., Fisher, M. & Knobe, J. (2012). Moral structure falls out of general event structure. *Psychological Inquiry, 23*(2), 198–205.

Sunnafrank, M. (1983). Attitude similarity and interpersonal attraction in communication processes: In pursuit of an ephemeral influence. *Communications Monographs, 50*(4), 273–284.

Thomsen, L., Frankenhuis, W. E., Ingold-Smith, M. & Carey, S. (2011). Big and mighty: Preverbal infants mentally represent social dominance. *Science, 331*(6016), 477–480.

Thornberry, T. P., Ireland, T. O. & Smith, C. A. (2001). The importance of timing: The varying impact of childhood and adolescent maltreatment on multiple problem outcomes. *Development and Psychopathology, 13*, 957–979.

Tizard, B. & Hodges, J. (1978). The effect of early institutional rearing on the development of eight-year-old children. *Journal of Child Psychology and Psychiatry, 19*(2), 99–118.

Toch, H. (1992). *Violent men: An inquiry into the psychology of violence.* Washington, DC: American Psychological Association.

Toobin, J. (2008). Death in Georgia. *The New Yorker*, February 4. Retrieved July 24, 2018, from: www.newyorker.com/magazine/2008/02/04/death-in-georgia.

Trevarthen, C. (1993). The self born in intersubjectivity: An infant communicating. In U. Neisser (Ed.), *The perceived self: Ecological and interpersonal sources of self-knowledge* (pp. 121–173). New York: Cambridge University Press.

Tronick, E. Z. (1989). Emotions and emotional communication in infants. *American Psychologist, 44*(2), 112–119. 10.1037/0003-066X.44.2.112

Tronick, E. Z. & Gianino, A. F. (1986). The transmission of maternal disturbance to the infant. *New Directions for Child Development, 34*, 5–11.

Tronick, E., Als, H., Adamson, L., Wise, S. & Brazelton, T. B. (1978). Infants response to entrapment between contradictory messages in face-to-face interaction. *Journal of the American Academy of Child and Adolescent Psychiatry, 17*, 1–13.

Turiel, E. (1983). *The development of social knowledge: Morality and convention.* Cambridge: Cambridge University Press.

Turiel, E. (2006). The development of morality. In N. Eisenberg (Ed.), *Social, emotional, and personality development. Volume 3 of the handbook of child psychology* (6th ed., pp. 789–857). Hoboken, NJ: Wiley.

Uleman, J. S. (2005). Introduction: Becoming aware of the new unconscious. In R. R. Hassin, J. S. Uleman & J. A. Bargh (Eds.), *The new unconscious.* (pp. 3–18). New York: Oxford University Press.

Walker, J. (1967). "Moral" versus "aesthetic." *Crítica: Revista Hispanoamericana de Filosofía, 1*(3), 21–40.

Walker, L. J. (1984). Sex differences in the development of moral reasoning: A critical review. *Child Development, 55*(3), 677–691.

Warneken, F. (2013). The origins of human altruistic behavior: Evidence from children and chimpanzees – invited paper symposium. American Psychological Association Annual Convention, Honolulu, HI.

Warneken, F. & Tomasello, M. (2006). Altruistic helping in human infants and young chimpanzees. *Science, 311*(5765), 1301–1303. 10.1126/science.1121448

Warneken, F. & Tomasello, M. (2007). Helping and cooperation at 14 months of age. *Infancy, 11*(3), 271–294.

Warneken, F. & Tomasello, M. (2008). Extrinsic rewards undermine altruistic tendencies in 20-month-olds. *Developmental Psychology, 44*(6), 1785–1788.

Warneken, F. & Tomasello, M. (2009). Varieties of altruism in children and chimpanzees. *Trends in Cognitive Sciences, 13*(9), 397–402.

Warneken, F., Hare, B., Melis, A. P., Hanus, D. & Tomasello, M. (2007). Chimpanzees altruistically help conspecifics in a novel situation. *PLOS Biology, 5*(7), 1414–1420.

Webster, R. J. & Saucier, D. A. (2013). Angels and demons are among us: Assessing individual differences in belief in pure evil and belief in pure good. *Personality and Social Psychology Bulletin, 39*(11), 1455–1470.

Webster, R. J. & Saucier, D. A. (2015). Demons are everywhere: The effects of belief in pure evil, demonization, and retribution on punishing criminal perpetrators. *Personality and Individual Differences, 74*, 72–77.

Webster, R. J. & Saucier, D. A. (2017). Angels everywhere? How beliefs in pure evil and pure good predict perceptions of heroic behavior. *Personality and Individual Differences, 104*, 387–392.

Weinberg, L. (1991). Infant development and the sense of self: Stern vs. Mahler. *Clinical Social Work Journal, 19*(1), 9–22.

Weiner, B. (2006). *Social motivation, justice, and the moral emotions: An attributional approach.* Mahwah, NJ: Erlbaum.

Whalen, P. J. (1998). Fear, vigilance and ambiguity: Initial neuroimaging studies of the human amygdala. *Current Directions in Psychological Science, 7*(6), 177–188.

Wilson, T. D. (2002). *Strangers to ourselves: Discovering the adaptive unconscious.* Cambridge, MA: Harvard University Press.

Wilson, T. D., Lindsey, S. & Schooler, T. Y. (2000). A model of dual attitudes. *Psychological Review, 107*(1), 101–126.

Winnicott, D. W. (1946/2012). Some psychological aspects of juvenile delinquency. In C. Winnicott, R. Sheperd & M. Davis (Eds.), *Deprivation and delinquency* (pp. 97–102) New York: Routledge.

Winnicott, D. W. (1956/1975). The antisocial tendency. In *Through paediatrics to psycho-analysis* (pp. 306–315). London: International Psycho-Analytical Library.

Winnicott, D. W. (1957). *The child and the outside world.* London: Tavistock.

Winnicott, D. W. (1958). Psychoanalysis and the sense of guilt. In J. D. Sutherland (Ed.), *Psychoanalysis and contemporary thought* (pp. 15–32). New York: Grove Press.

Winnicott, D. W. (1963). The development of the capacity for concern. *Bulletin of the Menninger Clinic, 27*, 167–176.

Winnicott, D. W. (1963/1990). Morals and education. In *The maturational process and the facilitating environment* (pp. 93–108). London: Karnac.

Winnicott, D.W. (1963/2012). The psychotherapy of character disorders. In C. Winnicott, R. Sheperd & M. Davis (Eds.), *Deprivation and delinquency* (pp. 208–220) New York: Routledge.

Winnicott, D. W. (1965). Classification: Is there a psycho-analytic contribution to psychiatric classification. In *The maturational processes and the facilitating environment* (pp. 124–139). London: Hogarth Press.

Winnicott, D.W. (1971/2005). *Playing and reality.* New York: Routledge.

Wittgenstein, L. (1953/2001). *Philosophical investigations*. Oxford: Blackwell.

Wolin, R. (2014). Thoughtlessness revisited: A response to Seyla Benhabib. *Jewish Review of Books*. Retrieved July 24, 2018, from: https://jewishreviewofbooks.com/articles/1287/in-still-not-banal-a-response-to-seyla-benhabib/.

Woodward, A. L. (1998). Infants selectively encode the goal object of an actor's reach. *Cognition, 69*, 1–34.

Woodward, A. L. (1999). Infants' ability to distinguish between purposeful and non-purposeful behaviors. *Infant Behavior and Development, 22*, 145–160.

Woodward, A. L. (2013). Infant foundations of intentional understanding. In M. R. Banaji & S. A. Gelman (Eds.), Navigating the social world: What infants, children, and other species can teach us (pp. 75–80). New York: Oxford University Press.

Wynn, K. (1992). Addition and subtraction by human infants. *Nature, 358*, 749–750.

Youniss, J. & Damon, W. (1992). Social construction in Piaget's theory. In H. Beilin. & P. Pufall (Eds.), *Piaget's theory: Prospects and possibilities* (pp. 267–286). Hillsdale, NJ: Erlbaum.

Zahavi, D. (2005). *Subjectivity and selfhood: Investigating the first-person perspective.* Cambridge, MA: MIT Press.

Zahavi, D. (2010). Empathy, embodiment and interpersonal understanding: From Lipps to Schutz. *Inquiry, 53*(3), 285–306.

Zebrowitz, L. A. & McDonald, S. M. (1991). The impact of litigants' baby-facedness and attractiveness on adjudications in small claims courts. *Law and Human Behavior, 15*(6), 603–623. 10.1007/BF01065855

Zhong, L. (2013). Internalism, emotionism, and the psychopathy challenge. *Philosophy, Psychiatry, & Psychology, 20*(4), 329–337.

Index